# BEYOND CONFRONTATION

**Praeger Series in
Transformational Politics and Political Science**

The Politics of Transformation: Local Activism in the Peace and Environmental
Movements
*Betty H. Zisk*

The Latino Family and the Politics of Transformation
*David T. Abalos*

Mediation, Citizen Empowerment, and Transformational Politics
*Edward W. Schwerin*

Strategies of Transformation Toward a Multicultural Society: Fulfilling the Story of
Democracy
*David T. Abalos*

# BEYOND CONFRONTATION

## *Transforming the New World Order*

### CHARLES HAUSS

*Praeger Series in Transformational Politics and Political Science*
*Theodore L. Becker, Series Editor*

PRAEGER

**Westport, Connecticut**
**London**

**Library of Congress Cataloging-in-Publication Data**

Hauss, Charles.
    Beyond confrontation : transforming the new world order / Charles
Hauss.
        p.    cm.—(Praeger series in transformational politics and
political science ISSN 1061–5261)
    Includes bibliographical references and index.
    ISBN 0–275–94615–0 (hc : alk. paper).—ISBN 0–275–95391–2 (pb)
    1. International relations.  2. Peace.  3. World politics—1989–
I. Title. II. Series.
JX1391.H38  1996
327.1'7—dc20      95–30656

British Library Cataloguing in Publication Data is available.

Library of Congress Catalog Card Number: 95–30656
ISBN: 0–275–94615–0
        0–275–95391–2 (pbk.)
ISSN: 1061–5261

First published in 1996

Praeger Publishers, 88 Post Road West, Westport, CT 06881
An imprint of Greenwood Publishing Group, Inc.

Printed in the United States of America

The paper used in this book complies with the
Permanent Paper Standard issued by the National
Information Standards Organization (Z39.48–1984).

10 9 8 7 6 5 4 3 2 1

*To Art Ledoux and Winslow Myers*

# CONTENTS

# PREFACE

It took a long time to write this book. My progress was slowed by other projects and the normal interruptions that keep us academics from writing as quickly as we'd like. More important, events like the end of the Cold War made me wonder if I was writing a book that was either years ahead or years behind its time. There were times when I thought about abandoning the project altogether.

I was in one of those frames of mind on November 8, 1994.

Like most political junkies, I turned CNN on when the first polls closed, stayed with the networks until they abandoned their election coverage around midnight, and then listened to NPR and the BBC well into the morning.

The news was devastating. The right won in large part because its negative campaign tapped the alienation felt by many Americans, but the left had contributed heavily to its own defeat, because it was seen as having nothing constructive to offer.

Sometime in the wee hours of November 9, the BBC announced that it was also the fifth anniversary of the fall of the Berlin Wall. That only heightened my pessimism. Since I was in the final stages of writing this book, it was hard for me not to remember how much things had changed for the worse in international as well as domestic political life.

The euphoria and hope many felt in 1989 had already given way to concerns about a host of problems, old and new alike, which may prove even more daunting than those of the Cold War years. In the late 1980s, Presidents Bush and Gorbachev had spoken of a new world order. Now, bloody wars scattered around the world, ethnic conflict, environmental degradation, millions living in abject poverty and more had led pundits to speak of a new world *dis*order instead.

Oddly, as I drifted in and out of sleep that long night, the goals of and need for this book swung back into focus.

The time has come for a new approach to domestic and global politics that can give us real reasons for hope for a world that is in such a state of flux. This book is by no means a blueprint for what the next new left should be. Its scope is too narrow. So is my own perspective. What I have tried to write is an optimistic book which acknowledges the severity of the problems we face, but also sees the possibility and potential for significant and progressive change.

*     *     *

Any author accumulates a lot of debts. That's especially true in writing a book which covers this much ground.

In many ways I feel like an intellectual sponge. For a decade, I've been "soaking up" facts and ideas which have taken me intellectual light years away from my initial specialties in comparative and French politics.

The history of this book began in 1984, when I was teaching at Colby College. The dean asked me to take over the first year book program. The other committee members had already chosen Jonathan Schell's *The Fate of the Earth*, a book I would never have chosen. My job was to use the several thousand dollars the dean had given me to bring Schell to campus. But when I called, Schell said that he didn't like to give talks. Besides, he said we'd be better off bringing a series of cheaper speakers. Reluctantly, I took his advice and started scrambling to find people.

A few weeks later, a colleague called and said he'd met some interesting people who'd moved to Maine to work with a new peace movement called Beyond War. My first reaction was, "No, not another peace movement." I have to admit though that my interest was piqued when my friend said they'd be sending Gene Richeson, a former CIA officer who had founded the ROLM corporation and then retired in his late thirties to work on this stuff full time. I changed my mind. My stereotypes were being challenged, which I always take to be a good sign. Besides, Gene would come for free.

We hit it off immediately. I realized that I was spending time with someone who had truly revolutionary ideas and, even more important, was living and modelling them in his daily life. Those ideas and practices meshed with some reading I'd been doing in Eastern religion and the sciences as well as my growing misgivings with the confrontational aspects of leftist politics which had been a central part of my life since high school. I was hooked.

One of the things I did with Beyond War was write the first iteration of this book. Art Ledoux, Winslow Myers, and I began work on a much narrower version of it, focused all but exclusively on the threat of nuclear war and US-Soviet relations. Unfortunately for us, the Cold War ended before we finished the final draft. While this book goes much farther than our original manuscript, I could not have written it had I not worked with Art and Winslow. This book is every bit as much theirs as mine, and it is thus dedicated to them.

Lots of other people outside Beyond War helped solidify the ideas that follow. Rushworth Kidder of the Institute for Global Ethics, in particular, was a great sounding board and source of emotional support, especially in the early stages. Bob Clark, Louise White, Fran Harbour, Jonathan Gifford, Jim Barry, Barbara Knight, and other colleagues at George Mason helped me see the importance of chaos theory, ethics, and other issues I had downplayed in earlier versions. Clark Baxter, the editor of a textbook I did on comparative politics, urged me to keep working on these ideas for that book, even though many of the anonymous reviewers he had recruited doubted they had anything to do with the subject.

On this front I am especially pleased to thank Angela Harkavy. I first met Angela when she was a student in one of my classes. That was her third career. After a stint as a television news anchor and years as an environmental activist which had taken her as an NGO delegate to the Rio Summit (where she helped draft many of the final documents), she finally returned to get her B.A. and, now, her Ph.D. She quickly passed from being one of my best students to one of my most valued colleagues. Her B.A. thesis on the Rio Summit was the basis for much of Chapter 12. More importantly, I have benefited tremendously from her insights and support over the last three years.

I am also delighted to acknowledge a number of critics. I could not have written this book without confronting qualms raised by dozens of people on both my left and right, whatever those terms mean these days. Roger Bowen, Vice President for Academic Affairs at Hollins College, and I spent fifteen years at Colby debating and never agreeing about our two visions of what the left should be and do. Ken Rodman came at me from the more traditional realism of international relations. Ken had so much trouble trying to assimilate what I was saying into his paradigm that I realized I had to take those traditional perspectives much more seriously than I had planned.

As usual, I owe a lot to my wife, Gretchen Sandles. Normally, we hold pretty similar views about the political issues we both work on. Normally, too, she shares my optimism. This time, I was able to benefit from her criticisms, especially about Chapter 11, since the organization she works for was being downsized, reorganized, and TQMed, but without achieving the results I was writing about so enthusiastically.

Also, I owe a lot to eight people most political scientists have never heard of and seven of whom I've never met.

Peter Senge (MIT) and Chris Argyris (Harvard) are two of the most important theorists behind new thinking in the organizational/business world, stressing, in particular, how groups of people can "learn" and grow by leaps and bounds. The third is Tom Chappell, founder and CEO of Tom's of Maine, the largest natural health care company in the country. His account of the development of his company as a result of his sojourn at the Harvard Divinity School helped convince me that this book, too, had to discuss our souls as well as the rational side of our lives, which social scientists tend to limit themselves to. Much the same can be said for Anita Roddick, cofounder of the Body Shop, who has done a lot to show us all how we can make money and act in a socially responsible way at the same time. Finally, I found out about many of the unconventional sources I've drawn on by listening to the talk shows hosted by Diane Rehm and Derek McGinty on WAMU, one of the public radio stations in Washington, DC.

The last details of the book were finished shortly after we moved to Britain where I am researching books on racism and the left. Right after we moved in, I read books by two of Britain's best political journalists, Andrew Marr of the *Independent* and Will Hutton of the *Guardian—Ruling Britannia* and *The State We're In* respectively. Both are stunning reappraisals of politics in a country Americans have odd views about. More important here, both helped me see that what was mostly a book about the US applied at least to all the industrialized democracies as well.

Last but by no means least are the members of the team at Praeger which helped turn a rough six page prospectus into a finished book. Ted Becker, editor of this series on transformational politics, kept encouraging me while feeding me powerful editorial suggestions which always magically seemed to arrive when I was most bogged down. Dan Eades and Terri Jennings did a wonderful job shepherding it through the drafting and production process. Among other things, Dan asked me to put the book through another draft and cut about 10% of the text, which meant I finished it after the 1994 elections and could incorporate my reactions to it and the decline (or demise?) of the traditional left into the manuscript.

In short, I have learned a lot and had a lot of fun writing this book. May it be the same for you in reading it.

# 1

# WHAT NEW WORLD ORDER?

You can never solve a problem on the same level you created it.
—Albert Einstein

The peoples and governments of the world today face a global *crisis*. War. A decaying environment. Economic uncertainty. Racial, ethnic, and religious strife. The list goes on and on.

Each of those problems will get its due in the pages and chapters which follow, but I want to start with that word I emphasized in the first paragraph, crisis. I chose it, because the word crisis has two very different connotations, each of which sums up half of what this book is about.

For most people in the West, crisis is not a pleasant word. It conjures up images of a problem with potentially dire consequences, which is why most of us try to avoid crises whenever possible.

On the other hand, the word's etymology yields a second and more intriguing meaning. It can be traced back to the Greek *krisis*, which simply meant "turning point." That's the way physicians use it today, defining a medical crisis as that moment when a patient's life hangs in the balance.

If anything, the ancient Chinese understood the nature of a crisis even better. In rendering the concept, they brought together two characters. The first, "danger," is consistent with the traditional western connotation. Like the Greek notion of a turning point, the second, "opportunity," is not. In this view, a crisis has its frightening and dangerous side but also brings with it new possibilities.

In the pages that follow, I will argue that very real opportunities accompany the very real dangers of the global crisis, because both are an outgrowth of the trend which makes our time different from any other in recorded history: the growing interdependence of all aspects of social, political, and economic life. The many problems we face represent the "down" side of that more interdependent world. The "up" side and the possible way out of the crisis may lie in seeing and seizing some alternatives which come to light when we base our thoughts and actions on interdependence.

There are lots of ways of portraying those dangers and opportunities. Here, I will do so around a single common denominator to both the problems and their possible solutions. If I'm right, we find ourselves in such deep trouble today because we rely on confrontation when we try to settle the disputes which are an inevitable outgrowth of life on this "shrinking" planet. To make matters worse, our reliance on confrontation carries with it increasing costs, which, under some circumstances, could include the end of human civilization as we know it. On the other hand, thinking interdependently can help us see ways of shedding confrontation and adopting more constructive and cooperative problem solving techniques.

## A NEW WORLD (DIS)ORDER?

In 1989, the reform-minded communist government in Hungary lifted the iron curtain, allowing a flood of East German "tourists" to escape to the West. Before the year was out, Germans had torn down the Berlin Wall, the most visible symbol of the forty-five year conflict between East and West. The Cold War was over.

Many observers expected that the end of the Cold War would usher in a more peaceful period. Global leaders and citizens alike would be able to turn their attention to other pressing problems that had defied solution for decades and probably received less tension than they deserved because of the Soviet-American rivalry.

Those hopes and expectations didn't last long. That the new world order wasn't going to be all that orderly became clear no later than August 1990, when Iraq invaded Kuwait. The invasion and the war that followed drove one stark lesson home. The Cold War may be over, but there is still plenty of conflict to go around.

Not all the news is bad, of course, The end of the Cold War removed the threat of a worldwide nuclear holocaust, at least for now. There are also signs that national governments are learning to cooperate more in solving some of their mutual problems. While each of these examples is highly controversial, the deepening integration of the European Union, the limited agreements reached at the 1992 Rio Summit on the Environment and Development, and trade pacts such as the General Agreement on Tariffs and Trade (GATT) and the North American Free Trade Agreement (NAFTA) all show us there is at least tremendous potential in international cooperation.

Most pundits, however, continue to stress the uncertainties and the dangers. That's the case not only because the dangers are real, but because they tend to view events from the perspective of a traditional international relations specialist (Kaplan 1994; Attali 1991; Mearsheimer 1990a, Mearsheimer 1990b; Cetron and Davies 1990; Rizopoulos 1991; Brzezinski 1993; Moynihan 1993; Kennedy 1993).

They continue to use models of conflict which stress the independence of states which pursue selfishly defined national interests in a largely anarchical international system. They still view the world in zero-sum terms, assuming that most forms of intense conflict will end up with a single winner and loser. Under those circumstances, it is hardly surprising that conflict typically turns into confrontation and, all too often, violence.

I will make the case that such win-lose approaches to conflict resolution are counterproductive and downright dangerous today. In their place, I'll suggest that interdependence helps us see the importance and possibility of positive-sum or win-win outcomes in which no one loses and all parties benefit.

Before sketching out that position, I should point out that I do agree with today's more conventional analysts in one critical respect. Their assumption that there will be more continuity than change is warranted *as long as* we stick with the traditional approaches to international conflict they describe. Indeed, like some of the most pessimistic among them, I am convinced our problems will get worse to the degree that we continue to rely on business as usual.

I part company with them because my reading of the evidence has convinced me that the world *could* be different and better. There are grounds for optimism and for seizing the opportunities rather than the dangers, but only *if* we can learn to handle our difficulties differently by making interdependence the organizing principle in the way we think and act. Doing so will require making some fundamental changes, most notably making win-win conflict resolution the norm rather than the exception it is today.

That will be no easy task.

To make the argument seem even more sweeping (and perhaps also more implausible), I'll show that we can make that shift from win-lose to win-win only if we broaden the scope of the problem under investigation. It isn't limited to the kinds of conflict international relations experts study, but extends to the way we deal with our disagreements at all levels, from the international to the interpersonal.

To put it as bluntly as possible, if my argument is right, creating a more benign world order will probably require us to change more than humans have ever changed before. That said, there are historical precedents that suggest such change is possible. To use the currently fashionable term, history is filled with paradigm shifts in which people made intellectual and political quantum leaps (Kuhn 1969; Gilman 1988). They occur when a community or a society decides that its traditional ways of analyzing problems and devising solutions to them no longer work very well and then comes up with a new approach.

Those new analyses and solutions can emerge only when people dig deeply into the root causes of the problems. Further, they occur only when people are willing to shed their preconceived notions and explore new ones as implied by Einstein in the statement which begins this chapter.

Some of that work has already been done. We have some plausible sketches of what a world which has moved beyond confrontation would be like. That is something, for instance, former Soviet President Mikhail Gorbachev (1987, 1988) did very eloquently and effectively before his reforms and then his country began to unravel. Then Senator Al Gore (1992) laid out much the same kind of vision in his widely popular *Earth in the Balance*.

There is also some evidence that such a shift is already taking shape, albeit slowly and fitfully. Little of that change reaches the morning newspaper or the nightly news because it isn't very spectacular and doesn't include the violence and confrontation that attract most people's attention. But it is happening, most visibly at the individual level where millions have taken the clichéd slogan, "think globally, act locally," to heart. There are signs of it as well in organizational behavior, most notably in the management revolution going on inside many corporations which has also served as a stimulus for the Clinton administration's proposal for "reinventing government" (Osborne and Gaebler 1992; Gore 1993). There are even glimmers of it in the international arena, for example, with the growing use of supranational institutions and what political scientists call regimes.

I don't want to mislead the reader. This book is not going to lay out a simple, easy to follow road map to a more peaceful and just world. I am as aware of the pitfalls and obstacles in my argument as any of the critics who have dismissed the possibility of such a global paradigm shift, which is why so much of what follows will be couched in the conditional.

That said, I am convinced I'm right about two things. First, continuing to rely on our traditional, confrontational approach to conflict resolution amounts to a recipe for disaster. Second, change is possible, though by no stretch of the imagination is it inevitable.

In its broadest sense, this is a book about the next stage in human evolution. Physical evolution takes place over generations. Mental evolution need not. Because humanity is the one species with consciousness, we are also the one species with the ability to shape at least some aspects of our future development. Therein lies the optimism which will pervade this book.

## THE ARGUMENT

In developing the dangers and opportunities of the post Cold War world, I will be making a three-pronged argument.

**1. The Problem.** The issues that make up today's global crisis share six characteristics that set them apart from anything that came before:

*They transcend national boundaries.* That's not just the case for the obvious issues such as global warming or the depletion of the ozone layer, but also for many ethnic and economic problems, such as the growing gap between rich and poor or the migration of tens of millions of people from one country to another over the last twenty years.

*They all can have devastating outcomes.* The most obvious and frightening examples are environmental decay and the consequences of an all-out nuclear war. But, there are plenty of others (overpopulation, the spread of AIDS, high-tech conventional warfare) that could be devastating, even if they do not put civilization itself at risk.

*It seems difficult, if not impossible, to tackle one of these issues without addressing them all.* They are a lot like an onion. Peel away one layer (the environment) and you find yourself at another (poverty in the less developed part of the world). Peel that layer and there's yet another (the costs of militarization and war). The overlapping nature of global problems was the main reason why the UN planners had to turn the 1992 Rio Summit into a session on the environment *and* development. We face what Norman Myers calls a "risk spiral where one factor is worsened by others, whereupon it supplies its own adverse impact in turn but with increased force" (1993: 51).

*The world is changing at an unprecedented and accelerating rate.* Take personal computers rather than global political issues for an example here. Apple launched the Macintosh in 1984. The first Macs couldn't do much, but they cost a lot. Today's PowerPC driven Macs have the power of a 1960s mainframe computer, and most models cost less than the original ones did a decade ago. And, as dozens of observers have pointed out, plenty of us have trouble coping with all this change not just in technology but throughout our lives.

*The global problems do not seem amenable to traditional political solutions in which one side imposes its will on the other.* Take one of the most difficult cases considered below, the Gulf war. To be sure, Iraq was forced out of Kuwait. But, that came at tremendous cost, *and* none of the other underlying problems which led to the war (e.g., instability in the region, Arab distrust of the West, the Iraqi regime itself) were resolved nor probably could they have been militarily.

*Instead, global problems seem to require some sort of cooperative, win-win solution.* Cooperative solutions are required, because by their very nature, no one nation or group or individual can solve them on its own. Again, that is easiest to see with the environment, where, for instance, ending the destruction of the Amazonian rain forest seems to require joint action by North and South (e.g., debt for nature swaps).

2. **Interdependence.** To best understand the crisis, we should view it through a mental lens few of us have used up to now: interdependence. For some time now, most ecologists, systems engineers, chaos theorists, quantum physicists and other natural scientists have based their work on the assumption that every actor and action directly or indirectly affects everyone and everything else.

Such ideas are not completely new in political science and related disciplines. In the 1950s and 1960s, David Easton (1965) and others brought systems theory with its concepts of environment and feedback to our attention. More recently, scholars like Robert Keohane and Joseph Nye (1989) have begun exploring a complex interdependence as a factor shaping an international system still largely determined by nation states.

But this book goes further in one key respect. It makes interdependence the central, empirical, organizing principle in analyzing the global crisis. In that sense, it is a dramatic departure from works that focus on the interdependence as an explanatory factor in what is still seen as predominantly a system of independent states. Because they tend to stress such notions as feedback or extend analyses over longer lengths of time, models based on interdependence tend to downplay our autonomy and lead to a radical rethinking of such critical notions as self-interest which are at the heart of much current descriptive and prescriptive theory.

*Each issue in the crisis has many of its roots in a common cause: the values and assumptions we use in analyzing and dealing with intense conflict wherever and whenever it occurs.* Thinking interdependently thus takes us far beyond the confines of traditional analyses of international relations and its emphases on nation states and power politics.

*Those values and assumptions can be replaced with others consistent with the implications of interdependence.* Again, unlike traditional international relations analysts, I will argue that those values and assumptions are by no means set in stone and that we can adopt new ones which make more sense given the conditions in today's world.

The global crisis could turn out to be a fundamental turning point in human history. We *could*, and the emphasis will be on could, move beyond confrontation as the most common approach used for resolving intense conflict. Psychologists and social workers have developed sophisticated mechanisms for helping individuals and groups forge win-win outcomes that allow them to go beyond confrontation in daily life and which have broader implications for transforming the way we solve problems at all levels.

**3. Change.** People who have written about paradigms suggest that one can never paint a full-blown picture of what life under a new one will be like when its basic parameters and principles are still being worked out. All one can do is point to examples which illustrate the new paradigm's basic principles and lend partial support to its explanations or predictions.

That's especially the case now, when so much is changing so rapidly. As Max Singer and the late Aaron Wildavsky put it in their book on what they called the "real" world order, "speculating about a kind of world that has never been seen before cannot be a high-confidence activity" (Singer and Wildavsky 1993: 23).

That said, we can point to instances of change already taking place which suggest that such a transformation is possible. We must be careful not to read too much into them, however. Not everyone involved in them sees things as broadly as I do. And if we are in the midst of a paradigm shift, we are definitely at its beginning stages. Still, at least three bodies of evidence suggest that this part of the argument is not pure fancy:

*Many people have already adopted at least part of what I will call new thinking or similar value systems which revolve around interdependence.* Some evidence along these lines can be found in public opinion polls, especially in the extensive but controversial work on "post-material" values (Inglehart 1978, 1989). Less systematic, but perhaps more revealing, support can also be found in the activities of dozens of organizations which are trying to build support for ideas that mirror new thinking everywhere from San Francisco to Sri Lanka.

*There are also intriguing signs from what might at first seem to be an unlikely source: the business community.* Many successful corporations have implemented new management systems which stress team building, cooperation, and employee involvement in the operation of the enterprise (Peters 1993). In recent years, that same approach has been carried over into the public sector, most notably in David Osborne and Ted Gaebler's provocative book, *Reinventing Government* (1992) and the report of the National Performance Review chaired by Vice President Al Gore (1993).

*Most important of all are some geopolitical examples of countries cooperating in new and promising ways.* These are important in their own right, but they also offer insights into how conflict can be resolved without violence through what Kenneth Boulding (1988) called "stable peace." As noted a few paragraphs ago, none of these examples offers a complete guide to new thinking in action. Nonetheless, the histories of, say, European integration and environmental regimes illustrate what the search for win-win outcomes *can* lead to. And if the likes of Gregg Easterbrook (1995) are to be believed, we have already made major strides toward solving some of the environmental problems which, a decade or two ago, seemed unsolvable to many.

                              *     *     *

All this is another way of saying that this book has a vast agenda. The changes it discusses are more sweeping than most readers will think possible or probable.

One should remember, however, that the world has gone through other periods when rapid social changes brought equally dramatic political changes in their wake. No one has described the need for and process of large scale change more effectively than Alvin Toffler:

I fail to see how it is possible for us to have a technological revolution, a social revolution, an information revolution, sexual, epistemological revolutions, and *not* a political revolution as well. Simply put, the political technology of the industrial age is no longer appropriate technology for the new civilization taking form around us. Our politics are obsolete. (1969: xii-xiv)

Toffler's words are telling in and of themselves, but his passage carries a second and more cautionary message. A quarter century has passed since Toffler wrote *Future Shock*. The political revolution has not come, although the others continue unabated, as his three other books on the subject attest. This book will focus on why a political paradigm shift is needed and why one might be possible now. But it is written knowing that what could happen and what should happen in political life are often very different from what does happen.

## GAPS, VISION, AND LENSES

When I've made this case with a group of students or workshop participants, I've found that people easily get bogged down in examples. To help people see the big picture, I find it helpful to weave more "right-brained" approaches in along with the statistical and other factual evidence.

I start with another well-known sentence of Einstein's which he included in a telegram sent to about two hundred prominent Americans in 1946 urging them to stop the nuclear arms race before it had really begun: "The unleashed power of the atom has changed everything save our modes of thinking and we thus drift toward unparalleled catastrophe" (Einstein 1946). The sentence has been quoted by politicians of all stripes, including former Defense Secretary Casper Weinberger. It even found its way into Tenghiz Abuladze's surrealistic film about Stalinism, *Repentance*.

Most interpretations focus on the beginning and end of the sentence and on the fact that Einstein was among the first to warn about the dangers of nuclear weapons. For this book, however, the key to it lies in the four words in the middle, our modes of thinking, as outlined in Figures 1.1 and 1.2.[1]

Figure 1.1 focuses on the issue Einstein raised directly in the sentence, nuclear war. It was another decade before the Americans and Soviets had enough weapons to produce the "unparalleled catastrophe" he warned against. Nonetheless, as early as 1946, Einstein realized just how dramatically different the "reality" of the nuclear age would be, which I depict with the sharp step curve that shoots upward in 1945.

The unleashed power of the atom changed everything, that is, save our modes of thinking, represented here by the second, straight line. That leaves a huge "gap" between the reality of the nuclear age and the way we go about dealing with it. We persist in using a pre-nuclear mind set to deal with a radically changed world. More than anything else, that gap is the root cause of much of the global crisis.

Because that gap has not been closed, we drift toward the unparalleled catastrophe of a nuclear war. The word "drift" is also a remarkably powerful one, ironically because of the very weakness it conveys. The cowboy "drifter" wanders aimlessly from town to town. A sailboat is adrift, unable to move, because it cannot catch the wind. If this interpretation is correct, our current way of thinking leaves us aimless, powerless, and unable to take the steps that would allow us to cope with the danger of nuclear weapons and the other dangers of the global crisis.

Now, consider Einstein's statement as a comment about all the issues of the global crisis (remember, Einstein said "everything changed"). The sentence "looks" a little different. For the environment, for example, there is no single date equivalent to 1945. Rather, the reality of the world we live in has been

---

[1] Figure 1.1 was first developed for the 1985 National Seminar for Beyond War volunteers.

Figure 1.1

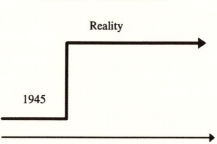

**Einstein: A Literal View**

changing continually at least since the beginning of the industrial revolution, as Figure 1.2 tries to portray. I've actually drawn the upper line rather conservatively, since one could argue that change should be a parabola or some other nonlinear curve to reflect the fact that it is occurring at ever-accelerating rates, as in the consumption of most natural resources or the emission of carbon dioxide and other "greenhouse" gases. In that case, the gap seems even wider than it appears in this figure.

Such discussions of gaps and changing modes of thinking are rarely found in academic circles. Political scientists, especially international relations specialists, tend to be pragmatists who focus on what policy makers can realistically hope to accomplish in reasonably short periods. Such concerns often lead them to criticize the kind of argument being made here as unrealistic or visionary. If the gap as depicted in either figure is narrow, they probably are right. Dramatic change isn't needed. If tried under those circumstances, it might well prove counter-productive.

When the gap gets as wide as I think it is now, we probably need to shed that so-called pragmatism and seek dramatically new alternatives. Central to that conclusion is a word realists have a lot of trouble with, "vision," which has two basic meanings. First is the often pejorative one used earlier: the visionary as someone who chooses to set far-reaching, idealistic, or even utopian goals for the future. Just as important is the second definition which an optometrist worries about: a person's ability to see things clearly.

This book is built on both definitions. To be sure, it is based on a vision of a future and, I believe, better world. Even more, it is an exercise in trying to improve our vision or understanding of political life as the twentieth century draws to a close.

Figure 1.2

**Einstein: A More General View**

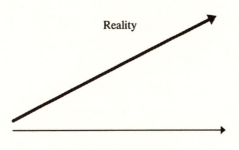

Reality

Modes of Thinking

Perhaps the best way to think about this book is as an examination of two mental "lenses" we could use to improve our political vision. When deciding which lens to prescribe, an optometrist always tries out a few. Consider this book as a session at an optometrist's office in which you and the doctor have to choose between two prescriptions, one based on the old way of solving problems and the other on an as yet not very fully tested new one. Each is actually for bifocals, because these "glasses" provide insights into both the way the world is today and what it could be like tomorrow.

## ON BIASES AND SOURCES

This is an unusual book for an academic to write because it constantly and consciously moves back and forth across the line between normative and empirical analysis. While you will have no trouble figuring out where this author stands, I take my responsibility to present my case in a fair and non-polemical manner seriously. I have therefore tried to write this book in a balanced enough way that a reader could reach any of its critical and controversial junctures and conclude that I'm wrong *on the basis of the evidence and argument I present.* I just hope that if that happens, I will have at least prompted you to think and question some of the values and assumptions you have about this material.

I thus make no claim that the pages which follow provide anything approaching definitive proof that my argument is right. It might not be possible to do so under the best of circumstances for a host of epistemological reasons. Even if one could, such proof would require a volume of material which could never be squeezed into a single book or mastered by a single author. Therefore,

I have chosen to present general trends and specific examples in order to illustrate rather than prove the argument.

You should also treat what follows skeptically for the simple reason that I am trying to project current trends into the reasonably distant future. Sometimes, writers do a pretty good job of predicting what will happen, as Jules Verne did in his recently rediscovered 1863 manuscript, *Paris au XXème siècle* (1994). More often (and I fear I fall into this category), we get much of it terribly wrong as in the following example:

In the thirties, the American president Franklin D. Roosevelt commissioned his administration to undertake a vast study of the coming technologies. When the study was published it made a very big impression. Indeed, it was enthralling. There was just one problem: it had not predicted the coming of television, nor that of plastic, or jet planes, or organ transplants, or laser beams, not even of ball-point pens. (cited in King and Schneider 1991: xxiii)

Finally, because this book draws on so many different subjects, a complete list of references at the end would have been too long and complicated. As a result, I have chosen two relatively unusual approaches to citing sources.

First, because most chapters cover dramatically different ground and only a few sources are brought into more than one of them, each chapter will have its own set of references. Second, I have not included every source I used but selected only those that bear most directly on the argument, are the most controversial, or are least well-known.

I should also point out that I have relied far less on academic sources than in anything else I have written. That is not a coincidence. We academics have a slow turn around time in our writing, which means our work on the subjects covered here is often dated before our books and articles are published. Also, given the way academic careers are built, we tend to focus on relatively narrow topics, meaning that one has to turn to journalists and others who often are more willing to look at the "big picture."

## REFERENCES

Attali, Jacques (1991). *Millennium: Winners and Losers in the Coming World Order.* New York: Times Books.
Boulding, Kenneth (1988). "Moving from Unstable to Stable Peace." In Anatoly Gromyko and Martin Hellman, eds., *Breakthrough: Emerging New Thinking: Soviet and Western Scholars Issue a Challenge to Building a World Beyond War.* New York/Moscow: Walker/Novosti, 157–167.
Brzezinski, Zbigniew (1993). *Out of Control.* New York: Scribner's.

Cetron, Martin, and Owen Davies (1991). *Global Reach: The Haves and Have-nots of the New World Order*. New York: St. Martin's.

Easterbrook, Gregg (1995). *A Moment on the Earth*. New York: Viking.

Easton, David (1965). *A Framework for Political Analysis*. New York: John Wiley.

Einstein, Albert (1946). Cited in Otto Nathan and Heinz Norden, eds., *Einstein on Peace*. New York: Avnel Books, 1981, 376.

Gilman, Robert (1988). "The Process of Change." *In Context*, Spring, 5–9.

Gorbachev, Mikhail S. (1987). *Perestroika*. New York: Harper and Row.

———. (1988). "A Road to the Future." Speech to the United Nations, December 7, 1988. Available either in the FBIS Daily Report, *Soviet Union*, 8 December 1988 or *A Road to the Future*. Santa Fe, NM: Ocean Tree Books.

Gore, Albert (1992). *Earth in the Balance: Ecology and the Human Spirit*. New York: Plume.

———. (1993). *Creating a Government That Works Better But Costs Less: The Report of the National Performance Review*. New York: Plume.

Inglehart, Ronald (1978). *The Silent Revolution*. Princeton: Princeton University Press.

———. (1989). *Culture Shift*. Princeton: Princeton University Press.

Kaplan, Robert (1994). "The Coming Anarchy." *The Atlantic*, February.

Kennedy, Paul (1993). *Preparing for the Twenty First Century*. New York: Random House.

Keohane, Robert, and Joseph Nye (1989). *Power and Interdependence*. 2d. ed. New York: HarperCollins.

King, Alexander, and Bertrand Schneider (1991). *The First Global Revolution: A Report by the Council of the Club of Rome*. New York: Pantheon.

Kuhn, Thomas (1969). *The Structure of Scientific Revolutions*, 2d ed. Chicago: University of Chicago Press.

Mearsheimer, John (1990a). "Why We Will Soon Miss the Cold War." *The Atlantic*, August.

———. (1990b). "Back to the Future: Instability in Europe After the Cold War." *International Security* 15: 5–56.

Moynihan, Daniel Patrick (1993). *Pandaemonium: Ethnicity in International Politics*. New York: Oxford University Press.

Myers, Norman (1993). *Ultimate Security: The Environmental Basis of Political Stability*. New York: W. W. Norton.

Osborne, David, and Ted Gaebler (1992). *Reinventing Government*. New York: Plume.

Peters, Tom (1993). *Liberation Management*. New York: Knopf.

Rizopoulos, Nicholas, ed. (1990). *Sea Changes: American Foreign Policy in a World Transformed*. New York: Council on Foreign Relations Press.

Singer, Max, and Aaron Wildavsky (1993). *The Real World Order: Zones of Peace/Zones of Turmoil*. Chatham, NJ: Chatham House.

Toffler, Alvin (1969). *Future Shock*. New York: Random House.

Verne, Jules (1994). *Paris au XXème siècle*. Paris: Hachette.

# PART ONE

# THE PROBLEM

# 2

# WAR

War truly has become a scourge, as was disease throughout most of human history.

—John Keegan

War is a fixture in human history. Scholars still debate how long it has been around and why our ancestors first turned to it, but there is widespread agreement that people have gone to war since the beginning of civilization, if not longer (Dwyer 1985; Keegan 1993).

There is also widespread agreement that war has played an important political role. Whatever their disagreements, most historians and political scientists have seen war the way the Prussian Karl von Clausewitz did, as one way of settling political disputes. There is always much more to any war than that, including the desire of (mostly) men to display their courage or of (often deranged) leaders to conquer new lands and peoples. But that Clausewitzean core was always there. However brutal, war has been something states could use to settle disagreements which could not be resolved otherwise. For most people, it provided solutions at acceptable costs, though both those key terms, solutions and acceptable costs, always carried with them a good bit of uncertainty.

Following the line of reasoning begun with Figures 1.1 and 1.2, I will argue that war has been rendered obsolete. As with many terms used in this book, I've chosen the term *obsolete* carefully. It does not mean that we cannot go to war. We obviously can, because we do. What it does mean is that war no longer serves that purpose of solving political disputes between nations.

Many people disagree and believe war continues to play the same role it always has. Take two examples I will focus on below, the Contra war against the Sandinista government in Nicaragua during the Reagan administration and the Gulf war following Iraq's occupation of Kuwait. In each case, there are analysts, and not just apologists, who claimed that there was no other way to dislodge morally unacceptable and dangerous rulers who were portrayed as threats to the national interests of many countries. By the same token, they argue that both wars were successful because the United States achieved its political goals: eliminating the Sandinistas from power and forcing Saddam Hussein's troops out of Kuwait.

My reading of the evidence suggests otherwise, especially as you look beyond the immediate fighting and its impact. Some political and other goals are still being met through war. The Iraqis were forced to leave Kuwait; the Sandinistas were never able to impose anything like total control over Nicaragua. Typically, however, the costs exceed the benefits (Cranna 1994). Many wars turn into bloody stalemates that drag on indefinitely without a decisive victory for either side. Meanwhile, the costs of fighting them have escalated beyond anything one could have anticipated a half century ago. And even when there is an apparent victor, wars rarely, if ever, result in lasting settlements of the political disputes which spawned them.

Thus, Saddam Hussein remained in power in Iraq after the Gulf war, and none of the long-term geopolitical problems which gave rise to it in the first place were any closer to being solved. And, the enduring socioeconomic inequalities and miseries in Nicaragua (for that matter in all of Central America) continue to plague the country's politics, sparking protests which have already brought it perilously close to civil war once again.


## NUCLEAR WAR

Had this book been written a decade ago, I would have given the threat of nuclear war far more attention. Heightened tensions between the United States and the Soviet Union had sparked a new arms race that would add a trillion dollars to American military expenditure and contribute heavily to the collapse of the USSR. Everything from President Reagan's famous "warning" that the bombs were to be launched in five minutes (made while rehearsing his weekly radio address and thinking the microphones weren't on) to the deployment of thousands of ever more accurate and deadlier weapons convinced people and policy makers alike that the threat of nuclear war was real indeed.

The end of the Cold War has dramatically reduced the likelihood of a major nuclear war for the foreseeable future. Nonetheless, it is important to recall four major lessons from the research and speculation on nuclear weapons, each of which remains important in what many analysts still call the "nuclear age."

First, books like *The Fate of the Earth* and television docudramas like *The Day After* and *Threads* drove home a point many of us have lost sight of with the end of the Cold War. The invention and then the deployment of some fifty thousand nuclear weapons meant that humanity had become the first species that could render itself extinct.

There were some highly macabre debates about what exactly would happen in an all out nuclear war. Estimates of deaths in the two superpowers were all over the map, but most experts predicted that the number of dead could easily top one hundred million people in both the Soviet Union and the United States. Hotly contested theories about the spread of radiation and, later, the climatic effects known as "nuclear winter" showed that the impact would spread far beyond the countries which actually fired missiles at each other. In the mid-1980s, New Zealand's Minister of the Environment acknowledged that his country would almost certainly not be a target but argued persuasively that it would be devastated anyway, because it would be cut off from its supply of many vital goods, including everything from insulin for its diabetics to spare parts for its machines.

Whatever their other differences, most authorities were convinced that although a substantial number of people would survive, civilization as we know it would be dealt a crippling and perhaps fatal blow. Humanity would not be rendered physically extinct as biologists think of the term, but we might well be "sociologically extinct." Survivors would face dreadful living conditions. There would be no electricity, running water, or modern medical services. They would have to cut down trees (without using chainsaws) to heat their homes, grow their own food, and care for their own illnesses. As Dr. Jack Geiger pithily put it in the powerful film *The Last Epidemic*, "the living would envy the dead."

The threat of what some experts euphemistically called a major nuclear "exchange" has all but disappeared for now with the end of the Cold War. Russia retains enough of the old Soviet arsenal to inflict the kind of damage we worried about in the early 1980s. With no Cold War, however, there aren't issues on the international horizon that could plausibly lead Russian and American leaders to contemplate using nuclear weapons on each other. In fact, in June 1994, the two countries stopped targeting their strategic missiles at each other.

But that doesn't mean we can stop worrying about nuclear weapons because of the second reason. As the world saw in Hiroshima and Nagasaki, any use of nuclear weapons brings unprecedented death and destruction. Those primitive bombs wiped out entire cities, and most bombs in today's arsenals pack a lot more firepower. One only has to think for a second about what would have happened had there been a nuclear warhead on one of the SCUD or Cruise missiles used in the Gulf war or had the terrorists who attacked the World Trade Center or the Federal Building in Oklahoma City used a primitive nuclear device rather than a truck filled with conventional explosives.

That leads to the third issue. The likelihood of such a "limited" war will increase if there is further proliferation of nuclear weapons.

So far, we have been lucky. In the early 1960s, experts predicted that there could be as many as fifty nuclear powers before the end of the century. For a variety of reasons, most notably the regime established by the Nuclear Non-Proliferation Treaty of 1968, that has not happened. However, that regime has always been imperfect, and those imperfections persist despite the fact that the signatories decided to renew its provisions indefinitely when they reviewed the treaty in 1995.

A number of countries are close to possessing nuclear weapons. Israel almost certainly has them. India has exploded a nuclear "device" and could quickly and easily put together a usable bomb if it has not already done so. Its long-time rival Pakistan is not very far behind and may well have a few bombs in its arsenal. South Africa did, too, before it abandoned its nuclear weapons program as part of its dismantling of apartheid. There is little doubt that Iraq was reasonably close to building its first bomb when the Gulf war broke out, as was North Korea before it reached its 1994 agreement with the United States to stop developing weapons grade fuel.

The breakup of the Soviet Union fueled fears about proliferation as well. Overnight, four new nuclear states were formed, and it took almost three years before all of them agreed to abide by the arms control agreements the USSR had reached before it collapsed. More worrisome now is the possibility that these new, fragile governments will lose track of the weapons and other nuclear material they now have or be tempted to sell technologies which could be used in building bombs in order to get desperately needed cash. There are already rumors that some unemployed Soviet nuclear scientists have gone to work in Iran and other countries interested in building a bomb.

The concern is not only about the spread of nuclear weapons to national governments, but to terrorist organizations as well. For a generation or more, there has been speculation about what terrorists could do with a bomb. Now, there is a growing possibility that terrorist groups could actually get their hands on one.

Hundreds of strategic nuclear weapons could not be accounted for in the first days after the failed coup attempt in Moscow in August 1991, and it is not clear yet that responsible officials control all the smaller, tactical ones. There have been recent reports, as well, of the theft of substantial quantities of fissionable material in the former Soviet Union. The FBI opened an office in the US Embassy in Moscow in 1994 in large part to monitor alleged attempts by Russian organized crime to steal and then sell fissionable material.

It is getting easier, not harder, for governments, terrorists, and others to obtain nuclear weapons. The technology is relatively simple. Undergraduates routinely design plans for atomic bombs in independent study projects. The hard part has always been obtaining the needed enriched plutonium or uranium as well as sophisticated enough delivery systems. Even that is becoming easier with the widespread use of nuclear power for non-military purposes and the global sales of increasingly sophisticated "dual use" hardware which could be used for nuclear as well as conventional weapons.

Finally, there is an important link connecting nuclear weapons, the Cold War, and the other issues that follow in the rest of Part One. The Cold War and the nuclear age marked the real globalization of geopolitical life. That had begun in earnest with imperial expansion from the sixteenth through the end of the nineteenth century. Still, there had never been a time when all major powers were concerned about what happened virtually everywhere in the world, even during the two conflicts we mistakenly label world wars. Now, with frightening speed and devastation, war could touch the entire planet.

## THE FIGHTING NEVER STOPPED

The period between 1945 and 1989 was the longest one in recorded history without a major war on European soil, which prompted the historian John Lewis Gaddis (1987) to call the Cold War "the long peace." Gaddis and other realists are no doubt right in arguing that deterrence and American foreign policy in general had a lot to do with keeping the superpowers and their allies from taking up arms against each other.

That doesn't mean that the world was free of war during those years. Quite the opposite. As the title of Patrick Brogan's book (1990) suggests, the fighting never did stop. It just occurred elsewhere. And got deadlier.

War has been getting a lot more gruesome for centuries. The weapons are more powerful and the wars more all encompassing. There were some devastating wars long ago, including the Thirty Years War (1618–1648), which cut the German population from some twenty one to fourteen million.[1] Toward the end of that century, the last of the great Indian Mughals, Alamgir, led a campaign to unite the subcontinent in which roughly a hundred thousand people died each year.

Those wars were the exception. Until the end of the eighteenth century, most wars were fought by small armies which saw combat for at most a few weeks a year. The rise of huge conscript armies and, later, newer and much deadlier weapons changed all that.

Ours has been a violent century marked by what Zbigniew Brzezinski calls "megadeath" (1993: 9–17). As Table 2.1 shows, the number of wars has remained about the same, but more than five times as many people died in the fighting in this century than in the last. As horrifying as these figures may seem, they were collected too early to include the recent fighting in Sudan, Somalia, Angola, many of the former Soviet republics, Iraq, Rwanda and the regions which used to make up Yugoslavia.

Researchers call the first and second world wars "total," because entire societies were mobilized and vast numbers of civilians as well as soldiers were killed and wounded. By that definition, most regional wars since 1945 have been total as well. In the most complete recent overview of wars in that period, Patrick Brogan (1990) estimates that at least twenty million people have been killed. John Keegan (1993) puts the number at more like fifty million.

The human cost of war can perhaps most easily be seen in the cheapest and most common weapon system, the land mine (Webster 1994). Land mines are cheap. Almost all models cost less than $50; some of the deadliest cost as little as $3. And, they are everywhere. There are tens of millions of them scattered under the world's current and former battlefields. The United Nations estimates there may be as many as one for every fifty people on earth. Some believe there are as many as a million in northern Somalia alone. The mines kill and maim tens of thousands of people each year, a good third of whom are children. Many are left from wars long over, because it is difficult, dangerous, expensive, and time consuming to remove them. The French government still has a crack team that tries to defuse the hundreds of mines left from the two world wars, which hikers, farmers, and children stumble across each year. Kuwait's government has appropriated over a billion dollars to remove mines left from the Gulf

---

[1] Statistics on casualties are uncertain estimates at best. I've drawn the numbers that follow from the previously cited books by Gwynn Dyer and Patrick Brogan plus Ruth Leger Sivard (1991) and the Stockholm International Peace Research Institute on SIPRI's yearbook (annual).

Table 2.1
Approximate Number of Deaths in Wars by Century

| Century | Number of wars | Deaths (millions) |
|---------|----------------|-------------------|
| Sixteenth | 66 | 1.6 |
| Seventeenth | 36 | 6.1 |
| Eighteenth | 55 | 7.0 |
| Nineteenth | 211 | 19.4 |
| Twentieth | 227 | 107.8 |

*Source:* Sivard (1991: 20).

war. Most war-ravaged governments, however, including Iraq's, don't have that kind of money, and so the mines sit there.

There is one overarching reason why wars have been so much deadlier since World War II. Until 1991, the United States and the Soviet Union intervened directly or indirectly in just about every conflict. Most of the time, the superpowers did not use their own troops but simply armed both sides, magnifying the carnage in what amounted to proxy struggles between them. On a few occasions (Korea, Vietnam, Afghanistan) one of the superpowers did send its soliders into wars that killed hundreds of thousands and took a terrible toll not only on the countries in which the fighting occurred but on the superpower's society back home.

The Cold War also helped create a booming arms trade with a clear and depressing pattern. As Table 2.2 shows, with the exception of Brazil, the top ten exporters were "northern" countries, and all but two of the leading importers were LDCs. Much of the industrialized world may have become what Max Singer and Aaron Wildavsky (1993) call a "zone of peace" in which countries are not likely to go to war with each other. On the other hand, they have done a lot to make the rest of the world an even deadlier "zone of turmoil" than it had been before.

The end of the Cold War changed remarkably little on this score (Klare 1994, 1995; Renner 1993). True, regional conflicts are no longer part of a global battle between two superpowers. Nonetheless, the United States and many of its allies still feel the need to be involved in all or most of them. Most are still being fought using arms left over from the Cold War era, and, in most cases, the arms are still flowing from the countries which have come to depend on that trade economically.

Table 2.2
Global Arms Sales

| Exporter | Value (billions of constant 1990 dollars) | Importer | Value (billions of constant 1990 dollars) |
|---|---|---|---|
| Soviet Union | 61.3 | India | 17.6 |
| United States | 60.0 | Saudi Arabia | 10.6 |
| France | 11.2 | Iraq | 10.3 |
| Britain | 9.1 | Japan | 9.8 |
| China | 7.9 | Afghanistan | 8.4 |
| West Germany | 6.1 | Turkey | 6.4 |
| Czechoslovakia | 3.3 | Egypt | 5.5 |
| Italy | 1.9 | Spain | 5.0 |
| Netherlands | 1.8 | Czechoslovakia | 4.7 |
| Brazil | 1.6 | North Korea | 4.0 |

*Source:* Renner (1993: 147).

Most important, these wars have not produced the kind of lasting solutions one assumes Clausewitz had in mind when he wrote about war as politics through other means. For Americans, the most obvious example is Vietnam. Half a century after the Indochinese rebellion against the French began, much of the peninsula, especially Cambodia, is still in turmoil. Economically, most of Vietnam is as bad off as it was before the United States got deeply involved in the fighting in the mid-1960s. The United States has yet to heal its own wounds, as we saw in the protests during the 1992 election campaign against candidate Bill Clinton for opposing the war and avoiding the draft twenty-five years earlier.

It's not just Vietnam. It is hard to identify even one example of a recent war in which one side clearly won, ending the conflict that had spawned it in the first place in the way the Allied victory did in 1945. Instead, wars usually result only in limited victories and a temporary end to the fighting.

Some wars, including Grenada or the Falklands/Malvines, stand out because they were relatively minor conflicts, often pitting one very strong combatant against a far weaker one. More typical, however, are examples such as the on-again/off-again conflict between India and Pakistan or Israel and its Arab neighbors in which the end of one war does little more than intensify the resentment between the two sides and sow the seeds for the next one.

That will be clearer if we move away from the general level and consider two recent cases in more detail.

### Nicaragua

For a number of reasons which changed over the years, American policy makers have long considered Nicaragua and its neighbors vital to our own security. For more than a century, that involvement has fanned the flames in that tiny country and throughout Central America.

In the middle of the nineteenth century, Nicaragua was divided among loose groupings of politicians who called themselves Liberals and Conservatives, though they represented competing regional more than different ideological interests. The conflict among them intensified with the growing involvement of the United States and Great Britain in Nicaraguan affairs once the discovery of gold in California heightened interest in building a canal linking the Caribbean and the Pacific.

The first direct American intervention came in 1854. The Liberals were losing one of the periodic power struggles and turned to an American soldier of fortune, William Walker, who took over the country with his band of fifty-some "Immortals." Walker ran Nicaragua on and off until 1860, when he was captured and executed by the British.

American involvement in Nicaraguan affairs continued. Early in this century, the US government intervened to see to it that no second canal was built to compete with the one in Panama. American marines for all intents and purposes occupied the country from 1912 until 1925 and 1926 until 1933.

American intervention and its impact reached a peak later in the 1930s once Anastasio Somoza Garcia solidified his control over the National Guard and then assumed the presidency. He and his two sons would control the country until the revolution of 1979. Their corrupt and dictatorial rule is well enough known not to need recounting here. So, too, was their relationship with the United States, which President Franklin Delano Roosevelt once pithily summed up as, "Somoza might be an S.O.B., but he is our S.O.B." (Walker 1991: 108).

Opposition to the United States and its Nicaraguan "pawns" mounted as well, beginning with the movement headed by the wonderfully named Augusto Cesar Sandino. Sandino's execution in 1934 by Somoza's troops (if not Somoza himself) and the severity of the new regime's repression kept the lid on most protest until the 1970s. Then, the Sandinistas (FSLN—Sandinista Front for National Liberation) and other opposition groups expanded quickly. So did the fighting. Before the Somozas were finally thrown out of power and then out of the country in 1979, between ten and thirty thousand people had died.

The Sandinista victory settled little, and there would have been considerable resistance to their government whatever happened. But, the combination of Sandinista policy and the anti-communism of the newly elected Reagan administration led to the Contra war which lasted throughout the 1980s. The US-funded Contras, consisting of former Somoza loyalists and some of the old regime's opponents, fought the well-armed Sandinista regime. Estimates of the number of soldiers and civilians killed in the 1980s vary tremendously, from a low of ten to as many as seventy thousand.

This round of fighting ended when the Sandinistas called an election for February 1991, which they lost to a broad coalition of organizations which represented many of the Contra groups as well as other opponents of the regime who had not taken up arms. Even though Daniel Ortega handed the presidency over to Violetta Chamorro, there was no definitive resolution to the conflict.

The cost of the two most recent wars has been immense for Nicaragua and its people. If we take the most widely accepted estimate of about twenty thousand deaths as a proportion of Nicaragua's population and extrapolate it out to a country the size of the United States, that would be the equivalent of about 1.8 million people.

And the cycle continues. The Sandinistas remained the single largest party and continued to control the army and police well after losing the presidency. Little has been done to alleviate the country's poverty which had been worsened by nearly a generation of warfare. By mid-1991, perhaps as many as a thousand Contras had taken up arms, while the Sandinistas were threatening armed rebellion once again. The year 1993 saw a peculiar twin hostage crisis in which Sandinista-controlled forces and remnants of the Contras each held captives. Since then, there has been sporadic fighting, and yet another major conflagration remains a possibility.

Even this brief overview of Nicaragua's sorry history reflects the basic argument being made here. The stakes and the costs of the conflict keep growing, but any kind of lasting solution to the poverty, inequality, and underdevelopment that spawn the wars in the first place seems as elusive today as it was in the days of William Walker (for a conservative argument along these lines, see Hirschmann 1991).


### Iraq and the Gulf War

Much the same can be said for Iraq and the Gulf war. In early 1990, most Americans did not know who Saddam Hussein was or even where Iraq is. A year later, we were all fixated on events in Iraq because of its invasion and annexation of its small, oil-rich neighbor, Kuwait, on August 2, 1990.

Americans quickly learned about one of the more personalized and authoritarian regimes in the world. In the more than twenty years they had ruled Iraq, Saddam Hussein and the Baath party had assumed what came close to totalitarian power. While one could cite statistical and other sources about the repression, this single statement made by a taxi driver to *New York Times* reporter Ellen Sciolino tells it all. "One taxi driver explains the attitude of many Iraqis toward their President this way: 'This is car,' he says, patting his hand on the dashboard. 'But if Saddam says this is bicycle, it is bicycle.' He looks around anxiously and adds: 'he could kill me for saying this' " (cited in Denoeux 1994: 379).

Iraq spent the bulk of the 1980s fighting Iran. At least a half million people died in a war which settled next to nothing. In fact, the battle lines never moved more than twenty miles or so in the eight years of fighting.

By the time the war finally ended, Iraq had the fourth largest military in the world, funded in part by the United States out of its hostility toward Iran. In other words, the familiar logic of supporting one's enemies' enemies led American policy makers to give at least tacit support and sell arms to one of the most ruthless governments in the world, one of the very few to have used chemical and/or biological weapons on its own citizens.

The war also left Iraq on the verge of bankruptcy, which made oil rich Kuwait attractive to the Iraqi leadership. Over the years, many Iraqis had argued that what became Kuwait should have been made part of their country when the Ottoman Empire collapsed, though such views were rarely taken seriously.

Iraq renewed those claims during the first half of 1990, while also accusing the Kuwaitis of taking oil illegally from fields which lay below its territory. By summer, they were acting in ways which led some observers to believe they might try to take over Kuwait.

The situation was very confusing. American intelligence officials were divided. Some thought Iraq was planning to invade, while others thought Saddam and his colleagues were bluffing. The United States and other interested outside powers sent what the Iraqis took to be mixed messages about how a take-over would be received. For instance, the Iraqis assert that in a now infamous meeting, Ambassador April Glaspie told them that the Bush administration did not particularly care about what happened between them and the Kuwaitis.

Iraqi troops finally moved on August 2 and occupied tiny Kuwait in a matter of hours. Then, in an unprecedented display of international cooperation, most of the world community, including both superpowers and several Arab states, denounced Iraq's actions and called for its immediate and unconditional withdrawal. Within days, the first contingent of American and other troops were heading to the region in what then-President Bush called Operation Desert Shield.

During the fall and early winter, the US-led coalition issued a series of ultimatums and invoked tough economic sanctions in its attempt to force Iraq out. By January, Bush had become convinced that the sanctions were not going to work, Operation Desert Shield turned into Desert Storm, and the Gulf war began (Gordon and Trainor 1995).

Many Americans are convinced that this was not a particularly devastating war. Our images of it are dominated by television pictures of "smart" bombs accurately finding and destroying their targets, which some observers believe were a harbinger of technologically sophisticated and less bloody future wars (Toffler and Toffler 1993). The public focused on American casualties, which were very low, especially given the fears many had had about highly trained and dedicated Iraqi forces.

In fact, the war was very destructive for Iraq (Heidenrich 1993; Chomsky 1991). In all, the allied air forces flew eighty eight thousand sorties, relatively few of which included the widely publicized and highly accurate "smart bombs."

As is usually the case in warfare, casualty figures are quite uncertain. It seems that at least a hundred thousand Iraqis died in the fighting itself, the vast majority of whom were civilians. Much of the Iraqi infrastructure was destroyed, including most of its urban water supply, which led to the deaths of thousands more as a result of diarrhea and other diseases. Estimates are that it will take $70 billion to clean up the damage in Kuwait and $200 billion in Iraq.

And, one has to ask if the war really was worth the price.

To be sure, the allies achieved their most important stated goal by forcing Iraq out of Kuwait. However, they accomplished little else.

Saddam Hussein and his Baath colleagues remained in power (Kelly 1993). As the war ended, their government brutally put down revolts from the Shiite community in the southern part of the country and the Kurds in the north. It continued to resist international efforts to curtail its nuclear and other weapons research programs. In the summer of 1993, press reports suggested that the government had found the money to start a new missile program and keep alive some of its projects to develop weapons of mass destruction.

Saddam himself seems as confident as ever. On his fifty-sixth birthday, Iraqi television showed him eating a giant cake and riding in what the commentator called a "pure gold, horse-drawn chariot—a gift from his palace staff members" (Murphy 1993).

Meanwhile, the Iraqi people continue to suffer from war-related damage and the continuing sanctions. Most people cannot afford to buy the sugar needed to bake a birthday cake of any size. Government rations cover only about three quarters of people's daily caloric needs, medicine is in short supply, and inflation is eroding the value of what little money people have.

As one civil servant put it to Caryle Murphy of the *Washington Post* (1993): "People don't think about democracy or freedom. They think just about food. That's the way he [Saddam Hussein] wants it, so people can't do anything. People are not thinking about tomorrow. They can do nothing. There is no one to lead them. No one can get him out. No one. Even if the Americans landed in Baghdad, they couldn't remove him."

*     *     *

I could go on to explore other examples, but there is no need, because the point would be the same. The costs of war have risen dramatically, while the benefits that even the victor receives have shrunk.

## THE COST OF PREVENTING WAR

The people who are killed and wounded or the buildings and roads which are destroyed in the fighting are not the only casualties of war. We all are because the money preparing for war is eaten up.

The nations of the world spend a lot of money on "defense." During four years in the 1980s, global expenditures topped $1 trillion and then declined to "only" $934 billion in the early 1990s (Renner 1992). Total military expenditures have increased by a factor of four since the end of World War II and twenty five times since the beginning of this century (King and Schneider 1991: 48). In some LDCs, defense can account for as much as a third of GNP.

There are tremendous trade-offs or opportunity costs associated with defense spending. Ruth Leger Sivard estimates that the cost of a single ballistic missile firing submarine would be enough to double the education budget of eighteen of the poorest countries in the world, which have to educate about 130 million children (1991: 5). Similarly, the industrialized countries spend ten times as much on defense as they do on foreign aid.

Harry G. Schaffer eloquently summed up how we could use the trillion dollars spent globally each year on defense, instead, to meet social needs in this country. Schaffer wrote in Republic Airline's in-flight magazine, and thus focused on the area that now defunct airline flew to the most. I leave it to your imagination to figure out how that sum could be used elsewhere, where the needs are even greater:

With that amount of money, we could build a $75,000 house, place it on $5,000 worth of land, furnish it with $10,000 worth of furniture, put a $10,000 car in the garage—and give all this to each and every family in Kansas, Missouri, Iowa, Nebraska, Oklahoma and Arkansas. After having done this, we would still have enough out of our trillion dollars to build a $10 million library for each of 250 cities and towns throughout the six state region. After having done all that, we would still have enough money left out of our trillion to put aside, at ten per cent annual interest, a sum of money that would pay a salary of $25,000 per year for an army of 10,000 nurses, the same for an army of 10,000 teachers, and an annual cash allowance of $5,000 for each and every family throughout that six state region—not just for one year but forever. (Schaffer 1986: 24)

Many people claim, though, that we have to keep up our military spending, because it is good for the economy. After all, millions of people work in the defense industries, and technological breakthroughs from the military often have highly useful civilian spinoffs.

Recent evidence suggests that spending on the military is of limited value, even in this respect. As the wrenching experience of people being laid off from weapons plants shows, defense is an important sector in this and just about every other country's economy. There are plenty of examples of technologies being transferred to the civilian sector, including, for instance, the flat screen display on notebook computers.

On balance, however, the costs probably outweigh the benefits by quite a bit. The countries which devote the most money to defense (e.g., the United States, the former Soviet Union, Great Britain) have slower growing economies than those that spend less (e.g., Japan, Sweden, Germany), though military spending is obviously not the only reason why that's the case. Moreover, roughly a third of the money spent on research and development in the United States goes to defense related projects, which have fewer and fewer benefits for the economy as a whole.

When we spend billions on new weapons systems, the money goes into machinery that sits idly by (or so we hope). As a result, such spending generates relatively little additional economic activity. Invest the same amount, say, in a rapid transit system, and the "multiplier effects" generate jobs for the system's staff, spare parts manufacturers, taxi drivers, and so on.

One estimate from the 1980s predicted that if an additional $1 billion were invested in the defense sector, it would yield about 28,000 new jobs. On the other hand, if that same amount were put into public transit, there would be 32,000 jobs. A comparable investment in education could produce as many as 71,000.

## DOES WAR WORK?

In exploring warfare, my point has not been to criticize American policy, though there is plenty to be critical of. Instead, I have tried to make a broader point. Even if one accepts the premises that have led policy makers to turn to war, there is good reason to question the very mind set which holds that security can be achieved militarily.

Yet, most policy analysts and makers have not focused their attention much on the growing costs and difficulties discussed above. In many ways, the misperception that the Gulf war was relatively painless has reinforced the notion that one can still use warfare as an effective geopolitical tool, a point made most eloquently by the poet and essayist Wendell Berry:

Perhaps the most depressing development of this latest war is the idea, creeping into editorials and commentaries, that war is inevitable, that it will be inescapably a part of our national life as long as we are a nation, and that we can continue to be a nation only by going to war. We must be prepared to fight on and on, for we will inevitably meet competitors who will become enemies, and some of these enemies will be madmen or madwomen. Surely it is too soon to come to such a desperate conclusion, for there is one great possibility that we have hardly tried: that we can come to peace by being peaceable. (1991: 27)

It's not just long-time peace activists like Wendell Berry who are beginning to question war's purported benefits. In discussing recent efforts at peace making, John Keegan, perhaps the most eminent military historian of our day, argued:

This is not mere idealism. Mankind does have the capacity, over time, to correlate the costs and benefits of large and universal undertakings. Throughout much of the time for which we have a record of human behavior, mankind can clearly be seen to have judged that war's benefits outweighed its costs. Now the computation works in the opposite direction. Costs clearly exceed benefits. Some of these costs are material. The human costs of actually going to war are even higher. War truly has become a scourge, as was disease throughout most of human history. The scourge of disease has, almost within living memory, been very largely defeated and, though it is true that disease had no friends as war had had friends, war now demands a friendship which can only be paid in false coin. (1993: 59)

The problem, thus, is with what war actually accomplishes, whatever one thinks of the moral or strategic logic which leads to it, or of our unwillingness to use our creative abilities to develop those "peaceable" alternatives Berry refers to. For centuries, national security has been viewed as a country's ability to protect its territory, people, and possessions. For good or ill, war and the threat of war have been mechanisms national leaders believed they had to rely on in order to ensure that security.

Traditional techniques are by no means useless. The American policy of deterrence certainly had a lot to do with the end of the Cold War and the collapse of communism in Eurasia. But the benefits are declining and the returns diminishing.

## THE COMING ANARCHY?

The discussion in this chapter only tells part of the story. That's always the case when covering the first in a series of overlapping problems.

This chapter was written from the conventional geopolitical perspective used by most political scientists in analyzing international conflict. In this day and age, however, one cannot limit the scope of the analysis that much.

In 1994, Robert Kaplan wrote a remarkable article on what he called "The Coming Anarchy." In it, he combines the insights from his travels in more than sixty countries with his reading of some of the best academic writing since the end of the Cold War to paint a bleak picture of a world in which war and violence extend far beyond the state-centered domain of the traditional analysis of international relations.

He saw societies and governments decaying in Africa, Asia, the Middle East, and the Balkans. He has seen crime become increasingly indistinguishable from war; the environment, ethnicity, and impoverishment sow the seeds of intense conflict; and maps bear less and less resemblance to the realities of life. He expects things to get worse as, for instance, more and more people move to the filthy, overpopulated, and unhealthy shantytowns that surround virtually every city in the LDCs. He expects even more fighting as ethnic identity becomes more important to people and central governments can exert control over their populations. In his words:

To understand the events of the next fifty years, one must understand environmental scarcity, cultural and racial clash, geographic density, and the transformation of war. The order in which I have named these is not accidental. Each concept except the first relies partly on the one or ones before it.

If he's even half right, any attempt to deal with security today requires dealing with those issues which have not traditionally been part of policy makers' or professors' calculations. The consequences of not doing so could be tragic.

## REFERENCES

Berry, Wendell (1991). "What the Gulf War Taught." *The Progressive*, November, 26–29.

Brogan, Patrick (1990). *The Fighting Never Stopped: A Comprehensive Guide to World Conflict since 1945*. New York: Vintage.

Brzezinski, Zbigniew (1993). *Out of Control*. New York: Scribner's.

Chomsky, Noam (1991). "Aftermath: Voices from Below." *Zeta Magazine*, October, 19–28.

Cranna, Michael, ed. (1994). *The True Cost of Conflict: Seven Recent Wars and Their Effects on Society*. New York: New Press.

Denoeux, Guilain (1994). "Iraq." In Charles Hauss, *Comparative Politics: Domestic Responses to Global Challenges*. St. Paul: West Educational Publishers, ch. 14.

Dwyer, Gwynn (1985). *War*. Homewood, Ill.: Dorsey Press.

Gaddis, John Lewis (1987). *The Long Peace*. New York: Oxford University Press.

Gordon, Michael and Bernard Trainor (1995). *The Generals' War: The Inside Story of the Conflict in the Gulf*. Boston: Little, Brown.

Heidenrich, John (1993). "The Gulf War: How Many Iraqis Died?" *Foreign Policy* 90: 108–125.

Hirschmann, David (1991). "Nicaragua's Failed Coup: The Slow Pace of Reform." *The World and I*, November, 116–121.

Kaplan, Robert D. (1994). "The Coming Anarchy." *The Atlantic*. February.

Keegan, John (1993). *A History of Warfare*. New York: Knopf.

Kelly, Michael (1993). *Martyr's Day: Chronicle of a Small War*. New York: Random House.

King, Alexander, and Bertrand Schneider (1991). *The First Global Revolution: A Report by the Council of the Club of Rome*. New York: Pantheon.

Klare, Michael T. (1994). "Adding Fuel to the Fires: The Conventional Arms Trade in the 1990s." In Michael T. Klare and Daniel C. Thomas, eds., *World Security: Challenges for a New Century*. 2d ed. New York: St. Martin's.

————. (1995). *Rogue States and Nuclear Outlaws*. New York: Hill and Wang.

Murphy, Caryle (1993). "Sanctions, Saddam Wearing Iraqis Down." *Washington Post*, June 8, A17.

Renner, Michael (1992). "Military Expenditures Falling." In Lester Brown, Christopher Flavin, and Hal Kane, *Vital Signs 1992: The Trends that are Shaping our Future*. New York: W. W. Norton, 84–85.

————. (1993). "Preparing for Peace." In Lester Brown, ed., *The State of the World 1993*. New York: W. W. Norton, 139–157.

Schaffer, Harry G. (1986) "What a Trillion Dollars Would Buy." *Republic Airlines Magazine* (October), 24.

Singer, Max, and Aaron Wildavsky (1993). *The Real World Order*. Chatham, N.J.: Chatham House.

Sivard, Ruth Leger (1991). *World Military and Social Indicators*. Washington: World Priorities Institute.

Stockholm International Peace Research Institute (annual). *Yearbook.*

Toffler, Alan, and Heidi Toffler (1993). *War and Anti-War: Survival at the Dawn of the Twenty First Century.* Boston: Little Brown.

Walker, Thomas W. (1991). *Nicaragua: The Land of Sandino*, 3d ed. Boulder, Colo.: Westview.

Webster, Donovan (1994). "It's the Little Bombs That Kill You." *New York Times Magazine*, January 23, 26–33, 42, 51.

# 3

# THE ENVIRONMENT

It is time to understand "the environment" for what it is: the national-se-
curity issue of the early twenty-first century.

—Robert Kaplan

ester Brown (1988) introduced the Worldwatch Institute's 1988 *State
of the World* by describing the book as the world's annual physical exam.
Its "vital signs" weren't very good. Environmental deterioration had put
the earth into a kind of global intensive care. It was approaching the terrestrial
version of the medical crisis discussed in Chapter 1 when the very life or death
of the patient is determined.

There is a lot of debate in the scientific community about just how serious
the dangers are. Some think we are close to reaching what the Club of Rome
called the "limits to growth" a generation ago (Meadows et al. 1972, 1992)
and that we are causing such damage that the fabric of life and human
civilization will be damaged forever. Others think those limits are still far off
and that both people and the ecosystem itself are far more adaptable than the
more extreme environmentalists think (Bailey 1993). In their recent books,
Gregg Easterbrook (1995) and Frances Cairncross (1995) have made an even
more powerful argument about the striking progress which has been made on
the environmental front since the first Earth Day in 1970.

Even accepting those revisionist views, there is something approaching a
consensus among scientists and activists alike on the four main points to be

made in this chapter. Those points are important in and of themselves, but they are critical here, because they will take us far deeper into the argument about the global crisis outlined in Chapter 1 and provide a first look at what Einstein may have had in mind when he wrote about being able to solve a problem only by tackling it on a different level.

First, environmental degradation threatens us every bit as much as war. Environmental decay will lead to the extinction of thousands of species (though no one can predict how many with any degree of precision), the disruption of many aspects of human life, and perhaps the unraveling of civilization as a whole. Other environmental problems, like conventional wars, may not put the earth in the balance as Vice President Gore (1992) put it, but they have already taken a heavy toll, which seems bound to rise for the foreseeable future.

Second, the environment drives home the idea that a global crisis exists better than any of the other issues considered in Part One. Many environmental problems, such as global warming or the depletion of the ozone layer, touch each and every person and place on the planet. Most of the other seemingly "smaller" ones also transcend national boundaries in both their causes and consequences.

Third, combining the environment with war will give us a first glimpse at how the various problems discussed in this book intersect with each other. Ecologists frequently talk about "synergisms" or the complex and often unpredictable ways changes in one area, like the environment, lead to changes in others, such as the economy or international relations. Seeing the environment along with war here and with economics and race in the next two chapters will make it clear that it is all but impossible to study or try to change any one of these issues on its own.

Fourth and most important of all, considering the environment makes it hard not to question the very notion of security, which has been at the heart of most international relations and conflict resolution theory up to now. Already, environmental issues are sparking violent conflict around the world, and all the signs point to more of it to come. Environmental issues also help us see that the traditional way of looking at security as something a person or group or country seeks against others no longer makes much sense, because I cannot be environmentally secure if you aren't as well.

This last point opens the door to the new way of thinking which I will focus on in Parts Two and Three. Here, it's enough to see that it involves, first, putting interdependence at the heart of our analyses and actions and, second, fundamentally broadening what we mean by such key notions as security, self-interest, and winning or losing.

In writing this chapter, I have mostly used material from the Worldwatch Institute. Worldwatch is one of the leading organizations monitoring environmental and related trends. Some critics would argue that it is "overly" environmentalist. That may be, but there is little debate over the accuracy of its statistics, most of which are drawn from "mainstream" organizations (e.g., its petroleum and natural gas figures come from the American Petroleum Institute). Moreover, Worldwatch is one of the few organizations to provide a reasonably complete "run" of consistently and systematically gathered evidence. If you think this evidence is exaggerated, simply discount the material presented here by whatever fraction you feel is appropriate. Or, for a radically different perspective, see Ronald Bailey's acerbic, polemical, but extremely well researched *Eco-Scam* (1993).[1]

## LIKE BOMBS GOING OFF GRADUALLY

There is nothing new to the assault on our physical surroundings. At least since the beginning of the industrial revolution, people have been concerned about the ecological consequences of human actions. Read a novel like Charles Dickens' *Bleak House*, and you will see that even in Victorian England people knew what the soot from thousands of coal furnaces was doing. The United States' first environmental movement during the Progressive years at the beginning of this century was in large part a response to the horrid conditions in the cities about which the aptly named muckraking journalists had written. But it is only in the last few years that the destruction of the environment has reached globally dangerous proportions.

Today, people wield technological powers that take a far greater toll than anything the muckrakers of Theodore Roosevelt's day could have imagined. Back then, people had little impact on the whole system. When they cut down trees, depleted the soil, polluted the rivers, or poisoned the air, some people paid a price for those actions, and some species were rendered extinct. But the system as a whole was able to replenish itself. In the 1990s, we produce and waste a lot more, and we are therefore doing much more damage to the environment.

[1] The literature on the environment is voluminous, and much of it is fairly technical. However, there are plenty of good sources for a non-technical reader to turn to. Though recent research leaves much of his data dated, the best descriptions of these processes for a non-technical reader are found in the two books by John Gribbons (1988, 1990). Vice President Gore (1992) and the ecologist Norman Myers (1993) have effectively explored the environmental crisis and its broader implications.

The direst predictions anticipate climatic and other changes that would undermine civilization every bit as much as an all out nuclear war. The difference is that it would take the better part of a century to occur. It would be as if all those bombs went off a few at a time, not in the hours, days, or weeks of a thermonuclear "exchange."

At least three environmental problems are of a magnitude that they might have such an impact: the depletion of the ozone layer, global warming, and overpopulation. We will put off discussing the population explosion until the next chapter, where we will consider it as a link between the environment and underdevelopment. The dangers posed by the other two are summed up in Table 3.1.

Although ozone is dangerous to humans when mixed with the air we breathe as a major component of smog, we couldn't live without the layer of it in the stratosphere which keeps most harmful ultraviolet (UV) rays from reaching the earth.

There is no debate about the harm UV rays can do. They cause skin cancer and cataracts. Although we don't understand all the details, UV rays also disrupt the human immune system, leaving people more vulnerable to almost all diseases.

**Table 3.1**
**The Two Big Hazards**

| Years | Average Global Temperature (Degrees Celsius) | Global Carbon Emissions (millions of metric tons) | Global CFC Production (thousands of metric tons) |
|---|---|---|---|
| 1950–1955 | 11.99 | 1,807 | 65 |
| 1956–1960 | 12.03 | 2,334 | 119 |
| 1961–1965 | 11.95 | 2,814 | 250 |
| 1966–1970 | 11.98 | 3,576 | 512 |
| 1971–1975 | 11.99 | 4,425 | 842 |
| 1976–1980 | 12.10 | 5,015 | 882 |
| 1981–1985 | 12.20 | 5,059 | 970 |
| 1986–1991 | 12.33 | 5,697 | 1047 |

*Source:* Brown et al. (1992: 59, 61, 63).

Possibly more devastating are the effects UV rays have on some of the plants and animals in the human food chain. Soybeans, peas, barley, and cauliflower apparently would be among the crops most affected. Microscopic oceanic phytoplanktons are highly vulnerable, and any significant reduction in their population would alter the entire ocean-based part of our food supply.

Natural processes created the ozone in the first place and have continued destroying and creating it over the millennia. Now, as with so many aspects of the ecosystem, humanity is altering that balance.

The "culprits" are mostly CFCs, which were invented in this century and have been widely used in aerosols, cleansers, foams, and refrigerants. CFC molecules escape from such everyday products as Styrofoam cups and the freon in refrigerators and air conditioners. Eventually, they reach the ozone layer, where their chlorine is released. That chlorine begins breaking down the ozone, converting it into molecules that cannot block the UV rays.

There has already been considerable ozone loss above Antarctica and most likely a good bit above the Arctic and the northern midlatitudes, including the United States. Given the normal seasonal and geographical variation in the amount of ozone in the stratosphere, it is hard to estimate just how much ozone has disappeared. Indeed, it was only in 1990 (and only widely reported in 1993) that scientists could measure the atmospheric dynamics responsible for those seasonal variations. NASA estimates that there has already been a 4 to 6 percent loss of ozone in the midlatitudes which has allowed 8 to 12 percent more UV rays to reach the earth's surface (Pollock-Shea 1991). Each 1 percent of lost ozone translates into a 4 percent increase in cases of skin cancer. The loss of 10 percent of the ozone layer would mean that exposure levels in New York would be roughly those in Caracas, Venezuela today.

The human impact is already being felt under the ozone holes. In northeastern Australia, almost everyone over sixty-five has some form of skin cancer. A new law requires children to wear hats and scarves on their way to and from school.

In 1990, ninety-three nations agreed to phase out most CFC production before the end of the century. Although the averaging used in creating Table 3.1 doesn't show it, global production of CFCs was cut almost in half between 1988 and 1991. Despite that remarkable progress, we may not be able to reverse the damaging impact any time soon, since the CFC molecules already up there will continue destroying the ozone for up to another hundred years, during which time each one may destroy one hundred thousand ozone molecules. Meanwhile, we are still producing halons and other dangerous chemicals which may prove to have the same kind of impact on the ozone layer.

The dangers are as easy to see in the environmental issue that is receiving the most attention today, the anticipated rise in temperature known as global warming or the greenhouse effect. Put as simply as possible, carbon dioxide ($CO_2$) and other molecules rise, but do not escape the earth's atmosphere. Eventually, they come to act like a greenhouse, letting the sun's rays in, but blocking the heat reflected off the earth from going back off into space.

Until the industrial revolution, natural mechanisms regulated the amount of $CO_2$ and other potentially toxic compounds which would continue sustaining plant and animal life indefinitely. Since then, the burning of fossil fuels and other human actions have put more and more of them into the atmosphere. As Table 3.1 suggests, their presence has increased dramatically in the last generation. Given current projections, sometime between 2025 and 2050, there will be twice as many greenhouse gases in the atmosphere as there were before the industrial revolution.

The most commonly cited cause is the cutting down of trees in tropical rain forests, which reduces the number of organisms that take $CO_2$ out of the atmosphere. The damage is magnified because many of the trees are then burned, thereby creating even more $CO_2$ for the atmosphere to absorb.

In fact, the industrialized nations are by far the biggest producer of greenhouse gases, because they are the largest consumer of fossil fuels. The United States alone produces almost a quarter of them even though we make up less than 5 percent of the world's population. Each American puts about five tons and each car contributes the equivalent of its own weight in $CO_2$ into the atmosphere each year.

The accumulation of these gases is widely believed to be one of the reasons that the surface of the planet is gradually heating up. Six of the warmest years on record occurred in the 1980s. Scientists are not sure how much of this warming is due to the greenhouse effect. Nonetheless, there is almost no chance that all of it is due to random fluctuations in the global climate.

Similarly, no one knows how much warmer it is going to get. Many scientists believe the initial models of global warming overstated the rate at which the world's temperature will rise because, for instance, oceans can probably absorb more carbon dioxide and deforestation may not yield as much of it as previously estimated (Stevens 1993).

Most mainstream estimates now suggest that the greenhouse gases already in the atmosphere could produce an increase of as much as five degrees Fahrenheit in average annual global temperatures. If their emission continues at the current rate, the figure could easily reach twelve. To get a sense of how significant such a change could be, the best estimates are that during the last ice age, global temperatures averaged only about fifteen degrees below what they are now.

The number of ninety-degree days in Washington, DC could triple to nearly ninety a year. Enough of the polar icepacks could melt to raise the oceans by as much as seven feet. If so, most coastal areas, much of the Washington, DC region, and the entire Maldive Island chain would be permanently flooded. The Great Plains might be too hot and dusty to live in. Rainfall and ocean current patterns would be drastically altered, which could leave the British Isles dryer and colder but the Russian steppes warmer and wetter. The tropics would be especially hard hit, because their biota are most vulnerable to even minor climatic changes.[2] People might flock to the Yukon and Siberia looking for jobs and a hospitable climate. Like the great ice ages, the global warming could so disrupt things that untold but unpredictable numbers of species would simply disappear. *Homo sapiens* probably wouldn't be on that list, but it certainly would include many forms of plant and animal life that we now depend on.

There is a lot of uncertainty in the models and the predictions they render. Nonetheless, it seems certain that average temperatures are going to increase, which will lead to even wider fluctuations from year to year than we currently experience. As Christopher Flavin points out, "it is not the averages that kill, it is the extremes" (1991: 82).

The climate has changed dramatically and rapidly in the past. But that's not particularly good news either. Two teams of scientists have drilled deep into the ice in Greenland and discovered that the ten thousand years of relative stability in global temperature during which humanity has flourished have probably been the exception rather than the rule. They found that natural factors have produced shifts of as much as ten degrees centigrade in as little as two decades. Were that to happen now, there almost certainly would not be enough time for the world's farmers to change what and how they planted fast enough to feed all the world's people.

As with CFCs, no matter what policies are adopted, they cannot do all that much good in the short run. We have already sent enough of those gases into the atmosphere to produce a substantial greenhouse effect for years to come. It would take a reduction of at least 60 percent in greenhouse gas emissions to stop global warming. The most sweeping proposals put forth at the Rio Summit anticipate no more than a 12 to 15 percent cut.

---

[2]This point seems counterintuitive to many people. However, tropical plants and trees have evolved over the millennia under conditions in which average annual temperature swings are much smaller than they are in the midlatitudes where life has had to be far hardier in order to survive.

While the ozone layer and global warming have gotten the most attention, they are by no means the only environmental problems that threaten global security. The others may not have quite the worldwide consequences, but they are frightening nonetheless, something we can see by examining the extinction of countless species noted earlier.

Each and every day, between fifty and a hundred species are rendered extinct, at least one of which is due to logging operations in tropical rainforests (Myers 1993: 179ff; Ryan 1992). More than two thirds of all primate species and one fourth of the forty thousand known invertebrates in Germany are endangered, as are most species of wild cats and bears. In all, extinctions are occurring one hundred twenty thousand times more rapidly than they were before humanity started leaving its traces on the earth.

It is widely assumed that many as yet unstudied species in the tropics could have important biomedical uses, but not if they become extinct. It's not just human health that's at risk. The genetic ancestors of modern corn and coffee are found only in Mexico and Ethiopia respectively, and each is threatened with extinction. Such early versions of more recent natural "creations" are sometimes the only source of new strains which would protect existing ones against blight and other plant diseases. Their extinction thus might jeopardize two of the most important food crops in the world.

We really do not know very much about what so many extinctions will mean for those ecosystems, but the results *could* be catastrophic, and there is little doubt that they are already putting future evolution into question. As the remarkable popularity of dinosaurs reminds us, there were plenty of other periods with massive numbers of extinctions. In those cases, the so-called bounce back time before some new ecological balance was reached often lasted millions of years. This time, even more extinctions will probably occur over a briefer period, hence the importance given the pending biodiversity treaty negotiated at the 1992 Rio Summit on the Environment and Development.

The threat of massive extinctions brings us to a final, overarching point about the potential dangers human civilization and the ecosystem face: synergisms or the impact of one kind of change on the rest of the system. Such changes often amplify or multiply the impact of each other in the process.

That's the case because an organism or ecosystem already weakened by one environmental trauma is more vulnerable to others as well. The destruction of phytoplankton through exposure to UV rays is likely also to worsen global warming, because those tiny organisms are major absorbers of $CO_2$. It is also widely known but poorly understood that such environmental problems as polluted drinking water or air lead to diseases in humans. There are likely to be even more pathogens in a noticeably warmer world, which people will have to face with immune systems weakened to some degree by exposure to increased doses of UV radiation. Indeed, Norman Myers goes so far as to claim that "probably the biggest environmental problem of all on the horizon will turn out to be that of the interactions between lesser problems" (1993: 204).

To make matters worse, synergisms will not be limited to the environment but will almost certainly extend to all the issues included in Part One. Much of the rest of this first part of the book will explore their unpredictable, poorly understood, but extremely important connections. For our purposes here, a single example can make the case powerfully enough.

As of this writing, the Sudan is embroiled in a horrible civil war. Each night, government run television includes a half hour show glorifying a Sudanese (Muslim) soldier who has sacrificed his life in the struggle against the largely Christian southerners. The war had a number of causes, but the fighting and the tensions that led to it were all worsened by a severe drought in the southern part of the country in 1994 (Lorch 1994). The rains never came, and authorities anticipated a famine perhaps as bad as the one in 1988 in which close to three hundred thousand people died. In the meantime, the fighting picked up, and refugee camps and relief stations were among the targets. At least a hundred thousand people fled to Uganda and Kenya, joining the four hundred thousand Sudanese already in countries which can ill afford such an influx of economic and environmental as well as political refugees.

Western donors could only raise about 40 percent of the food Sudan needed to avoid mass starvation. The government and the rebels could not reach an agreement that would allow even these inadequate supplies to get through. Given the difficulties faced by Western forces in neighboring Somalia, no direct intervention seems likely. As one Western diplomat put it: "It is the forgotten war, the tragedy that is often swept under the rug. There isn't the political will in the US or Europe" (Lorch 1994: A3).

## IS THE AGE OF NATIONS PAST?

In 1936, Pierre Teilhard de Chardin claimed "The Age of Nations is past. The task before us now, if we would not perish, is to shake off our ancient prejudices, and to build the earth." The tragic history of the last sixty years suggests how much it has cost us not to have learned Teilhard's lesson. The environmental crisis, however, may best drive it home for us, because more than any of the other issues considered in Part One, these problems are transnational in origin and will all but certainly require transnational solutions.

The nation-state unquestionably remains the world's most important geo-political unit. On the other hand, the major environmental problems increasingly transcend national boundaries and cannot realistically be resolved by any one nation acting on its own.

Plenty of environmental problems are not transnational. The smog that makes the air unhealthy in dozens of British cities or the wastes that left every single river in Connecticut polluted in the 1960s have their sources and impacts in a single country. My region of northern Virginia has a monstrous solid waste disposal problem, despite a rather effective recycling program. New sites will have to be found, most likely in West Virginia. Our wastes will despoil our poor neighbor's land, but they are probably not going to have much of an effect on the environment of any other country.

But, that is not true of most serious environmental problems. All countries emit CFCs and greenhouse gases, though the industrialized countries, especially in the former Soviet bloc, do so disproportionately on a per capita basis. Much of the deforestation of the rain forests in the Amazon and Southeast Asia occurs to supply meat and tropical hardwoods respectively to "northern" markets. Recent research has shown that the increase in the carbon dioxide level over Hawaii, where there is relatively little industry, has been almost as rapid as over industrial regions of North America or the former Soviet Union. Similarly, the first hole in the ozone developed over Antarctica where no CFCs have ever been produced. The best-documented measures of severe depletion have been made in sparsely populated southern Argentina, though it should be noted that there is at least one major CFC-producing factory in the area.

Chernobyl is probably the best symbol of the transnational nature of the environmental crisis. Except for the area immediately surrounding the reactor, the worst impact of the world's worst nuclear disaster was not felt in that part of Ukraine. The greatest damage to crops in the short run and to human health in the longer term will probably occur in neighboring Belarus. Within a matter of weeks of the accident, enough radiation had spread throughout Europe to make the grass the reindeer eat in northern Scandinavia so radioactive that it was unsafe for humans to eat their meat, thus depriving the Lapps of a major source of income. Similarly, many fruits and vegetables were deemed unsafe in France, Germany, and Italy. After a few months, upper atmosphere winds had carried radiation from Chernobyl throughout the northern mid-latitudes, which means that people throughout the Northern Hemisphere will suffer from higher than normal rates of leukemia and other diseases, just as they did from fallout emitted as a result of above ground nuclear testing.

The transnational side of environmental decay is also easy to see in what is commonly called acid rain. Industrial plants emit large amounts of sulfur dioxide, which combines with water in the atmosphere to form sulfuric acid. The prevailing winds then carry the acid for hundreds of miles until it returns to earth as part of the rainfall. The acidic rain then poisons trees and other plant life and alters the pH level of lakes, making them unsafe for fish.

In the United States, emissions from midwestern industrial plants wreak havoc on the ecosystem of northern New England but have an even greater impact on Canada. Similarly, it is not only German acid rain which is destroying the Black Forest in Bavaria. Pollution from factories in several countries is damaging medieval buildings in Poland, hundreds of miles from its source. In the mid-1980s, over half of the emissions from eleven of the twelve leading European industrial nations were "exported" across national boundaries (Renner 1993; Feshbach and Friendly 1992). In perhaps the most spectacular example, emissions from a *single factory complex* in Russia are responsible for the death of about a quarter of the trees along the Arctic Circle in Finland.

In the long run, acid rain probably pales in comparison with the combined impact of deforestation and desertification. Every year, more than forty million acres of forests are lost (the equivalent of half of Finland) and another fifteen million acres (the size of West Virginia) turns into desert which cannot be reclaimed. Fifty million acres are so badly damaged that they can no longer be used for farming or grazing.

As with these other problems, some of the land loss is restricted to a single country, but much isn't. Take the spread of the Sahel for example. It has seemingly simple causes, including the work of women who cut down more and more trees for firewood needed to support a population growing at the rate of 3 to 4 percent per year. With fewer trees, there is less water in the atmosphere, which means that it rains less. The fragile ecosystem turns, and once marginal forests become deserts which inch southward year after year. The trees may be cut in Mali or Kenya, but the desert spreads across the continent.

A wide variety of forms of global pollution also imperils the world's oceans and other parts of the global water supply. As Nicholas Lenssen put it,

The last few years have been rough on the oceans. Hundreds of beaches along the Italian Adriatic were off limits due to an infestation of algae. Medical waste washing ashore closed beaches in many areas of the eastern United States. Thousands of seals died in the North Sea, possibly due to a combination of disease and pollution. A similar fate befell dolphins off the U.S. Atlantic coast. And in Alaska, a supertanker hit a reef and dumped a quarter million barrels of oil into one of the world's richest fishing grounds. Once thought to be so vast and resilient that no level of human insult could damage them, the oceans are now crying out for attention. (1991: 43)

There are many causes and consequences of all this pollution. Accumulating amounts of human sewage lead to algal "blooms" and other organisms which foul the beaches and reduce the yield of fisheries. Twenty-one million barrels of oil "accidentally" enter the oceans each year through leakages, runoff from streets, or ships flushing their tanks. As many as thirty thousand seals a year die from getting caught in plastic nets and bags, many of which were simply dropped by sailors who choose to use the oceans as a solid waste dump. Chemists have found that those same phytoplankton which are being devastated by UV radiation are also being killed off by toxic chemicals which reach the oceans from land and air. Once those toxins get into the water, it is very difficult to get them out. PCB, DDT, mercury, and other pollutants of human origin have been linked to tumors, ulcers, failed immune systems, and other fatal illnesses in whales.

Even more important here are the oceans' dynamics. While pollutants may have a single source, they do not have a single destination. Once they enter the oceans or any of the lakes and streams which ultimately feed into them, they become part of an interdependent system. Tides, winds, and currents move the water and the pollutants it contains all around. While that dilutes the pollution in the short run, in the longer run it gradually spreads it around the world. Eventually, the oceans could well run out of the capacity to absorb the pollution safely, just as it seems to be losing the ability to absorb excessive carbon dioxide from the atmosphere.

This last paragraph drives home the most important point of this section and perhaps of this entire book. The environment demonstrates not only that our problems are transnational, but that we live in a single, completely interdependent ecosystem. We will return to the broader implications of that interdependence in Parts Two and Three. Here, it is enough to note just how interdependent the environment shows our planet to be.

One does not have go as far as the most extreme chaos theorists, who argue that a butterfly flapping its wings over the Pacific could lead to a hurricane in the Atlantic (Gleick 1987), to see that our actions affect the entire system of which we are part. Sometimes, that system is quite small, as we have seen countless times as we have tried to deal with toxic compounds seeping into groundwater systems or the solid waste problems plaguing almost every part of the industrialized world. Sometimes, the system is planetary, as we are increasingly seeing in the most dangerous and visible environmental issues discussed here. The common point in each of these cases is that the impact of all of our actions ripple out until they affect everything and everyone else in the system.

## SECURITY

Most international relations experts date the modern state system from the Treaty of Westphalia in 1648. Since then, we have lived in a world in which the nation-state has been the most powerful actor, and security has been defined in geopolitical terms. Now, we are beginning to have to question the equation of security with geopolitical strength in part because of the importance of environmental issues.

The link between the environment and security actually has two dimensions. Each dramatically broadens what we mean by the idea of "security" itself, something relatively few political scientists but a substantial number of journalists and environmentalists have focused on (e.g., Myers 1993; Kaplan 1994; Meadows et al. 1972, 1992; Homer-Dixon 1991, Homer-Dixon et al. 1993; Kidder 1988).

The first dimension is the way environmental issues have become part and parcel of the kind of geopolitical disputes at the heart of international relations. That was hard to miss in the closing days of the Gulf war when retreating Iraqi soldiers set fire to hundreds of Kuwaiti oil wells. Millions of gallons of oil spilled onto the land and into the water. For days and weeks, the fires pumped clouds of sooty black smoke into the air, which the prevailing winds carried eastward toward the Indian subcontinent.

Scientists fresh from studying the Exxon Valdez oil spill and making projections about the atmospheric dynamics which might lead to nuclear winter and global warming began worrying about a possible environmental disaster here as well. It turned out that the long-term impact of the Iraqi destruction was not all that great, but who knows what will happen in the next war?

Environmental issues are already at the heart of a number of violent international and domestic disputes. Rarely are they the only cause, but they can be a major one, as we can see by considering a single set of environmental issues: how limited access to water complicates the already complicated conflicts wracking the Middle East.

Something like 40 percent of the world's population depends on water for drinking, electricity, or irrigation from one of the 214 major transnational river systems (Renner 1989: 32–34). That dependency is even more acute in regions like the Middle East in which there was a shortage of water to begin with, a shortage which is now exacerbated by rapidly increasing populations and the desertification in the headwater areas of many of those rivers.

Iraq, for instance, depends on the Tigris and Euphrates rivers for much of its water, the flow of which is largely controlled at dams in Turkey. In the months before the Gulf war started, the allies discussed cutting off Iraq's oil supply as part of their attempt to force it out of Kuwait. Even without that crisis, however, the two rivers have been a source of dispute. Turkey has been building a series of twenty-two dams on the rivers which are turning its Harran Plain into a lush agricultural region (Cooley 1984; Vesilind 1993). The problem is that when these dams are completed, less water will flow into Iraq and Syria, and the water which does get there will have a much higher salt content.

Similarly, Israel and Jordan essentially rely on a single, already heavily burdened aquifer for their water. Water-supply systems have frequently been targets in the many wars in the region since the state of Israel was formed. In the last few years both countries have had to accommodate huge new groups of migrants, more than four hundred thousand former Soviet Jews and three hundred fifty thousand Palestinian refugees from the Gulf war respectively. That means that ever more pressure is likely to be put on the water which is already in short supply, thereby increasing the likelihood of conflict.

Much the same can be said of the Nile. Egypt relies on the river to irrigate land it needs to feed a population which grows by a million every nine months. On the other hand, so do the other seven riparian nations, which together account for about 10 percent of Africa's population, including some of those most threatened by desertification. More and more demands are being placed on a finite water supply. In recent years, the Undugu group, which includes seven of the eight riparian countries, agreed on an annual supply of 55.5 billion cubic meters of water at Egypt's Aswan dam, but even that can't be guaranteed because Ethiopia is home to 85 percent of the Nile's headwaters but is not a party to the agreement.

These are by no means the only water disputes. France, Switzerland, Germany, and the Netherlands cannot agree about industrial pollution policy for the Rhine. A series of dams built along the Danube before the collapse of communism in 1989 divides Romania, Bulgaria, the Czech Republic, and Slovakia. Even the United States has problems with its two neighbors about the use of the water in the lakes and rivers that it shares with Canada and Mexico.

As Thomas Homer-Dixon and his colleagues (1991, 1993) see it, there is an important link between the environment and geopolitical security as we have traditionally defined it. The environment adds another source of tension that reinforces existing social and economic stresses and may be reinforced by them in turn. To return for a moment to the example of Sudan, the drought of 1993–1994 and the environmental refugees it produced made a bad economic, ethnic, and political situation worse. One cannot say for sure just how much worse the fighting is because of the drought and the refugees. The causal webs in such conflict are typically extremely complicated. Nonetheless, at the very least, environmental issues are in the causal mix and are creating geopolitical as well as environmental synergisms.

What's more, environmental issues have become part of the international process of "blaming" (Chapter 6 and Frank and Melville 1988). Thus, in the debate on global warming, northern leaders criticize southerners for cutting down trees in the rain forests, while they, in turn, point their finger at the North and its enormous use of fossil fuels. Similarly, northerners complain about rapid population growth in the South, while southerners do the same with northern consumption patterns (Durning 1993; MacNeill et al. 1991: 57). Both conveniently "forget" their own region's role while laying the blame on the other. This "habit" of putting the blame for one's problem on someone else's shoulders, which has long been a major force in international relations and will be a central part of the analysis of our modes of thinking in Part Two, is anything but constructive.

Jim MacNeill (chief advisor to Maurice Strong, Secretary General of the 1992 Rio Summit), Pieter Winsemius, and Taizo Yakushiji summed the situation up in their 1991 report to the Trilateral Commission, a group rarely thought of as a bastion of environmentalism:

Environmental changes at the regional and global level are anything but trivial. They form a class of issue for which there are few precedents. Every situation is driven by its own dynamics, but environmental changes that threaten peace and security are all rooted in economic and physical realities. History is in fact full of examples of nations fighting to gain control of, or to stop another nation from gaining control of, raw materials, energy supplies, water supplies, sea passages, and other key environmental resources. This type of conflict is likely to increase as certain resources become scarcer in face of growing demand, and as competition for them grow. (MacNeill et al. 1991: 54)

The second dimension takes the whole notion of security to a different level altogether by redefining what the very idea of security itself means (Myers 1993; Mathews 1989, 1994; Gore 1992; Lanier-Graham 1993; Kaplan 1994). As Michael Renner put it,

National security is a meaningless concept if it does not include the preservation of livable conditions within a country—or on the planet as a whole. Increasingly, countries are finding their security undermined by environmental threats emanating from other nations. Military means are not only impotent in the face of environmental security threats but are an obstacle to their resolution. Weapons production can directly cause environmental damage. And the military consumes much of the resources needed to stem environmental degradation. (1989: 6)

From this perspective, we cannot be geopolitically secure without being environmentally secure as well. What's more, environmental security is rarely something one country or group can achieve by exerting its power over someone else. There is no way Finland can force Russians to stop emitting so much sulfur dioxide or northern bankers can force the Brazilians to stop cutting down the rain forest or poor people in the shantytowns of the LDCs can force American drivers to stop putting that five tons of carbon dioxide each into the atmosphere each year.

In almost every case, solutions can only be found through cooperative outcomes that benefit all parties in the medium to long term, if not right away. Chapter 12 will explore some instances in which tremendous strides have been made through international cooperation, most notably with the Montreal Protocol on CFC production. But, it must be noted that while more and more people are seeing the value of such cooperation, it remains very much the exception rather than the rule.

## POLITICAL WILL

Lester R. Brown and Edward C. Wolf (1988) ended the 1988 volume of *The State of the World* with a chapter which is as powerful as the image of the earth in intensive care which begins it. They did an inventory of global needs in the following environmental areas: protecting topsoil on croplands, reforesting the earth, slowing population growth, raising energy efficiency, developing renewable energy, and retiring third world debt.

They made two remarkable discoveries (1988: esp. pp. 183 and 186). First, we know how to solve these problems. Second, doing so would be surprisingly cheap. They estimate what it would cost to solve these problems and achieve a sustainable economy using the period from 1990 to 2000 as their hypothetical example. Annual costs would have started at about $46 billion and reached a peak of $150 billion at the end of the period. The total cost would been under $1.4 trillion (of course, it would be a bit more were the program to start today given inflation and further environmental degradation since 1988).

That might seem like a lot of money, but given the total wealth generated around the planet over the course of a decade, it really isn't all that much. Take but the most obvious example. Assuming these funds could be taken from global military expenditures of (also assumed) $900 billion a year, the fate of the earth could be taken out of the balance and still leave $750 billion a year for defense.

Here is one place where Worldwatch figures have to be taken with a grain of salt. I'm certainly not enough of an expert to say that these estimates are accurate. But, even if they are off by 100 percent, that still leaves us with a bill the people and countries of the world should be able to handle. Similarly, even if these clean-up efforts would not lead us to a wholly sustainable economy which could yield lives of dignity for all, these programs would certainly make a major dent in the environmental problems discussed in this chapter and those of underdevelopment we will encounter in Chapter 4.

What's missing is the will, political and otherwise, to make it happen. That's what Parts Two and Three of this book are about.

## REFERENCES

Bailey, Ronald (1993). *Eco-Scam: The False Prophets of Environmental Apocalypse.* New York: St. Martin's.

Brown, Lester R. (1992). *Vital Signs 1992.* New York: W. W. Norton.

———. (Annual). *The State of the World.* New York: W. W. Norton.

Brown, Lester R., Christopher Flavin, and Sandra Postel (1991). *Saving the Planet: How to Shape an Environmentally Sustainable Global Economy.* New York: W. W. Norton.

Cooley, John K. (1984). "The War Over Water." *Foreign Policy* 54, Spring.

Durning, Alan (1993). *How Much Is Enough.* New York: W. W. Norton.

Easterbrook, Gregg (1995). *A Moment on the Earth.* New York: Viking.

Feschbach, Murray, and Fred Friendly (1992). *Ecocide.* New York: Basic Books.

Flavin, Christopher (1991). "The Heat Is On," In Lester Brown, ed., *The Worldwatch Reader.* New York: W. W. Norton, 75–96.

Frank, Jerome D., and Andrei Y. Melville (1988). "The Image of the Enemy and the Process of Change." In Anatoly Gromyko and Martin Hellman, eds., *Breakthrough: Emerging New Thinking: Soviet and Western Scholars Issue a Challenge to Build a World Beyond War.* New York/Moscow: Walker/Novosti, 199–208.

Gleick, James (1987). *Chaos: The Making of a New Science.* New York: Viking.

Gore, Albert (1992). *Earth in the Balance.* New York: Plume.

Gribbin, John (1988). *The Hole in the Sky: Man's Threat to the Ozone Layer.* New York: Bantam New Age.

———. (1990). *Hothouse Earth: The Greenhouse Effect and Gaia.* New York: Grove Weidenfeld.

Hawken, Paul (1993). *The Ecology of Commerce: A Declaration of Sustainability.* New York: Harper/Business.

Homer-Dixon, Thomas (1991). "On the Threshold: Environmental Changes as Causes of Acute Conflict." *International Security* 16: 76–116.

Homer-Dixon, Thomas, Jeffrey H. Boutwell, and George W. Rathjens (1993). "Environmental Change and Violent Conflict." *Scientific American*, 268, 38–45.

Kaplan, Robert D. (1994). "The Coming Anarchy." *The Atlantic*, February.

Kidder, Rushworth (1988). *Reinventing the Future*. Cambridge: MIT Press.

Lanier-Graham, Susan D. (1993). *The Ecology of War: Environmental Impacts of Weaponry and Warfare*. New York: Walker.

Lenssen, Nicholas (1991). "The Ocean Blues." In Lester Brown, ed., *The Worldwatch Reader*. New York: W. W. Norton, 43–59.

Lorch, Donatella (1994). "Drought and Famine Imperil 2 Million in Sudan." *New York Times*, February 10, A3.

Lovelock, James (1979). *Gaia: A New Look at Life on Earth*. New York: Oxford.

————. (1988). *The Ages of Gaia: A Biography of Our Living Earth*. New York: W. W. Norton.

MacNeill, Jim, Pieter Winsemius, and Taizo Yakushiji (1991). *Beyond Interdependence: The Meshing of the World's Economy and the Earth's Ecology*. New York: Oxford University Press.

Mathews, Jessica Tuchman (1989). "Redefining Security." *Foreign Policy* 68: 162–177.

————. (1994). "The Environment and International Security." In Michael T. Klare and Daniel C. Thomas, *World Security: Challenges for a New Century*. New York: St. Martin's, 274–289.

Meadows, Donella H. et al. (1972). *The Limits to Growth*. New York: Universe Books.

Meadows, Donella H., Dennis L. Meadows, and Jorgen Randers (1992). *Beyond The Limits*. Post Mills, Vt.: Chelsea Green Publishing Company.

Myers, Norman H. (1993). *Ultimate Security*. New York: W. W. Norton.

Renner, Michael (1989). *National Security: The Economic and Environmental Dimensions*. Worldwatch Paper #89. Washington: Worldwatch Institute.

Ryan, John (1992). "Conserving Biological Diversity." In Lester R. Brown, ed., *State of the World 1992*. New York: W. W. Norton, 9–26.

Stevens, William K. (1993). "Loss of Species Is Worse Than Thought in Brazil's Amazon." *New York Times*, June 29, C4.

Vesilind, Pritt (1993). "The Middle East's Water: A Critical Resource," *National Geographic* 183, May, 38–70.

# 4

# ECONOMICS

It's the economy, stupid.

—James Carville

J ames Carville wanted Bill Clinton and Al Gore to keep those four words on center stage throughout the 1992 presidential election campaign. He succeeded. In the process, Carville became something of a campaign legend, but his words turned quickly into a cliché as wags around the world played with them. Critics of the administration who doubted its ability to change the economy wrote articles with such titles as "It's *Not* the Economy, Stupid." Pundits used it to explain the French Socialists' defeat the following April. Others rewrote it to "it's the corruption, stupid" in assessing why the Miyazawa government fell and the LDP lost its first election ever that summer in Japan.

If we take a step back from the one liners, Carville's words seem anything but a cliché. The global economy itself is increasingly interconnected, and economic issues overlap with all the others that make up the global crisis. While other issues in the global crisis may get more ink or air time, it's hard to argue that economic interdependence is not one of the defining characteristics of our time.

Tangible signs of that interdependence are all around us. We wear shirts from Hong Kong, shoes from Italy. We eat bananas from Honduras, beef from Argentina, lamb from New Zealand, tuna from Ecuador. We drink coffee from Colombia, tea from Sri Lanka, cocoa from Nigeria, wine from France. We use tin cans from Chile, aluminum foil from Jamaica, televisions and VCRs from Japan and Korea, oil and gas from Saudi Arabia. We drive cars made by American, German, Japanese, and Korean companies which have factories scattered all over the world. Everywhere, people have come to rely on other countries and other peoples to supply their basic needs.

As was the case with the last two chapters, I am not going to try to give anything like a comprehensive overview of the "shrinking" global economy. I simply want to add the economy to the argument and illustrate some of the links between it and the issues considered in the last two chapters: security and the environment. For the former, I will concentrate on relations among the industrialized democracies, especially the changing role of their giant corporations. For the latter, the focus will be on the connection between economics and the environment in the developing world.


## THE ECONOMY AND NATIONAL SECURITY

There has always been a connection between the economy and national security. To cite but the most obvious historical example, the search for riches and new markets ("gold") was one of the three "g's" (along with "God" and "glory") that led Europeans to build their colonial empires in the last third of the nineteenth century.

If anything, economic issues have become more important in this century. In some respects, of course, the Cold War was a dispute between advocates of two sharply different and antagonistic economic systems. In the post-Cold War world, all the signs are that economic issues will be intertwined with the traditional "war and peace" questions of international relations more than ever.

Again, one example should suffice. Many think the Gulf war was really about a single economic issue: oil. The Iraqi invasion of Kuwait was widely seen as a moral outrage, but there have been plenty of comparable acts which have not elicited anything like the international response of Operations Desert Shield and Storm, as the tragic "ethnic cleansing" in Bosnia so horridly attests.

But what's more important today is the growing realization that economic strength itself is an indicator and even a determinant of national power. Americans see that most clearly in what many take to be our weakening relationship with Japan and, to a lesser extent, the fifteen members of the European Union (Prestowitz 1989; Tyson 1993; Sbragia 1992; Krause 1992).

Some go so far as to claim that economic power is or will soon be more important than military might in determining a nation's influence. No less a geopolitical expert than Michael Crichton had a protectionist senator proclaim in *Rising Sun*, his novel about Japanese influence in the United States:

Yes, I can tell you exactly why I'm disturbed about the extent of Japanese ownership of American industry. If we lose the ability to make our own products, we lose control over our destiny. It's that simple. We're now dependent on Japan—and I believe we shouldn't be dependent on any nation. (1992: 109)

While Crichton drew on some of the more extreme works on American-Japanese relations in researching *Rising Sun*, there is no denying that he was describing an important trend which is undermining American power to some degree. Japanese companies have all but destroyed the American consumer electronics industry. Only one American company, for instance, makes televisions in this country, and there are no significant domestic manufacturers of microwave ovens, stereo equipment, or VCRs. Japanese investors have bought huge chunks of real estate, especially in Hawaii, California, Texas, and New York. Japanese firms now own such American cultural icons as the Radio City building in New York and what used to be Columbia Pictures and Records in Hollywood.

By contrast, Japanese markets for many goods, including many high tech ones, remain largely closed to American products, because of rules and regulation which amount to unfair barriers to trade—or so the critics claim (Tyson 1993; Fallows 1994; for a contrasting view, see Emmott 1993a). American rice imports are banned even though Japanese consumers would only pay about one eighth as much as they do for domestically produced rice. Three successive American administrations have struggled to convince Japanese governments to allow American companies to sell 20 percent of the semi-conductors they buy. As this was written, the U.S. government was getting ready to impose stiff tariffs on Japanese cellular telephones, because Japanese rules and restrictions kept Motorola from getting even 5 percent of the market in Nagoya and Tokyo, while it captured about 40 percent of the booming market in the rest of the world. The Japanese have even kept American metal baseball bats out, arguing that they do not meet their higher product-safety standards.

The connection between national corporations and national power dates at least to the beginnings of modern capitalism. From the time of the British East India Company on, governments have tried to support the overseas efforts of their major private companies, while those firms have often seen their role as, at least in part, to be economic patriots helping support what they and their governments took to be the national interest (for much of this section, see Reich 1991: esp. ch. 3–5). That sentiment was perhaps best summed up in the often but inaccurately cited statement by General Motors CEO Charles Wilson, "What's good for General Motors is good for America."

It has only been with the development and spread of the modern multinational corporation (MNC) that the connection has taken on global significance and inspired fear in the hearts and minds of those who felt they were losing out to foreign competition (Emmott 1993b, Woolridge 1995). A generation ago, that meant Europeans worrying about what Jean-Jacques Servan-Schreiber called the American challenge (1968). In those days, it was IBM and ITT and General Motors and the Chase Manhattan Bank which seemed to be such a threat to what many still thought were the fragile economies of western Europe.

Today's concern is not an American, but a Japanese challenge. Mitsubishi, Mitsui, Matsushita, Toyota, and Hitachi are the behemoths to be feared. Those fears are only magnified by the historically close relationship between the big trading firms and the powerful Ministry of International Trade and Industry (MITI).

Whether one's worries are Crichton's from the 1990s or Servan-Schreiber's from the 1960s, thinking about economic security mirrors that about national geopolitical security, which we will explore in more detail in Chapter 6. Here simply note that the novelists and polemicists as well as the political scientists who have written on the subject tend to see economic, like military, power in zero-sum terms. Be it in national defense or the economy, the traditional view defines security in national terms and measures it as a function of the resources one country can exert over another or others to see its will prevail. IBM's gains in the 1960s or Mitsubishi's in the 1990s must come at someone's expense. If the Japanese win, Americans or Europeans lose.

There is a tremendous amount of foreign investment in the United States. Direct foreign investment grew from 2 percent to 7 percent of the total in the 1980s alone and is expected to reach 15 percent by the middle of this decade. Much of that is Japanese, because most of its $200 billion trade surplus is invested here. By the end of the 1980s, Mitsui, for example, had bought at least a third of the stock of seventy-five American companies, which earned it something on the order of $17 billion a year in revenues (Attali 1991: 52).

It's also important to understand that at the same time, Americans are investing their capital abroad. Maquiladora factories along the Mexican-American border, data entry operations in the Philippines, computer component factories in India, major league baseballs made in Haiti—the list goes on and on. Along with the opening of these and so many other direct operations of United States-based firms abroad has been an even more rapid rate of growth in foreign investment by pension funds. In 1987, they invested slightly less than $40 billion. Six years later it had reached $140 billion. And, as they have in the United States, the pension funds have often played an active role in the way those companies were run.

Virtually all observers agree that MNCs are even more powerful than they were in Servan-Schreiber's day. The smallest of the fifty leading non-financial MNCs, Texaco, had $7.8 billion in foreign assets and $18.0 billion of foreign sales in 1990. As Table 4.1 shows, all have their headquarters in an OECD country, and the largest, such as General Motors, General Electric, Ford, and Royal Dutch/Shell, have assets of well over $100 billion, which is more than the GNP of all but the wealthiest LDCs. The hundred largest non-financial MNCs had about $3 trillion in assets, about a third of which were from overseas investment. The one finding which might surprise some readers is that there are only seven Japanese companies on the list and the largest, Mitsubishi, only ranks eighteenth in terms of total foreign assets.

What the critics do is put these data in a new light. Observers like Secretary of Labor Robert Reich or former president of the European Bank for Reconstruction and Development Jacques Attali (1991) are convinced that the nature of that investment and those corporations has changed and in the process at least begun a change in the relationship between a country's economy and its security.

In particular, they point out that the link between the MNC and its country of origin is disappearing. The Americanness of IBM and the Germanness of Volkswagen are becoming facades (Reich 1991: 81; Ohmae 1995). Instead, he describes them as international networks or webs of smaller operations with little in the way of national loyalty and a shrinking identification of any sort with their nation of origin.

Typically, any single product will be designed and manufactured in a number of countries. In other words, few products can really be thought of as American or Japanese or anything else.

The miniaturization that made Macintosh PowerBooks possible, for instance, was mostly Japanese, but the software and chip design for them were mostly American. Other components come from at least a half dozen Asian countries, and some of the computers themselves were assembled in Ireland. Apple's headquarters may still be in Cupertino, but does that make all that much of a difference any more?

The big companies have really become *multi*national, locating manufacturing, training, and management facilities wherever it makes the most sense to do so from a business perspective. To cite but one extreme example, German law prohibits research on genetic engineering. Does that mean that BASF doesn't do it? Of course not, it simply does it outside of Germany. Where did it choose to locate its facility? In Silicon Valley, of course, the global center for research and development in the field.

Table 4.1
The Top 50 MNCs in 1990

| Country | Number of MNCs | Foreign sales—$ billion |
|---|---|---|
| United States | 13 | 358 |
| France | 8 | 101 |
| Japan | 7 | 167 |
| Germany | 5 | 111 |
| Britain | 4 | 124 |
| Switzerland | 4 | 69 |
| Netherlands | 3 | 101 |
| Sweden | 3 | 44 |
| Italy | 3 | 33 |
| Australia | 1 | 5 |
| Belgium | 1 | 5 |

*Note:* The total number of MNCs is larger than 50 since some (e.g., Royal Dutch/Shell, Unilever) have headquarters in more than one country.

*Source:* Adapted from Emmott (1993b: 6–7).

Given the growing nonnational nature of the MNC, the very argument that we should "buy American" makes less and less sense even for those people who have protecting American industry at the top of their list of priorities. Again, Reich provides a telling example.

When an American buys a Pontiac Le Mans, he or she engages unwittingly in an international transaction. Of the $20,000 paid to GM, about $6,000 goes to South Korea for routine labor and assembly operations, $3,500 to Japan for advanced components (engines, transaxles, and electronics), $1,500 to West Germany for styling and design engineering, $800 to Taiwan, Singapore, and Japan for small components, $500 to Britain for advertising and marketing services, and about $100 to Ireland and Barbados for data processing. The rest—less than $8,000—goes to strategists in Detroit, lawyers and bankers in New York, lobbyists in Washington, insurance and health-care workers all over the country, and General Motors shareholders—most of whom live in the United States, but an increasing number of whom are foreign nationals. (1991: 113)

If Reich is right, a consumer would protect more American jobs by buying a Honda!

These companies abide by the rules and laws of the "host" country and, in fact, act like any "domestic" company operating in that market. Thus, Sony markets the music and films it got when it bought Columbia the same way RCA and Disney do.

The modern, truly multinational corporation is emerging alongside another extremely important development, the emergence of three increasingly integrated trading blocks in Western Europe, North America, and the Pacific Rim of Asia (see especially Attali 1991; Garten 1992; Kennedy 1993; Cetron and Davies 1991).

Of particular interest is the European Union (EU), if only because it is the most fully developed of the three in institutional terms. The EU itself will be dealt with in Chapter 12. Here, it is enough to note two things. First, the removal of trade barriers and the emergence of an increasingly common market have made corporations ever more transnational and have begun stimulating a series of mergers, at least some of which blend publicly and privately held firms. Second, it is increasingly difficult for a nation state to define its own economic policy, because that is increasingly being made by EU authorities in Brussels.

All these changes affect national security, but not in the ways one mostly sees in the popular press or the international relations literature. In particular, problems in international trade do not typically lend themselves to zero-sum outcomes. Some do, but that is less and less frequently the case for the most advanced products and markets (remember that we are restricting our attention to the industrialized capitalist countries for the moment).

It still matters somewhat who owns these companies. More profits from American transactions are heading to Japan or Europe, and more control is being exercised in boardrooms there. But, we should not overestimate the degree to which that happens or even that it is important.

It is more important to realize that these relationships cannot be as parasitic as Crichton's senator or any of the real-life Japan bashers would suggest. As we will see in more detail in Chapter 7, it is becoming harder and harder for countries to assure their own security, because they cannot do so without assuring that of their competitors as well. In this case, Japan's economic security is increasingly dependent on the ability of its companies to succeed abroad, which can happen only if those other countries are prosperous enough to buy their goods and services.

In other words the whole debate about winners and losers in trade among the industrialized democracies may be missing two even more important points about it, the growing interconnection or inter*dependency* among these economies and the declining importance of the nation state as an actor in determining when, where, and how that trade takes place.

## UNDERDEVELOPMENT AND ENVIRONMENTAL DECLINE

I now want to extend that argument by exploring the overlap between economic development and the environment, as I just did for economic trends and national security. But, rather than doing so by exploring the North again, we will shift gears and explore the LDCs, where the apparent trade off between economic growth and environmental preservation seems even more pronounced.

Most were born with tremendous hope and optimism in the postwar years. The reality has not come close to reaching those hopes. As Table 4.2 shows, most of these countries remain mired in poverty.

In the poorest countries, their average annual $300 GNP per capita income is roughly what it costs an American undergraduate to join a fraternity or sorority or barely half of what is spent on disposable diapers during an American baby's first year of life (Durning 1993: 44). Also well known is a syndrome of economic (overpopulation, spiraling debt, unemployment, urban congestion) and political (instability, military and other forms of authoritarian rule) difficulties.

There has been some progress. In the LDCs as a whole, life expectancy has risen by at least fifteen years, adult literacy is up by two-fifths, and infant mortality has dropped by even more. In these and some other areas, the gap between rich and poor has narrowed appreciably. But in the late 1980s, average income in the South was still only 6 percent of that in the North. A quarter of

Table 4.2
Basic Differences: Richest and Poorest Countries

| Type of Country | % Pop'n Growth | Pop'n in 1990 millions | GNP per capital 1990 US$ | % GNP Growth 1965–1990 | % Illiterate |
|---|---|---|---|---|---|
| Poorest | 2.0 | 3,058 | 350 | 2.9 | 40 |
| Richest | 0.6 | 816 | 19,590 | 2.4 | Under 5 |

Poorest countries: Mozambique, Ethiopia, Tanzania, Somalia, Bangladesh, Laos, Malawi, Nepal, Chad, Burundi, Sierra Leone, Madagascar, Nigeria, Uganda Zaire, Mali, Niger, Burkina Faso, Rwanda, India, China, Haiti, Kenya, Pakistan, Benin, Central African Republic, Ghana, Togo, Zambia, Guinée, Sri Lanka, Lesotho, Indonesia, Mauritania, Afghanistan, Bhutan, Kampuchea, Liberia, Myanmar, Sudan, Vietnam.
Richest countries: Ireland, Spain, New Zealand, Australia, Great Britain, Italy, Netherlands, Belgium, Austria, France, Canada, Germany, Denmark, United States, Sweden, Finland, Norway, Japan, Switzerland.
Source: Hauss (1994: Inside cover).

the people in the LDCs live in utter poverty without access to adequate housing, food, or health care (King and Schneider 1991: 20–21). Finally, note that despite these improvements, it would take thousands of years for most of them to catch up with the OECD countries at current rates of growth.

Less well known are the environmental consequences of development in many of these countries. The twin pressures of population growth and industrial development are taking a terrible toll on the ecosystem today and could well be the source of intense political conflict tomorrow.

The world's population is growing at an accelerating rate. As Table 4.2 suggests, that growth is not distributed evenly around the world. The industrialized democracies are growing quite slowly (and much of that growth is due to immigration from LDCs; see Chapter 5) at a rate their economies, if not their environment, can readily absorb. That's not the case for the poorest countries where, overall, the total population will double roughly every thirty-five years. Egypt's population grows at the rate of a million every nine months. India adds the equivalent of Australia to its population each year. Within two generations, there will probably be as many Nigerians as there are people in all of Africa today.

Even using the most conservative estimates of population growth, the strains on the economy and the environment are likely to be tremendous. Take, for example, urbanization and other forms of migration. In the last twenty years, more than a billion people have moved from the countryside to cities, while 2 percent of the total world population migrated from one country to another, with most moving from an LDC to the North. The urban share of global population is likely to reach two thirds as compared to the half it is today. Mexico City could well reach thirty million, making the serious air and water pollution and transportation problems it already faces all but unsolvable. One fifth of urban residents and a far higher proportion of the rural population do not have access to safe drinking water, and those figures will only get worse as populations mushroom.

In order to feed this growing population, the land is being pushed near its limits, especially in Africa. As we saw in Chapter 3, the search for ever more firewood has led to the loss of two to three million acres of woodlands each year and the spread of the major African deserts. Over 80 percent of African land has some drawbacks for use in agriculture and an even higher percentage of its grasslands are in the process of being desertified (Mathews 1991: 368).

The point is not that there is a simple one to one correspondence between population growth and worsening economic problems. Enough food is already produced to all but eliminate hunger, and we could improve distribution systems or provide the hungry with more money so that fewer would starve

(Collins 1991). There is every reason to believe, too, that unlike the most Malthusian predictions, scientists will develop new seed strains or new technologies which would yield an increase in food production (Bailey 1993). On the other hand, given the pressures already placed on the ecosystem, the limited resources available globally during these rough economic times and the relatively low priority given these issues by most global policy makers, it seems all but certain that population growth will lead to worsened economic and environmental conditions.

Much of the debate on the LDCs has been about how much development is occurring and whether it benefits these countries politically or economically. For a generation now, dependency theorists and others have drawn our attention to the uneven nature of that development. Western firms and the relatively small number of mostly well educated people who work for them have done well. Some have made so much money that Kenyans invented a new Swahili word to describe them, the *wabenzi*, literally, the people of the Benz.

What often goes unnoticed are the environmental costs. Although the LDCs make relatively minor contributions to the looming ecological crisis, they still face serious environmental problems which are byproducts of industrialization.

Northern companies have relocated many of their operations which generate the most pollution to the South, a trend we saw most clearly and tragically in the disaster at the Union Carbide plant in Bhopal, India. Also, one has to consider the ecological impact of domestically introduced development. For instance, expanded mining operations have dumped tons of mercury into the Amazon and radon gas into South African townships, while similar efforts are draining Botswana's most important nature reserve (Durning 1993: 97). Automobiles in Bangkok emit about a ton of lead per day, not all that much less than in Los Angeles (Hurtado 1990). A million and a quarter cubic meters of untreated waste a day are dumped into the Chao Phraya River, which Thai officials estimate will run out of oxygen (and thus kill all aquatic life forms in it) by 2000.

With more development is bound to come more mass consumption, which Alan Durning estimates is the world's second most dangerous environmental problem, after population growth. Today, the industrialized world consumes anywhere between three (fresh water, grains, fish, cement) and nearly twenty (chemicals and aluminum) times as much as the developing countries (Durning 1993: 50). The average American uses at least thirty times as much energy as the average Indian, Indonesian, Nigerian, or Bangladeshi. Most estimates suggest that if population remains stable (which, of course, it will not), the developing world would need to use at least five times as much energy over the next few decades (assuming there are no major technological breakthroughs on that front) to meet their people's basic human needs (MacNeill et al. 1991). The same holds for almost any commodity one can imagine, such as the number of automobiles, the amount of meat eaten, or the quantities of plastic used for packaging.

There is mounting evidence that the very process of development is taking a heavy toll on the environment. As with so much in this book, we could pile statistic upon statistic, but the point can be made just as forcefully by posing one simple, but vexing, question. What is going to happen as more and more people get what some Japanese call the "new three sacred treasures," a color television, a car, and an air conditioner?

Desertification, soil erosion, water shortages, and other damage to croplands plus the burgeoning rural population have put serious pressures on rural areas. During the 1980s, grain production declined in more than two-thirds of African countries and three-fourths of Latin America (Freeman 1990). There is some fear that there has been so much damage to the land and water supply that agricultural systems will no longer have the capacity to keep up with population growth given known or even anticipated agricultural technologies. Those same trends have created millions of what can only be termed "environmental refugees" who are flocking to cities in the LDCs and adding to that pool of frustrated and often desperate people who could well be the catalyst for conflict and war (MacNeill et al.: 57).

No one has shown that link any better than Roger Stone in his account of development projects and environmental problems from the late 1980s and early 1990s (1992). Stone does offer some instances in which developers and environmentalists have cooperated, but his book concentrates on the far more common tale of development harming the environment.

An all-too-typical example is the growth of Parauapebas in Brazil's Amazonia (Stone 1992: 12–21, 74–83). In the 1970s, very few outsiders visited the region, but that changed when iron and then gold were discovered. The mining itself did relatively little damage to the ecosystem, since the ore lay practically on the surface and the company that ran the mines did a pretty good job of cleaning up afterward. Its sixty-eight hundred workers lived in a well-maintained and self-contained community which Stone called a "tropical Levittown" (17).

The same cannot be said for the town of Parauapebas, which grew up overnight into an urban slum whose ten thousand residents lived without adequate shelter, sewage facilities, or health care. Poverty stricken families from elsewhere in the country were given tracts of forest land to farm, which of course meant cutting down the trees. As is often the case in rain forests, the soil isn't very rich, and after a year or two of good harvests, it was depleted. Now these families eke out at best a marginal existence.

The problems don't end in the immediate Parauapebas region. The city of Marabà to its south has pinned its developmental hopes on smelting the pig iron from Parauapebas. At the time of Stone's last visit in 1990, two factories were ready to begin operations and two others were under construction. Unfortunately for the environment, the factories will use the worst form of energy possible, charcoal, which means that even more trees will be cut and more pollution than necessary generated in the manufacturing process. Meanwhile, development took its toll on the indigenous peoples who had been living rather peacefully in the area. In what Stone calls the military government's policy of "unstated genocide," their population was reduced from several million to barely two hundred thousand in a couple of decades. Some were forced to migrate and blend into the larger Brazilian population. Many others died of mercury poisoning from the mines, infectious diseases brought by the people moving into the region, or from attacks by people who felt, as the military government did, that these groups stood in the way of development.

To make matters even worse, the economic and environmental problems are magnified by the fact that more money flows from South to North than vice versa. Despite the foreign aid and investment in the developing world, the combination of imports to the region and payment of massive debt tilts the balance away from the countries and people who need the money the most, to the tune of about $50 billion in 1989 alone (Speth 1990). The outflow of resources and other economic problems may be the most pronounced in the countries which have the most severe environmental difficulties. Thus, of the fourteen countries that were most responsible for deforestation, only one (Zaire) had a total external debt below $10 billion in 1987. India and Indonesia both owed close to $50 billion. Mexican debt exceeded $80 billion, and Brazil topped the list with nearly $110 billion (Speth 1990).

Finally, it is by no means clear that the global shift toward free trade will be a universal blessing. There is reason to believe that overall growth may rise, which may benefit entire societies over time. In the short run, however, the transition to freer trade and more open markets may actually exacerbate the problems mentioned here, because markets have never been very effective at promoting more equality or providing "collective goods" such as environmental protection.

All this led the men and women who planned the 1992 Rio Summit to argue that environmental protection and economic development are two sides of the same policy coin. Northern countries cannot expect the South to protect the environment at the cost of the very survival of its people. Similarly, northern countries cannot expect the South to protect the environment if the North doesn't first take the lead on such issues as global warming and the depletion of the ozone layer, because they are by far the biggest source of the problem.

While there is widespread agreement that this is the case and while there are plenty of constructive proposals on such things as debt for nature swaps, remarkably little progress has been made. Some tentative steps have been taken with the creation of the Global Environmental Facility and other decisions made at the Rio Summit, the Montreal Protocol on CFCs, and so on. There is reason to believe, too, that biotechnology or some other scientific break-through could alleviate many of the worst Malthusian predictions early in the next century, much as the Green Revolution did in India and elsewhere a generation ago.

But the key word here is tentative.

## WHAT IS THE ECONOMY, STUPID?

Carville's statement and the strategy that lay behind it seem simple enough. But if a growing group of economists, environmentalists, and political scientists are right, our conventional ways of looking at the economy are pretty stupid themselves. By seeing that, we can move one step closer to the new ways of thinking and acting that will be the focus of Part Two of this book.

Basically, these observers criticize mainstream analysts and policy makers for not including the full and long-term costs of production into the accounting systems used to measure profit, loss, growth, efficiency, and just about every other economic indicator.

Ecologically oriented economists are urging the rest of us to include the environmental costs of growth in such traditional measures as GNP (Cline 1992; World Bank 1991). Doing so will show that people in many other LDCs are actually 20 percent or so poorer than those statistics suggest (Mathews 1991: 376).

However, the former business executive Paul Hawken (1993) and the renowned economist Hazel Henderson (1991) think we need to go even further in incorporating the environment into economic calculations. Hawken approaches the subject as someone who organized one of the first organic food distribution companies in the United States and then a gardening supply company which won a number of environmental awards. As someone in business, Hawken tends to take a bottom-line approach to economic issues, but he is convinced we use a faulty and potentially disastrous bottom line.

Despite all the advantages that markets bring, Hawken claims they fail to take into account environmental and other long-term costs of production. The price of gasoline does not include the cost of the smog, greenhouse gases, and other pollutants it produces, let alone the cost of finding alternate sources of energy once the oil is gone (1993: 75ff). He cites a study that suggests that incorporating the cost of health care for smokers would add at least another $3 to the "real price" of a pack of cigarettes. Non-organic food costs less than most organic products in the supermarket in large part because the impact of pesticides and other inputs on the land and on humans are never factored in. In almost every area of production, the failure to include the cost of the natural resources themselves or that of sustaining the environment after production leads to a distorted picture of what economic life is really like.

Henderson goes even farther and questions the neo-classical economists' intellectual point of departure: individuals and firms acting independently and autonomously in pursuit of their self-interest in the relatively short run. The mounting evidence on the interdependence rather than the independence of life leads her to say we need to start again from scratch with a whole new paradigm.

What we see emerging today in all industrial societies are basic value and behavior shifts, new perceptions and an emerging paradigm, based on facing up to a new awareness of planetary realities and confirmed by a "post-Cartesian" scientific world-view based on biological and systemic life sciences, rather than inorganic, mechanistic models. (1991: 18)

Thinking in these new ways brings us back to what also seems to be the oldest way of thinking about the economy. Hawken tells us (1993: 58–59) that the English "economics" is derived from the Greek *oikonomia*. Oikonomia had nothing to do with short-term profit and loss, that apparently was the province of *chrematistics*. Instead, oikonomia dealt with the careful management of the household for the benefit of all its members. In Hawken's terms, "if we expand the concept of household to include the larger community of the land, of shared values, resources, biomes, institutions, language, and history, then we have a good definition of 'economics for community' " (1993: 59).

## REFERENCES

Attali, Jacques (1991). *Millennium: Winners and Losers in the Coming World Order.* New York: Times Books.
Bailey, Ronald (1993). *Eco-Scam: The False Prophets of Ecological Apocalypse.* New York: St. Martin's.
Brown, Lester (1994). *The State of the World 1994.* New York: W. W. Norton.
Cetron, Marvin, and Owen Davies (1991). *Crystal Globe: The Haves and Have-Nots of the New World Order.* New York: St. Martin's.

Cline, William R. (1992). *The Economics of Global Warming*. Washington: Institute for International Economics.

Collins, Joseph (1991). "World Hunger: A Scarcity of Food or a Scarcity of Democracy?" In Michael T. Klare and Daniel C. Thomas, eds., *World Security: Trends and Challenges at Century's End*. New York: St. Martin's, 345–361.

Crichton, Michael (1992). *Rising Sun*. New York: Ballantine.

Durning, Alan (1993). *How Much Is Enough: The Consumer Society and the Future of the Earth*. New York: W. W. Norton.

Emmott, Bill (1993a). *Japanophobia: The Myth of the Invincible Japanese*. New York: Times Books.

————. (1993b) "Multinationals: A Survey." *The Economist*. March 27.

Fallows, James (1994). *Looking at the Sun*. New York: Pantheon.

Freeman, Orville (1990). "Meeting the Food Needs of the Coming Decade: Agriculture vs. the Environment." *The Futurist*, November/December, 15–20.

Friedman, Milton (1962). *Capitalism and Freedom*. Chicago: University of Chicago Press.

Garten, Jeffrey E. (1992). *A Cold Peace: America, Japan, Germany, and the Struggle for Supremacy*. New York: Times Books.

Hauss, Charles (1994). *Comparative Politics: Domestic Responses to Global Challenges*. St. Paul: West Educational Publishers.

Hawken, Paul (1993). *The Ecology of Commerce: A Declaration of Sustainability*. New York: W. W. Norton.

Henderson, Hazel (1991). *Paradigms in Progress: Life Beyond Economics*. Indianapolis: Knowledge Systems, Inc.

Hurtado, Maria Elena (1990). "Green Economics: Growth Up in Smoke?" *South: The Third World Magazine* (London), June, 11–13,15.

Kennedy, Paul (1993). *Preparing for the Twenty-First Century*. New York: Random House.

King, Alexander, and Bertrand Schneider (1991). *The First Global Revolution: A Report by the Council of the Club of Rome*. New York: Pantheon.

Krause, Axel (1992). *Inside the New Europe*. New York: HarperCollins.

MacNeill, Jim, Pieter Winsemius, and Taizo Yakushiji (1991). *Beyond Interdependence: The Meshing of the World's Economy and the Earth's Ecology*. New York: Oxford University Press.

Mathews, Jessica Tuchman (1991). "The Environment and International Security." In Michael T. Klare and Daniel C. Thomas, eds., *World Security: Trends and Challenges at Century's End*. New York: St. Martin's, 362–380.

Ohmae, Kenichi (1995). *The End of the Nation State: The Rise of Regional Economies*. New York: Free Press.

Prestowitz, Clyde (1989). *Trading Places*. Paperback edition. New York: Basic Books.

Reich, Robert (1991). *The Work of Nations: Preparing Ourselves for 21st-Century Capitalism*. New York: Knopf.

Sbragia, Alberta (1992). *Europolitics*. Washington: Brookings Institution.

Servan-Schreiber, Jean-Jacques (1968). *The American Challenge.* New York: Atheneum.
Speth, James Gustave (1990). "Coming to Terms: Toward a North-South Compact for the Environment." *Environment,* June, 16–20, 40–43.
Stone, Roger D. (1992). *The Nature of Development: A Report from the Rural Tropics on the Quest for Sustainable Economic Growth.* New York: Knopf.
Tyson, Laura d'Andrea (1993). *Who's Bashing Whom?* Washington: Institute for International Economics.
Woolridge, Adrian (1995). "Big is Back: A Survey of the Multinationals," *The Economist,* June 24.
World Bank (1991). *The World Bank and the Environment: A Progress Report. Fiscal 1991.* Washington: World Bank.

# 5

# MINORITIES

People, can't we get along?

—Rodney King

On October 21, 1993, Tutsi soldiers in Burundi attempted a coup. The newly elected Hutu President Melchior Ndadaye and five other officials were killed. Fighting between the Tutsi and Hutu spread around the country in a matter of hours. There are still no reliable estimates of how many people died, but all observers agreed that the number easily topped the twenty thousand killed in 1988, the last time the two clashed. In all, about two hundred thousand people, or five percent of the country's current population, have died in ethnic clashes in the first thirty years since Burundi gained its independence. During the first week of fighting in 1993 alone, nearly six hundred thousand refugees fled to neighboring countries with perhaps another hundred thousand displaced within Burundi.

In April 1994, the Presidents of Burundi and Rwanda were flying into Kigali, the latter's capital, after a negotiating session in Tanzania. Their plane crashed under what are still mysterious circumstances. Everyone on board was killed. The crash touched off a massive wave of violence in Rwanda in which Tutsis killed Hutus and vice versa once again. As many as two hundred thousand people were killed before the month was out. At least that many refugees fled into neighboring Tanzania in a single day. As this book went to press, there was still sporadic fighting and periodic reports of torture, murder, and other human rights abuses in the refugee camps. No one dares predict what might happen next, but another round of bloody fighting is certainly a possibility.

Burundi and Rwanda, of course, are not alone. In April 1993, the editors of *Current History* counted some forty-seven violent ethnic conflicts taking place around the world (*Current History* 1993). No more than twenty of the 185 member states of the United Nations are ethnically homogeneous, if by that we mean minority groups make up less that 5 percent of the population. And if ethnic tensions continue to rise, so, too, will the violence they spawn (Kaplan 1994).

Ethnic conflict is also spreading internationally as we also saw so tragically in Burundi and Rwanda. Few ethnic groups are confined to a single country. Most instances of ethnic conflict also create a flood of refugees who often magnify existing tensions in the countries they come to settle in.

No single conflict over race, religion, or language could wreak the havoc of an all out nuclear war or of global warming. Taken together, however, the cumulative impact of multiple conflicts could be nearly as devastating because of the chaos these struggles leave in their wake. As the eminent French student of international relations, Pierre Hassner, recently put it:

It is not only the order of Yalta (bipolarity and the Cold War) and the order of Versailles (the borders and states that emerged from the Ottoman and the Austro-Hungarian Empires) that are being challenged. The order of Westphalia—the idea of a system based on territoriality and the sovereignty of states—is also being called into question. (1993: 129)

Ethnic conflict is all the more important to our understanding of the global crisis because, until recently, many observers had expected it to decline. In the academic world, scholars like Daniel Lerner (1958) argued that spread of the mass media and other modern technologies would incorporate not just the Turkish he studied but the LDCs as a whole into the "twentieth century." Sometimes explicitly, sometimes implicitly, people like Lerner assumed that as people learned more about the outside (i.e., western) world, they would shed their traditional values, which would give way to a more cosmopolitan attitude in which one's racial or ethnic or religious identification would matter less and less.

It didn't take long for the optimism to fade.

In the week after President Johnson signed the Voting Rights Act of 1965, a riot broke out in Watts. By the end of the decade, virtually every major city had been hit. Dr. Martin Luther King's dream of an integrated United States was replaced by black power and then a worrisome backlash among "Reagan

Democrats" in the white community which has been a powerful political force since then, including in the 1994 Republican landslide (Edsall and Edsall 1991).

Within another year or two it was impossible to miss the role that ethnicity and related issues continued to play in the rest of the world. In 1967, Israel and its Arab adversaries went to war again. Then, Nigeria, once seen as the most promising of the new African states, was beset by civil war when the predominantly Igbo east declared its independence and sought to create the new state of Biafra. The resurgence of racial, ethnic, linguistic, and religious concerns was driven home for Americans when Islamic fundamentalists overthrew the Shah in Iran and then a group of young activists occupied the United States Embassy in Tehran and held sixty-seven Americans hostage for 464 days.

We had come full circle. Rather than breaking down parochial attitudes, the spread of modern technologies often *reinforced* them. "Cosmopolitanism" increasingly gave way to what Robin Wright (1985) so aptly calls "sacred rage." In the Islamic movements she studied, the rage was religious in origin. In others, it is based on racial or ethnic identity. In every case, the operative term is rage, be it of the fundamentalists who exploded a bomb under the World Trade Center, the dozens of ethnic groups who are fighting it out in what used to be the Soviet Union, or the Israeli doctor who stormed into a mosque in Hebron and killed upwards of fifty Palestinians shortly after the PLO-Israeli peace accords were signed.

Ethnicity and related issues are by no means a new force in international or domestic political life (Moynihan 1993; Lauren 1988; Goldberg 1990). They figure in the conflicts enumerated in the Bible and other sacred texts. They were, of course, a primary force behind classical imperialism and the arrogant desire to take on Rudyard Kipling's "white man's burden." What's new is the more general role these issues are playing in the global crisis, especially their severity and their connection with the other daunting problems countries around the world face (Brown 1993).

No one put it better than the then eighty-two year old Sir Isaiah Berlin in an interview he gave the *New York Review of Books* in 1991. "In our modern age, nationalism is not resurgent; it never died. Neither did racism. They are the most powerful movements in the world today, cutting across many social systems. I am glad to be as old as I am" (Berlin 1991: 19, 23).

## THE SCOPE OF THE PROBLEM

Of all the issues considered in this book, the problems faced by minorities are the hardest to document, because the study of them is filled with all kinds

of intellectual confusion. The very notion of what a "minority" is lends itself
to tremendous uncertainty, because the groups people identify with as well as
the way they are identified by outsiders varies over time (for a jargon-free
version of what is often a highly abstract discussion, see Pfaff 1993: ch. 2).

Consider this simple example. In the 1920s, the curator of the Bronx Zoo,
Madison Grant, published his influential book, *The Passing of the Great Race*.
In it, he lamented the fact that such inferior "races" as the Nordics, Slavs, and
Mediterraneans made up a larger and larger part of the American population.
He wrote at a time when many people thought that Jews or Poles or the Irish
constituted separate and inferior races and the Ku Klux Klan attacked Catholics
as well as African Americans. Today, just about everyone lumps all these groups
of European extraction together as whites, and there are undoubtedly some
Catholic members of the Klan's several branches.

In short, simply determining who the minorities are is no mean feat.

The most recent attempt to do so was coordinated by Ted Robert Gurr
(1993) of the University of Maryland. Gurr used relatively strict criteria in
identifying what he calls "minorities at risk." His team of researchers gathered
information only on groups that had at least one hundred thousand members
in a country with at least a million people. To be included, a group also had to
have been the object of systematic discrimination and have mounted some sort
of protest or organization in defense of its interests at some time between 1945
and 1990. That set of criteria left out a number of important communal groups
which did not meet Gurr's criteria for the time period in question but certainly
would now, including Francophones in the Flemish region of Belgium and
literally dozens in the formerly communist countries of Eurasia.

In all, Gurr identified 233 minorities groups at risk in 93 of the 127
countries that met his criteria (Gurr 1993: 10ff). The groups include over nine
hundred million people or a bit over 17 percent of the world's population.
They fall into five types: "ethnonationalists" who have experienced a degree of
political autonomy in the past and are demanding more now, "indigenous
peoples" who are descendants of conquered groups who typically live on a
country's periphery, "ethnoclasses" who are usually immigrants or descendants
of them, "militant sects" who base their claims on religious grounds, and a
looser group, "communal contenders," made up of culturally distinct groups
in heterogeneous societies which make claims on political power, some of
whom may actually be wealthier and more influential than the country's
majority group.

Gurr's research suggests that there is tremendous variation in what different
types of groups have done in the nearly half century he studied. Nonetheless,
there are two overarching trends in his data. First, economic, demographic,

and environmental forces are major causes of most ethno-political conflict (esp. 87). Second, there has been a tremendous increase in the amount of conflict and protest involving these minorities in the last half century (esp. 101–112).

Gurr's project has demonstrated the links between ethnicity and the other issues considered in Part One here. As is always the case with such statistical studies, it's hard to see how these various issues tie together in the "real world." Therefore, the rest of this chapter will explore specific examples that illustrate those broader trends Gurr and others have uncovered.

## RACE AND THE ENVIRONMENT

Drawing the link between race and the environment is the hardest element of Part One to document. That's not because the link isn't there, but is simply a function of the fact that it has received less attention than any of the others, especially outside the United States.

More attention is being paid today to what the activists call environmental racism in the United States (Bullard 1990, 1993; Bryant and Mohai 1992). It is now quite clear that members of minority groups suffer from environmental decay more than white Americans do.

Because African Americans occupy the oldest and worst share of the housing stock, they are exposed to higher levels of lead paint and asbestos than the rest of the population. They also are more likely than whites to hold jobs in which they are exposed to other dangerous substances. They tend to live in or near city centers where they breathe more of the dirtiest air and drink more of the most polluted water. The area of South Central Los Angeles' zip code is the most polluted one in California (Bullard 1993: 17). They also have the poorest health care, which means the pollution takes an even greater toll on their bodies.

The National Wildlife Federation, the African American Environmentalist Association, and the National Association of Neighborhoods released a study of the link between the environment and race in Washington, DC (Cohn 1994). Washington is often thought of as a relatively clean city, because there is so little heavy industry in the metropolitan area. This study, however, found alarming rates of pollution which were "profoundly worse" in the overwhelmingly black neighborhoods, while the predominantly white Ward 3 is by far its cleanest. Similarly, the Anacostia River which runs through predominantly black neighborhoods is far dirtier than the Potomac.

It's not just an urban or an African American problem. Hispanics are worse off than African Americans at least as far as exposure to polluted air is concerned. About 90 percent of migrant farm workers, who are most exposed to harmful pesticides, are members of minority groups. A quarter of the country's petrochemical industry is located in the heavily black, largely rural "cancer alley" between Baton Rouge and New Orleans. In rural areas, toxic waste dumps, smelters, and other highly polluting installations tend to be located in areas with large minority populations. Hispanics have suffered disproportionately from mining in Southern Colorado and Native Americans from the testing of nuclear weapons.

Table 5.1 summarizes some of the most revealing of the data on this front. The rows cover the counties and independent cities that failed to meet the EPA's air quality standards in 1990 for one, two, and three or more different pollutants.

Environmental racism is often hard to pin down. Nonetheless, a series of studies has shown that minorities suffer far more from environmental decline than whites even after holding other factors such as income and location constant.

The disproportionate burden minorities bear for our environmental woes, of course, is not simply an American phenomenon. Racial and religious minorities tend to live in the unhealthiest neighborhoods and work in the most polluted environments in western Europe as well. When urban planners redesigned the Caen (France) metropolitan area in the 1960s, they sought to turn the city proper into a *ville verte* (green city), while moving the Renault truck factory and the public housing projects which most immigrant workers live in to the bleak suburbs, which one activist called "people silos" (Hauss 1991: 105–107, 120–121).

Research on Eurasia suggests that the former communist regimes located a disproportionate number of their most polluting installations in minority dominated regions of Eastern Europe and the former Soviet Union (Feschbach and Friendly 1992). The relocating of much heavy industry from the indus-

Table 5.1
**Exposure to Air Pollution by Race**

| Number of pollutants below EPA standards | % of total white population | % of total black population | % of total Hispanic population |
|:---:|:---:|:---:|:---:|
| 1 | 57 | 65 | 80 |
| 2 | 33 | 50 | 60 |
| 3 | 12 | 20 | 31 |

*Source:* Adapted from Wernette and Nieves (1992: 16–17).

trialized democracies to the LDCs means that people of color there will have greater exposure to the environmental hazards those factories will generate. Similarly, the dozens of struggles led by and/or waged against indigenous peoples often take on environmental overtones, since many of them live in ecologically fragile regions.

## RACE AND THE ECONOMY: THE "NEW EUROPE?"

To see the link with the economy, one simply needs to examine the recent manifestations of racism in Europe, which have taken on a degree of violence and have been expressed with a degree of openness we have rarely seen in the United States since the 1960s. While Germany has received the most attention in the last few years, racism has spread across the continent and has probably had a greater political impact in other countries, most notably Great Britain and France.

In Europe, racial issues revolve largely around immigration. During the postwar period, the seventeen western European countries have seen so much immigration that their populations are now all at least 5 percent nonwhite.[1]

Immigration was not a serious political issue until the 1960s. European economies were booming, and millions of formerly poor people were quickly climbing the "ladder" of upward social mobility. Corporations and governments therefore encouraged immigrants to come fill the jobs Europeans no longer wanted or needed.

Beginning in Britain, however, opposition to immigration and other forms of racism took on new prominence once the economy began to deteriorate in the early 1960s. Many British workers became convinced that immigrants were taking jobs away from now unemployed whites, drawing too many benefits from the social service system, and eroding traditional values.

Riots broke out in a number of cities where large numbers of immigrants lived either in the same or abutting neighborhoods with poor whites (Solomos 1993; Gilroy 1987). Police officers routinely stopped young black men on the street on "sus" or the mere suspicion that they might have done something wrong, in ways almost any young African-American man would understand.

So, in 1962, the Conservative government passed the first in a series of laws that closed down most opportunities for nonwhites to enter Britain legally. In 1992, for instance, only fifty-two thousand people legally moved to Britain,

[1] As in the United States, there are no accurate figures for illegal immigrants, making the overall estimates of the size of the minority populations uncertain at best.

most of whom either were joining family members already there or had badly needed job skills (Darnton 1993).

Even so, immigration remains a hot political issue. As Thomas and Mary Edsall (1991) have persuasively shown in their study of America's "Reagan Democrats," politicians do not often display openly racist attitudes, but they use "coded language" about some other issue, in this case immigration, which everyone understands has racial overtones and plays on people's racist fears and other emotions.

The most famous of those politicians was Enoch Powell, a prominent Conservative cabinet member in the 1960s. In April 1968, Powell gave his (in)famous "rivers of blood" speech in Birmingham in which it is impossible not to see the "codes":

As I look ahead, I am filled with foreboding. Like the Romans, I seem to see "the River Tiber foaming with much blood." The tragic and intractable phenomenon which we watch with horror on the other side of the Atlantic, but which there is interwoven with the history and existence of the States itself, is coming upon us here by our own volition and our own neglect. (cited in Solomos 1993: 55–56)

Powell went on to predict what life might be like for the next generation of Britons:

They found their wives unable to obtain hospital beds in childbirth, their children unable to obtain school places, their homes and neighborhoods changed beyond recognition, their plans and prospects for the future defeated.

Powell went too far for most British politicians and voters. He soon was driven out of the Conservative Party and later served as a Member of Parliament for one of the extremist, Protestant-based Unionist parties representing a constituency in Northern Ireland.

Immigration didn't disappear from center stage with him, however. Though few systematic studies have been done and though it is difficult to get people to talk openly about such sensitive subjects using conventional social science research techniques, race does seem to be an important political flash point, especially for working class men without many skills, who are most threatened economically and socially by nonwhites. One only needs to take the underground or sit in a pub in a working class neighborhood to see how wide the gulf between black and white still is in Britain (Ali 1991, 1992).

Despite the fact that there has been very little immigration in more than twenty years, immigration remains the way most politicians pose the issue.

Margaret Thatcher weighed in and gained considerable support with her "swamping" speech in 1978, the year before she became Prime Minister.

That is an awful lot, and I think it means that people are really afraid that this country might be swamped by people of a different culture. The British character has done so much for democracy, for law, and done so much throughout the world that if there is any fear that it might be swamped, then people are going to be rather hostile to those coming in. (Solomos 1993: 129)

As recently as May 1993, Winston Churchill (grandson of the wartime Prime Minister) made a speech in Parliament in which he called for an end to what he called "the relentless flow of immigrants." While newspapers and politicians criticized Churchill, he claimed that mail showed his constituents strongly supported him.

In 1993 alone, there were several thousand racial incidents in Britain, ranging from insults to the kidnapping and assault of numerous young black and Asian men. That September, an avowedly racist candidate was elected to the British equivalent of an American city council in the east end of London.

In France, race and immigration became important issues a decade later than in England. In part, that reflected the policies of the Gaullist government which prided itself on its good relations with the emerging countries of the third world. In part, it was due to the fact that the French economic boom continued into the early 1970s.

By then, France had become a diverse society (Amar and Milza 1990). At least 5 percent of the population is nonwhite, most coming from former French colonies in the Caribbean, Africa, and Asia. That percentage is far higher in working class neighborhoods and public housing projects.

Over the last twenty years, France has seen its share of racist incidents (Monzat 1992). Cemeteries have been desecrated. Arab men have been murdered simply because they were Arabs. Muslim girls have been denied the right to wear veils to school. Stereotypes about hard-drinking Arab men chasing French women abound.

Two anecdotes from my last research trip to France give some indication of the depth of racist feelings.

One evening, I was riding the subway home. I had eaten dinner with friends who gave me a copy of a book one of them had written, *Les immigrés devant les urnes (Immigrants at the Ballot Box)*, which advocated giving the equivalent of American resident aliens the right to vote in local elections. The car was filled with Arabs and blacks, three of whom happened to notice the book that was sitting on my lap. They couldn't believe that a white person would read such a book or support such a proposal. Their surprise only deepened when they found out I was American.

The next day, I was sitting in a cafe across from the Gare du Nord, waiting for my train to leave. A couple sat down at the next table, realized I was American, and struck up a conversation. They told me that they were both members of the CGT trade union, which is affiliated with the Communist Party. They also told me they were returning from a vacation to Florida, where they had been "scared by every black we saw."

In France, the racism's political impact is mostly electoral. The all but avowedly racist *Front National* (National Front) routinely wins around 10 percent of the vote in national elections (Mayer and Perrineau 1992, 1993; Perrineau 1993). Its peak came in the 1988 and 1995 presidential elections when its leader, Jean-Marie Le Pen, won about 15 percent of the vote (Marcuse 1995, Gaspard 1995). Momentum toward the FN continued later that year when it won control of several large cities for the first time.

Le Pen stresses themes such as "France for the French" which echo the xenophobic movements which tried to keep Jews, Poles, Italians, and others out early in the century and then fed the powerful fascist movements of the 1930s (Birnbaum 1993). Like his counterparts in Britain, Le Pen denies being a racist, but there is little doubt that his slogans and his attacks on immigration are the same kind of coded language which evokes the same fears as "rivers of blood" and "swamping." The SOFRES public opinion polling firm has been asking the following question since 1984: "Would you say that you completely agree, somewhat agree, somewhat disagree, or completely disagree with ideas supported by Jean-Marie Le Pen?"[2] Expressed support for Le Pen has never dropped below 16 percent and reached a high of 32 percent in 1991.

As Table 5.2 shows, the Front does gain support from virtually every socioeconomic group in France, but there are some patterns which overlap with what we know about the distribution of racism in industrialized democracies in general. The Front does especially well among the groups who feel most threatened by the immigrants or their native-born children: poorly educated men who lack job skills and are either unemployed or are at least threatened by unemployment and those who live in the big cities where people of color are concentrated.

Racism has already had a substantial political impact. The same Gaullists who had been among Europe's most enlightened leaders in the 1960s passed legislation three decades later that will make it harder to get into the country

[2]Diniez-vous que vous êtes tout à fait d'accord avec des idées défendues par Jean-Marie Le Pen, assez d'accord, plutô en désaccord ou tout à fait en désaccord?

Table 5.2
A Statistical Profile of Le Pen Voters in 1988

| Category | % of Total Population | % Le Pen Voters |
|---|---|---|
| Men | 47 | 57 |
| Less than high school education | 55 | 62 |
| Live in cities of more than 100,000 | 36 | 45 |
| Shopkeepers | 7 | 10 |
| Blue collar workers | 24 | 29 |

*Source:* Mayer and Perrineau (1992): 129.

and, if one does, to obtain French citizenship. Then Interior Minister Charles Pasqua proclaimed the goal of "zero immigration." Another measure makes it easier for police to stop foreigners and check their documents.

While overt instances of racism itself rarely appear in parliamentary debates, stump speeches, or newspaper columns, it is there just below the surface. There has been next to no criticism of European Union provisions which allow the citizens, almost all of whom are white, from the fifteen member countries to move, take jobs, and vote in local elections throughout the community. The target of the new legislation on immigration and police power is clearly the minority population. As an Algerian doctor working in France put it, "They just go by the color of the face."

That impact is only likely to grow. As of May 1995, France has a Gaullist President and parliament, the first time the right has controlled both in fourteen years. Moreover, the Gaullists and their allies realize they owe their victory to National Front voters, which means that they will have to adopt some policies to please them, no matter how distasteful that proves to be. Moreover, the Front shows no signs of moderating. Right after it won a number of city halls the next month, it announced policies which seemed only likely to heighten tensions (e.g., giving preference to native born French men and women in hiring).

## ETHNICITY AND UNDERDEVELOPMENT: INDIA

Virtually all observers agree that the LDCs have had a hard time. Few have been able to escape the wrenching poverty that has left a quarter of their citizens without adequate food, clothing, or shelter. Few of their governments are effective, no matter how one chooses to define the term. Most are wracked by conflict which, in many cases, threatens to literally tear the country apart. At the heart of most of those problems in most of those countries are racial, ethnic, linguistic, and/or religious differences (Horowitz 1993; de Nevers 1993).

That should come as no surprise given the way most of these countries were initially created during the colonial era. The imperial powers drew arbitrary and artificial boundaries, which typically were retained when the colonies gained their independence. All too often, groups which had traditionally been antagonists were thrown into the same geopolitical entity. Similarly, many groups were divided into two or more colonies and, now, countries. In short, here as in so many other ways, colonialism has proved a recipe for disaster.

One of the most respected historians of Africa, Basil Davidson (1992), recently argued that there had been a kind of civil society in much of Africa before the white man arrived. Colonization, however, destroyed it by creating those artificial geopolitical units. In many of them, a decidedly non-civil society has emerged based around what he calls "modern tribalism" which has little or nothing to do with traditional culture or society but at the same time leaves most African countries all but ungovernable. While most true of Africa, something like this pattern can be found virtually everywhere the European or American empires spread.

As we saw in Chapter 2, Iraq was a British creation that lumped together Sunni Arabs, Shiite Arabs, and Kurds (themselves spread over five countries). Kurds and Shiites have opposed the dominant Sunni Arabs ever since Iraq was created after World War I. Most recently, both rose up in revolt in the aftermath of the 1991 Gulf war.

Similarly, the British brought three main ethnic groups (plus hundreds of smaller ones) into the entity they called Nigeria. Conflict among them has been one of the reasons that the country saw two republics fail and experienced six successful military coups in its first quarter century of independence.

The explosive potential of ethnicity and religion when mixed with the equally explosive potential of underdevelopment can perhaps best be seen, however, not by examining countries like Iraq and Nigeria, which are all but textbook examples of how not to put a country together. Instead, we will concentrate on India, because it is one of a handful of LDCs which has been able to sustain a reasonably successful democracy and a considerable degree of intercommunal tolerance for most of its post-independence history. That success, however, has been put in jeopardy for the last fifteen or twenty years because of increased religious and ethnic tensions. The fact that both Prime Minister Indira Gandhi and her son, Rajiv Gandhi, who had also been prime minister, were assassinated by members of dissatisfied religious or ethnic groups is but the tip of an iceberg which seems to be getting larger by the day. As Atul

Kohli put it in summing up his anthology of ethnic and other sources of India's problems, "Sooner or later all third world countries become difficult to govern, and over the past two decades, India has been moving in that direction" (Kohli 1990b: 317).

India is one of the most diverse countries in the world. Nearly 60 percent of the population grew up speaking one of the Indo-Aryan languages of the north. About half of those speak Hindi. But even though all the Indo-Aryan languages are related, they are less similar than Russian, Ukrainian, and Belorussian, for example. People who speak Hindi, Bengali, and Gujarati cannot readily understand one another. Most of the thirty percent of the population which lives in the south speak one of the Dravidian languages, which have little or nothing in common with the Indo-Aryan tongues. About 5 percent of the population (mostly Sikhs) speak Punjabi, an offspring of Persian and Urdu.

India also has three main religious groups. Slightly over 80 percent of the population is Hindu, but each major regional and linguistic group practices a different version of that religion. A bit more than 10 percent are Muslim, but they run the full range of belief from fundamentalists to highly assimilated and secularized people who have for all intents and purposes stopped practicing their religion. Finally, about 2 percent of the population are Sikhs who follow a religion begun by the Guru Nanak in the early sixteenth century as an attempt to blend Hindu and Muslim traditions emphasizing peacefulness and other-worldliness, even though Sikhs today are known for their ferocious fighting ability and their dissatisfaction with their status in the Punjab.

Finally, India is divided along caste lines, even though the constitution adopted at independence supposedly outlawed the system. There are four main castes and hundreds of subcastes, stretching from Brahmins who still dominate much of Indian life to untouchables or outcastes who are still struggling to achieve some semblance of social, political, and economic equality. While it has not received as much attention as linguistic and religious differences in recent years, it may well be that caste is the most influential of all the divisions.

India is the country of Mahatma Gandhi, where nonviolent action was the most popular and effective. It is, today, probably the world's most violent democracy, and much of that violence grows out of religious and ethnic tensions. Its first prime minister, Jawaharlal Nehru, noted in 1950, "In a country like India, no real nationalism can be built up except on the basis of secularity. Narrow religious nationalisms are relics of a past age and are no longer relevant today" (in Buultjens 1986:101–102).

India has never really lived up to Nehru's hopes. Independent India was born in communal violence when perhaps as many as fifty million Muslims desperately tried to leave India for Pakistan while roughly as many Hindus fled in the other direction. Gandhi traveled the country trying to use his moral force to stop the riots that broke out, but to no avail. As many as five hundred thousand people or more were killed, including Gandhi himself.

For the first twenty-five years after independence, communal violence was not a major problem. Then, for reasons which would take us beyond the scope of this book, Indira Gandhi's government centralized power and acted in an often heavy-handed and arbitrary way, antagonizing regionally based religious, ethnic, and linguistic groups along the way (Kohli 1990a, 1990b; Gupte 1992).

Since then, there have been so many and such different forms of communal violence in India that they could not be adequately described in a book, let alone a small part of one chapter. Still, a quick glimpse at two communities, the Sikhs and the militant Hindus, should provide a good sense of the scope of the problem that is, today, shaking Indian democracy to its core.

The Sikhs only make up about 2 percent of the Indian population and were not even a majority in the original state of Punjab where most of them lived. Nonetheless, they have been important on the national level in part because of their role in the military and security services. They have also been remark-ably successful as farmers, merchants, and industrialists. Not surprisingly, Sikh frustrations grew, because they were one of the few major minority groups not to have a state in which they would be dominant. Thus, how the government responded to the Sikhs' demands was bound to have a profound impact not just on the Punjab, but throughout India.

Little was done to accommodate the Sikhs during Indira Gandhi's first years in power. To be sure, the old Punjab was split into three states with a new and smaller one keeping the name and having a Sikh majority. Once that was done, the Delhi government threw up a stone wall against further Sikh demands.

Gandhi never dealt with anyone who disagreed with her gently. Her qualms about the Sikhs grew when their Akali Dal party proved to be among the most effective opponents of the Emergency Rule of 1975–1977. As support for the Akalis grew in the late 1970s, Gandhi's Congress party threw its support behind Sant Jarnail Singh Bhindranwale and other Sikh extremists in an attempt to undermine her immediate opponents.

Politically, the problems in Punjab came to a head following the collapse of the first non-Congress government and Gandhi's return to power in 1980. Among the losers were the Akalis, who won a mere 27 percent of the Punjabi vote.

Gandhi chose to dawdle in negotiations with the Sikhs over a number of issues, including water rights and incorporating the symbolically important city of Chandrigarh into Punjab as its capital. Meanwhile, Bhindranwale had broken with Congress and begun developing an independent base of support of his own. Along with dozens of other leaders, he called for a sovereign, Sikh dominated Khalistan and openly advocated the use of violence.

Its earlier support for Bhindranwale and other extremists ended up backfiring on Congress. In 1981, Bhindranwale was accused of murdering a political foe. But, because he also played off the various factions within the Akali Dal, the state government allowed him and his men to move into the Golden Temple at Amritsar, the Sikhs' holiest shrine. Violence mounted, and in October 1983, Gandhi ousted the elected Akali government in Punjab, imposed presidential rule, and sent one of her most trusted lieutenants to oversee the arrest of the alleged "terrorists," although Bhindranwale and most of the radicals remained free and seemingly safe in the Golden Temple complex.

The government then responded with even more repressive measures. In March 1984, the AISSF (All India Sikh Student Federation) was abolished. A hundred fifty companies of police troops were stationed in the Punjab, including ninety at the Golden Temple alone. In response, AISSF members occupied more and more Sikh temples and turned them into warehouses for arms and sanctuaries for terrorists. Meanwhile, in neighboring Haryana, Congress Chief Minister Bhajan Lal at the very least condoned what could only be described as organized mob violence directed at Sikhs in his state.

Finally, in June 1984, Gandhi ordered troops to storm the temple. Bhindranwale, at least five hundred of his supporters, and eighty-three soldiers were killed. In the aftermath of what came to be known as Operation Bluestar, the surviving Sikh leaders, including most prominent Akali Dal officials, were arrested. Sikh soldiers in other units mutinied and rioted in the most serious breach of army discipline since independence. Then, on October 31, Sikh members of Gandhi's own security detail assassinated her. To close the circle on the assassination, Hindus in Delhi lashed out in a wave of violence that, in turn, left hundreds of Sikhs dead.

Rajiv Gandhi set out to do things differently when he succeeded his mother as prime minister. Almost immediately after taking office, he began negotiations with the Akali Dal government, and the two sides reached an agreement on the Anandpur Sahib Resolution which, among other things, would have given Chandrigarh to Punjab and given the state some control over vital water resources its farmers claimed they needed.

By 1987, however, Gandhi had to back down. His Hindu constituents throughout North India were not prepared to go along with such sweeping concessions to the Sikhs. If anything, Congress found it to its electoral advantage to fan anti-Sikh sentiment among Hindu voters.

The 1989 Congress election campaign featured footage of Indira Gandhi's funeral pyre with a sobbing Rajiv standing nearby, with the clear implication that the Sikhs were to blame. Gandhi was challenged in his own constituency by his brother's widow Maneka, who is half Sikh. One of his party's most widely used slogans during the campaign was, *"Beti hai sardar kee, desh ke gaddar ki"* (The daughter of a Sikh, traitor to the nation).

Since then, the violence has continued. In every year since 1986, at least six hundred people have been killed. The situation in Punjab was so intense following Rajiv Gandhi's assassination during the 1991 election campaign (by a Tamil nationalist, not a Sikh) that elections there had to be put off for months.

It is hard to tell exactly what Sikhs feel today, since the state is mostly off limits to academic researchers and foreign journalists. The impressionistic evidence suggests that given the tragedy of the last decade, the Sikh community is more divided than but as angry as ever.

Support for the more extremist wings of the movement has probably declined. Nonetheless, the violence continues. On March 1, 1993, for instance, police officers killed Gurbachan Singh Manochabal, head of the significantly named Bhindranwale Tiger Party of Khalistan. Extremist Sikhs are generally held responsible for a September 11, 1993 car bomb attack on the president of the ruling Congress Party's youth wing, Maninder Singh Bitta, himself a Sikh. He escaped with minor injuries, but eight people were killed and at least thirty-five seriously wounded. To what end? None of the issues that sparked the violence in the first place have been resolved in a way that satisfies either the Sikhs or the central government.

Communal politics has also taken root among the Hindus. That's all the more remarkable and revealing because, as noted above, Hindus are not a minority, but make up about 80 percent of the population. Nonetheless, they share many of the feelings of oppression commonly found among minority groups.

Organized Hindu fundamentalism dates from the early years of this century and the formation of the RSS (Rashtriya Swayamsevak Sangh). By the mid-1920s, the RSS was engaging in military training. Through the 1950s and 1960s, the RSS and other Hindu organizations led a series of campaigns against cow slaughter, Christian missionaries, and other alleged evils.

Into the 1980s, however, Hindu fundamentalism had not been an important force in Indian politics. In the last decade, all that has changed with the emergence of the rather fundamentalist BJP.

The BJP (Bharatiya Janata Party) burst onto the scene in 1984 when it won 7.4 percent of the vote. Since then, it has become the second most powerful national party, winning 19.9 percent of the vote and 119 seats in the Lok Sabha in 1991.[3]

At the symbolic heart of Hindu fundamentalism is the clash over a building in the northern city of Ayodhya. Hindus claim their ancestors built it as a temple to honor one of their most important deities. Muslims claim that the first Mughal conqueror, Babur, built it as a mosque in the sixteenth century. Architecturally, it looks something like a temple, something like a mosque.

The building has been a source of controversy between the two groups from time to time ever since. For most of the last century or so, however, a modus vivendi had been worked out in which Muslims used the shrine on their sabbath, Friday, while Hindus were free to pray there during the rest of the week.

Controversy broke out again in 1986 after a judge's ruling closed the building to everyone. The rapidly growing VHP (Vishwa Hindu Parishad or Worldwide Hindu Brotherhood), which made the "freeing" of such properties its highest priority, entered the scene. It could routinely gather a hundred thousand devout Hindus along the banks of the river next to the temple/mosque. Within two years, the VHP gathered enough support to convince a judge to open the facility for Hindus. That, in turn, led to Muslim counter-protests.

In one typical 1989 incident, a riot broke out after the VHP announced it would add onto the building using specially consecrated bricks. More than one hundred fifty people were killed.

Later that year, Congress was defeated at the polls and replaced by a government which convinced the VHP to postpone building the new temple. Pressures around Ayodhya then eased until what can only be called a Hindu mob destroyed the mosque and started building a new temple in December, 1992.

The violence spread far from Ayodhya. Hindu revivalist movements, such as the Shiv Sena in Bombay, took to the streets, demanding vengeance and attacking individual Muslims who obviously had nothing directly to do with the situation in Ayodhya. At least seventeen hundred died in Bombay alone.

Two BJP leaders, Primkumar Sharma and Ramesh More, were assassinated. On February 25, the BJP planned a rally to demand the resignation of Prime Minister P. V. Narasimha Rao and new elections in the four states in which BJP governments had been removed by the central government after the

[3] The fact that parties which compete nationally only won about 60 percent of the vote in 1991 tells us a lot about India. The rest went to regional parties, which typically only contested the vote in a single state and drew their support from a single linguistic or ethnic group.

rioting. The government banned the rally and arrested over a hundred thousand BJP members, including at least one hundred elected officials. Small groups of demonstrators gathered anyway, but eighty thousand troops were able to keep them from coming together at a single site.

Those events illustrate the growing linguistic, religious, and ethnic antagonisms the country faces (Anderson 1993; Naipaul 1990). Consider, for instance, Bal Thackeray, the head of Shiv Sena (literally Lord Shiva's Army, named after a Hindu deity) who is currently the most powerful politician in Bombay. A former cartoonist, Thackeray is also a reputed mobster and openly patterns his appeals on Adolph Hitler's. He has summed up Shiv Sena's goals as follows. "My Hinduism is nationalism. My fight is against pro-Pakistan Muslims. The Pakistani extremists, the Bangladeshi Muslims, and the Muslims staying in this country for years together, giving shelter to them—all these people must be kicked out. Even if he is a Hindu giving shelter to these kinds of Muslims, he also must be shot dead" (Anderson 1993: A 14).

Like Le Pen and other politicians who build on racial fears, Thackeray denies that he hates Muslims or urges his supporters to engage in violence. Still, statements like this one are yet another example of coded language designed to play on popular fears and prejudices, which lurk just below the surface of this sprawling, impoverished city of more than twelve million. His protestations aside, there can be little doubt that Thackeray like so many Indian politicians is fanning ethnic flames in order to build his own base of support and, in the process, rendering his city and country ever harder to govern.

While India remains a functioning democracy, it is also one whose political life is increasingly violent. In 1989, over five hundred people were killed in communal riots that broke out in seven states, including some in cities and villages that had never seen this kind of protest before. The violence continued into the election campaign of 1991, in which at least seventeen hundred people died in communal riots. A Muslim writer and former member of Parliament from Bombay put it this way to John Ward Anderson of the *Washington Post*: "Never before have I felt so hopeless as I do today, when Muslims are just not wanted in this country. There is a whole campaign of hate going on. A systematic effort is being made to show how intolerant, how regressive, how almost primitive and barbaric Muslims are" (Anderson 1994: 16).

## CAN WE GET ALONG?

Two years after Rodney King asked his plaintive question, Clyde Ford (1994) published the latest in the "fifty things you can do about this or that" genre of books. It bore the title *We Really Can Get Along*.

It includes all kinds of seemingly simple and constructive suggestions: Understand. Explore your own personal experience with race and racism. Develop communications skills that enable you to cross cultural barriers. Celebrate holidays of other ethnic groups as part of an attempt to embrace diversity in your home. Create a support group in your neighborhood or community. Communicate with national and international decision makers.

This book's suggestions, however, are not quite as simple as those of The Earth Works Group's *50 Simple Things You Can Do to Save the Earth* (1989) and other books of its type. As the title suggests, theirs is mostly a list of things to do. Most of the items on Ford's list require the reader to go further and question many of his or her preconceptions and values as well as those of society as a whole.

There's an implicit lesson in all that. Before we can treat each other better, we have to think about each other differently.

We could go on and consider other areas in which people do not get along very well. The link between gender and underdevelopment. AIDS. South Africa. Revolts of indigenous peoples. Doing so, however, would not add much to what is already a depressing argument about the nature and stakes of a global crisis.

Doing so would also divert us from the most important goal of this book: exploring one potential way out of it through a more generalized version of Ford's answers to King's question.

## REFERENCES

Ali, Yasmin (1991). "Echoes of Empire: Towards a Politics of Representation." In John Carner and Sylvia Harvey, eds., *Enterprise and Heritage: Cross-Currents in British Culture*. London: Routledge.

————. (1992). "Muslim Women and the Politics of Ethnicity and Culture in Northern England." In Gita Subgal and Nira Ympaul, eds., *Refusing Holy Orders*. London: Daniel Virages.

Amar, Marianne, and Pierre Milza (1990). *L'immigration en France au XXème siècle*. Paris: Armand Colin.

Anderson, John Ward (1993). "The Flame That Lit an Inferno: Hindu Leader Creates Anti-Muslim Frenzy." *Washington Post*, August 11, A14.

————. (1994). "India's Muslims Fear New Physical Threat." *Washington Post*, March 12, A16.

Berlin, Isaiah (1991). "Two Concepts of Nationalism: An Interview with Isaiah Berlin." *New York Review of Books*, November 21, 19–23.

Birnbaum, Pierre (1993). *La France aux français: Histoire des haines nationalistes*. Paris: Editions du seuil.

Brass, Paul, *The Politics of India since Independence.* New York: Cambridge University Press, 1990.

Brown, Michael D., ed. (1993). *Ethnic Conflict and International Security.* Princeton: Princeton University Press.

Bryant, Bunyan, and Paul Mohai (1992). *Race and the Incidence of Environmental Hazards.* Boulder, Colo.: Westview.

Bullard, Robert D. (1990). *Dumping in Dixie: Race, Class, and Environmental Quality.* Boulder, Colo.: Westview.

———. (1993). "Introduction" and "Anatomy of Environmental Racism and the Environmental Justice Movement." In Robert D. Bullard, *Combating Environmental Racism: Voices from the Grassroots.* Boston: South End Press, 7–40.

Buultjens, Ralph (1986). "India: Religion, Political Legitimacy, and the Secular State." *Annals of the American Academy* 483 (January).

Cohn, D'Vera (1994). "Blacks Bear Brunt of DC's Pollution, Report Says." *Washington Post,* June 14, B1, B3.

Collins, Robert W., and William Harris (1993). "Race and Waste in Two Virginia Communities." In Robert D. Bullard, *Combating Environmental Racism: Voices from the Grassroots.* Boston: South End Press, 93–106.

Current History (1993). "Ethnic Conflicts Worldwide." *Current History,* April: 167–169.

Davidson, Basil (1992). *The Black Man's Burden: Africa and the Curse of the Nation State.* New York: Times Books.

de Nevers, Renée (1993). "Democratization and Ethnic Conflict." In Michael Brown, ed., *Ethnic Conflict and International Security.* Princeton: Princeton University Press, 61–78

Earth Works Group (1989). *50 Simple Things You Can Do to Save the Earth.* Berkeley: Earth Works Press.

Edsall, Thomas and Mary (1991). *Chain Reaction.* New York: W. W. Norton.

Feschbach, Murry, and Alfred Friendly, Jr. (1992). *Ecocide.* New York: Basic Books.

Ford, Clyde W. (1994). *We Can All Get Along: 50 Steps You Can Take to Help End Racism at Home at Work in Your Community.* New York: Dell.

Gaspard, Françoise (1995). *A Small City in France.* Cambridge: Harvard University Press.

Gilroy, Paul (1987). *There Ain't No Black in the Union Jack.* London: Routledge.

Goldberg, David Theo, ed. (1990). *Anatomy of Racism.* Minneapolis: University of Minnesota Press.

Gupte, Pranay (1992). *Mother India: A Political Biography of Indira Gandhi.* New York: Scribner's.

Gurr, Ted Robert (1993). *Minorities at Risk: A Global View of Ethnopolitical Conflicts.* Washington: United States Institute of Peace Press.

Hacker, Andrew (1992). *Two Nations: Black and White, Separate, Hostile, and Unequal.* New York: Charles Scribner's.

Hassner, Pierre (1993). "Beyond Nationalism and Internationalism: Ethnicity and World Order." In Michael Brown, ed., *Ethnic Conflict and International Security*. Princeton: Princeton University Press, 125–142.

Hauss, Charles (1991). *Politics in Gaullist France: Coping with Chaos*. New York: Praeger.

Horowitz, Donald L. (1993). "Ethnic and Nationalist Conflict." In Michael T. Klare and Daniel C. Thomas, eds., *World Security: Challenges for a New Century*. New York: St. Martin's: 175–187.

Kaplan, Robert (1994). "The Coming Anarchy." *The Atlantic*, February.

Kohli, Atul (1990a). *Democracy and Discontent. India's Growing Crisis of Government*. New York: Cambridge University Press.

———. (1990b). *India's Democracy: An Analysis of State-Society Relations*. Princeton: Princeton University Press.

Lauren, Paul Gordon (1988). *Power and Prejudice: The Politics and Diplomacy of Racial Discrimination*. Boulder, Colo.: Westview.

Lerner, Daniel (1958. *The Passing of Traditional Society*. Glencoe, Ill.: Free Press.

Lippman, Thomas W. (1993). "Is the World More Violent, Or Does It Just Seem That Way?" *Washington Post*, July 1, A14, A18.

Marcus, Jonathan (1995). *The National Front and French Politics: The Resistible Jean-Marie Le Pen*. London: Macmillan.

Mayer, Nona, and Pascal Perrineau (1992). "Why Do They Vote for Le Pen?" *European Journal of Political Research* 22: 123–141.

———. (1993). "Le Lépenisme dans l'opinion." In Olivier Duhamel and Jérôme Jaffré, eds., *L'état de l'opinion 1993*. Paris: Editions du seuil, 63–78.

Monzat, René (1992). *Enquêtes sur la droite extrême*. Paris: Le Monde Editions.

Moynihan, Daniel Patrick (1993). *Pandaemonium: Ethnicity in International Politics*. New York: Oxford University Press.

Naipaul, V. S. (1990). *India: A Million Mutinies Now*. New York: Viking.

Perrineau, Pascal (1993). "Le Front national, la force solitaire." In Habert, Philippe, Pascal Perrineau, and Colette Ysmal, eds., *Le vote sanction: les élections législatives des 21 et 28 mars 1993*. Paris: Département d'études politiques du Figaro and Presses de la Fondation Nationale des Sciences Politiques.

Pfaff, William (1993). *The Wrath of Nations: Civilization and the Furies of Nationalism*. New York: Simon and Schuster.

Solomos, John (1993). *Race and Racism in Contemporary Britain*. 2d. ed. London: Macmillan.

Wernette, D. R., and L. A. Nieves (1992). "Breathing Polluted Air." *EPA Magazine*. March/April, 16–17.

Wolpert, Stanley, *A New History of India*. Third Edition. New York: Oxford University Press, 1989.

Wright, Robin (1985). *Sacred Rage: The Wrath of Militant Islam*. New York: Linden Press/Simon and Schuster.

# PART TWO

# INTERDEPENDENCE

# 6

# CONFRONTATION

The real reason for the West's successful defense, and subsequent victory over Islam, was not western military capacity. It was the ability of Europe in the Renaissance, and subsequently the Enlightenment, to reexamine the fundamentals of its own religion and civilization.

—William Pfaff

So far, I have not paid much attention to the key words in this book's title, beyond confrontation. That has not been an oversight. It made little sense to discuss the possibility of moving beyond confrontation until we saw the problems we face for what they are: a global crisis.

The rest of the book will.

The reliance on confrontation in our attempts to settle disputes is the common denominator that allows us to understand and possibly solve the global crisis. I am not trying to say that the economics stressed by Marxist analysts or the international anarchy of the traditional realists in international relations are unimportant. However, my reading of the evidence is that confrontation is the key that actually helps tie all those other pieces together.

My dictionary defines confront as "to face boldly, defiantly, and antagonistically." The word's roots lie in the Latin and French words for forehead and, not surprisingly, it has come to have the connotation of staring down one's adversary. To use one of ESPN's most popular promotion slogans of the early 1990s, it's "in your face" politics.

The next seven chapters will show that we can move beyond confrontation and adopt a more cooperative and successful approach to dealing with the conflict. The trajectory I'll lay out parallels the one found in the academic study of scientific revolutions or paradigm shifts (Kuhn 1969).

Paradigms are the mental lenses through which we view the world and make sense of what we see. They thus provide us with the thoughts and interpretations which guide our actions. As Kuhn and others have shown in their studies of scientific history, people can change their paradigms. Only when that happens does the scientific community make quantum leaps in our understanding of natural phenomena.

Skeptics argue that politics and science are not the same and that there are no political equivalents of the periodic table of elements or Einstein's general theory of relativity. Others are convinced that such sweeping change cannot be pulled off in a world with so many people, cultures, and conflicting interests.

I will argue that the skeptics *could* be wrong. In the next three chapters, I will try to show both that there is a paradigm that governs much of our behavior and that we can at least sketch out an alternative to it. In Part Three, I will move on to concrete evidence that this paradigm is already being put into practice by at least a few people in a few areas around the world.

If you limit your attention to international relations since the creation of the Westphalian system in 1648, it is easy to agree with the skeptics. That's not the case if you take a broader look at history and the rise and fall of empires and civilizations (Kennedy 1987; Pfaff 1993). What you see then is a constant ebb and flow of dominant countries, cultures, and ideas.

As William Pfaff points out in the statement that begins this chapter, the countries that thrive over an extended period of time are the ones that can reexamine the fundamental organizing principles underlying their government, economy, society, and value system when conditions change dramatically. Those which cannot or will not condemn themselves to decline, if not eclipse.

The skeptics are right on at least one count. Sweeping change is never easy to achieve. But, it seems to be easiest in times like ours, when the stability of an extended period comes to an end and change, in general, is occurring quite rapidly.

To be sure, there has been a lot of reexamining of foreign policy in the light of the end of the Cold War, the Gulf war, and everything else that has happened in the last handful of years. But, if I am right, the reassessment has to go far deeper and broader. The problem isn't just with our paradigm for foreign policy. If we restrict our analysis to it alone, we are not likely to make more than incremental change or escape the frustration that has been such a commonplace in this post-Cold War world.

## ON HUMAN NATURE

One of the first things skeptics bring up in any discussion of a more peaceful world is human nature. They argue that confrontation and violence are built in to all or most people and that it therefore makes no sense to try to build a world that defies the very essence of our being.

It turns out that human nature is one of the most hotly debated topics in psychology and biology these days. Few responsible scientists still claim that we are condemned to relatively unconstrained violence because of our human nature. Fewer yet would argue that our nature makes us completely compassionate or cooperative.

Most take positions along the continuum between those two extreme positions. People obviously have tendencies or proclivities which can lead them to be violent. But most scientists now agree with the authors of the Seville Statement (key passages can be found in Keegan 1993: 80) in which an international group of distinguished behavioral scientists emphatically claimed that such a propensity does not inevitably lead us to be violent. The part of our brains that lead to cooperative behavior can apparently control our violent tendencies most of the time.

Some propensity to violence may well be a part of our genetic makeup. However, the decision to go to war, join a riot, or engage in ethnic cleansing is not because it involves one of those collective choices.

The kinds of confrontation and violence at the heart of this book are not usually individual in nature. People rarely engage in collective acts of violence because one person has too much serotonin and can not block the urge to be violent. Rather, the shift to group based confrontation and violence involves a collective decision.

Most likely, human nature, like race, is largely a social construct. There is probably something biological to it, just as there are biological differences between the people we label black or white. But, they are social constructs, because we have to read a lot into them to reach the conclusions we do.

Like race, human nature is also a social construct with a history. If the likes of Barry Schwartz (1986) and Philip Selznick (1992) are to be believed, the conventional wisdom about human nature is a product of the same intellectual changes that brought us individualism, the nation state, modern economics, and the rest of the value system we will be exploring in this chapter. Before the Enlightenment and the other intellectual breakthroughs of the sixteenth through the eighteenth centuries, people were more commonly thought of as part and parcel of an integrated universe which St. Thomas Aquinas called the "great chain of being." Many traditional cultures never accepted the notion that people were separate and autonomous by nature. Indeed, as countless anthropologists' reports or Tony Hillerman's novels show, Navajo culture is based on the belief that individualism defies our real human nature, which is to be one with the teachings of the culture, other creatures, and the universe as a whole.

In the end, what our nature as humans is seems likely to remain one of those unanswered and unanswerable questions for years to come. Nonetheless, one conclusion does seem warranted from the perplexing studies done on the subject.

If you remain convinced we are really and inescapably Hobbesian, it probably doesn't make sense to keep reading this book, because everything that follows is based on the assumption that we are not.

## CONFRONTATION: REALITY AND METAPHOR

Given what we know (and don't know) about human nature, it seems highly unlikely that confrontation can be eliminated altogether. However, it does at least seem possible that our reliance on it and its costs for human civilization can be reduced appreciably.

To see that, we have to start by taking a step back from the issues in the global crisis and probe our confrontational habits by exploring the thought processes underlying the choice to be confrontational. At that point, it becomes easier to envision alternatives to confrontation.

If I'm right, the key to understanding the link between confrontation and the global crisis lies in the middle words of Einstein's famous sentence about the unleashed power of the atom, that everything had changed "save our modes of thinking." Again, if I'm right, it is our way of thinking that leads us into confrontation in the first place. Then, when, as the cliché so aptly puts it, "push comes to shove," we are left with few alternatives to fighting.

We don't resort to confrontation all the time. College roommates rarely square off while trying to decide which pizza delivery service to call. Mexico and the United States don't mobilize the troops every time smugglers sneak a drug shipment into Texas or California because a border guard failed to check thoroughly enough for hidden compartments in a car.

There's a reason why confrontation is rare in these cases. The conflict isn't intense enough. Neither side is all that worried about the outcome. Losing doesn't seem like the end of the earth. But, when conflict does get intense and it feels like a life and death struggle (itself a telling figure of speech), then confrontation becomes the norm, not the exception.

We could begin an exploration of the root cause of confrontation by jumping right into what scholars and other observers have said about it. My experience, however, is that it is easier to see this argument by beginning with a decidedly non-academic exercise, though it is one with at least some support in the writing of social psychologists and students of management (Boehnke et al.: 1993; Argyris 1985).

I start by asking the participants in the class or workshop why a divisive national or international crisis was not resolved peacefully. Invariably, the group comes up with dozens of reasons, most of which mirror what one finds in the scholarly literature.

I list them in two columns. The first includes what amount to the objective differences between the adversaries, such as the importance of oil, the historical factors that left Iraq and Kuwait separate countries, or the way slavery and other forces have created a system of institutionalized racism in the United States.

The second list is far more subjective or psychological. It includes such themes as the fear of losing jobs or face or territory, the "need" to be "number one," stereotyping by both sides, self-interest, and politicians' ego needs.

Then I lead the group through a discussion about a divorce or some other interpersonal conflict they know about. Almost always, two very similar lists emerge.

In the first column go the objective differences between the people. Mother wants to take daughter to the opera; daughter prefers sitting on curves at stock car races so she can have the best view of the crashes (I actually overheard that one during a break in an orientation session for first year college students). Husband wants to spend weekends at home watching every game on television; wife wants to go to the mall and check out all the sales. A young man wants his fiancée to stay at home and raise a family just as his mother did; she wants to have a career, just as her mother did.

I almost never have to write anything in the second column. The psychological dynamics the participants raise are the same ones they did in discussing the political one.

As the discussion proceeds, the group invariably reaches one more conclusion. While the "objective" differences produce the conflict in the first place, the "subjective" ones turn the conflict into confrontation and produce all the problems that come in its wake.

What these groups realize is something one rarely finds in the academic literature on international relations or domestic politics. While there are many reasons why different forms of conflict turn into confrontation and then violence, there is also a common denominator to them all, as depicted in Figure 6.1.

Figure 6.1

**Modes of Thinking and Conflict**

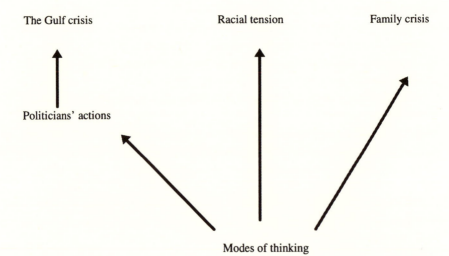

As the left side of the chart suggests, we political scientists tend to explain "high politics" through the actions of politicians. We focus on events in Washington or Baghdad or at the United Nations in trying to understand the Gulf war and, to a somewhat lesser degree, on Acts of Congress, the work of advertising executives working for the Republican party, or the statements of black leaders from J. C. Watts to Louis Farrakhan in exploring contemporary race relations.

The exercise shows us the need to also consider the psychological factors in my right hand column. The links between international or national and interpersonal conflict imply that the actors who make those life and death decisions are driven by values and assumptions that are not all that different from the ones average citizens use when they get into conflict with family members, fellow workers, or neighbors. In short, there seems to be a deeper set of causes that shape the way we deal with all forms of conflict, our way of thinking.

Obviously, one should not make too much of this or any other analogy based, single factor argument. Missing are such obvious things as the "evil" which most people would ascribe to American racists or Saddam Hussein. Missing, too, are the "accidents" of history such as the mixed message Saddam

Hussein apparently took from his meeting with Ambassador April Glaspie shortly before the invasion of Kuwait or the fact that, one day, Rosa Parks refused to give up her seat in the front of the bus.

Still, the fact that my workshop participants and students almost always get to these same ideas does suggest that there has to be something to my two columns. They are part of a way of thinking almost all of us assimilate as we grow up and which then gets reinforced during our adult years. Whether one starts with my exercise or with the academic literature on international relations or human nature, our paradigm for conflict resolution through confrontation can be summed up with the seven themes in Table 6.1.

To begin with, most people are convinced that there are not enough resources to go around. That's not hard to understand given the importance we attach to oil or material possessions[1] which certainly do seem to be in short supply. That's also typically the case for parents who have definite limits on the time, energy, or money they have to devote to their children.

Even more important, we tend to view each actor, be it an individual, class, or nation, as separate or autonomous. From the time Newtonian scientific principles were developed until quite recently, most scientists looked at everything from atoms to individuals as independent. Indeed, many of the most important scientific breakthroughs came in the "micro" wings of the relevant disciplines, for example in voting behavior in political science or the profit maximizing firm in economics. Today, few people would deny that interdependence is a critical fact of life, but typically the analytical starting point remains the individual actor.

Furthermore, we assume that those actors constantly try to pursue their self-interest. As we will see in a moment, traditional international relations theory defines that as the protection and/or extension of a country's power and influence. Micro-economists similarly see it as a firm's or an individual's desire to maximize profit and minimize loss.

It's important to note, as well, that most people make those kinds of cost-benefit analyses from a reasonably short term perspective. Of all the points in Table 6.1, this is the one that is least well developed in the academic literature. Nonetheless, it is a vital component of this way of thinking. In the debates leading up to the Gulf war, American attention was focused on getting

---

[1] For a remarkable but non-academic view of material possessions and their (mal)distribution, see Peter Menzel's *Material World* (1994). Menzel provides statistical data on the thirty countries he covers, but the key to the book is photographs of families standing outside their homes along with all their material possessions. The contrast between the middle class family in Pearland, Texas and the Bhutanese one on the book's dust cover tells more about the difference between the "haves" and the "have nots" than any table or scholarly text.

Table 6.1
Today's Core Values and Assumptions

| Area of Concern | Current Value |
|---|---|
| Availability of resources | Scarce |
| Nature of relationships | Independent |
| Motivations | Self-interest |
| Time perspective | Short term |
| Nature of conflict | We vs. they |
| Nature of power | Power over |
| Interpretation of conflict | Bad |

Iraq out of Kuwait as soon as possible, while not much was paid to the historical roots of the crisis or what the long term implications of our action would be. Similarly, in family disputes, the conflict is often over whether I'm going to miss the Giants-Redskins game today if I bow to my wife's demand that we go buy the new sofa bed we both know we need rather than on the longer term impact of that spat on our relationship.

Perhaps the most important of these ideas is what psychologists call the "image of the enemy" (Frank 1985; Frank and Melville 1988; Keen 1986). Conflict grows out of real differences between interests and groups and nations, the "objective" column in my foreign policy and divorce example.

This psychological dynamic, however, makes genuine, lasting resolution of conflict difficult if not impossible because of the way we view the people we disagree with. There is a common tendency to think of the people we agree with as all good and, more significantly, those we disagree with as all bad. People tend to think in we versus they terms and blame "them" for the problem.

Once that happens, we turn the people we disagree with into stereotypical caricatures. We filter out all but the worst information or interpretations about the other side. Because we make these worst case assumptions about the other side, we blow the real differences far out of proportion and practically stop thinking of those we disagree with as human beings at all.

Any kind of constructive response becomes difficult. Each side becomes convinced that the other is out to do it in. By saying someone else is at fault, we are also saying that she or he is the problem. We wait for the other side to take the first step, humble itself, make conciliatory gestures, or apologize. Meanwhile, each side is paralyzed, because it is waiting for the hated, feared other to take that first step.

The image of the enemy becomes mutually self-fulfilling. Assuming the other side is treacherous and cruel, each convinces itself it may well have to be treacherous and cruel in return.

Thinking this way also leads us to expect that intense conflict can only have a zero-sum or win-lose outcome. Since our enemy's interests are at odds with our own, we assume that anything it does to pursue or defend those interests will somehow be detrimental to ours. Disagreement becomes dangerous. If somehow "they" manage to win, that means "we" automatically have lost. If someone has to lose, we'd better strain every nerve and muscle to make certain it's not us. If our enemies seem to do something that could benefit us, we dare not trust them. Friendly gestures from them are probably just tricks designed to lull us into letting our guard down. We need to be eternally vigilant and suspicious.

Given all this, it is hardly surprising that the conventional definition of power, my ability to get you to do something *you otherwise wouldn't do*, includes force, if not always violence. At times of intense conflict, we see no other way of working things out. Each side struggles, perhaps not always to win, but certainly not to lose. Neither is likely to give in easily.

The four italicized words in that definition are critical. I assume that in order to get what I want, you will have to give something up and you won't want to do that. That means, in turn, that my side will have to exert power over yours in order to prevail. Again, that force need not be physical violence. It can include the threat of violence, economic and other forms of coercive sanctions, or even psychological pressure. Whatever form it takes, the important thing to note is that it is confrontation.

To see the power and destructiveness of this way of thinking, take an example most readers of this book will know all too well, a student who doesn't agree with the grade he has gotten and goes to complain to the professor. There is an obvious "objective" side to the conflict. The student thinks the paper deserves an A, while the professor thinks it's only worth a C.

Such an encounter rarely turns out well. The professor and student both come to it with predispositions about the other. The student assumes the professor thinks all football players are dumb. The professor assumes the student is only interested in getting a good grade to boost his GPA and doesn't care about the material at all. The student is likely to be afraid of the teacher. But the teacher who doesn't like confrontations in the first place may be afraid of the student in return. Besides, he'd rather be working on the article he needs to get out before his tenure decision next year.

The professor probably will point out some things the student could have done differently, but if he fails to convince the student that the grade was justified, he'll probably notice that the student is getting angry. Everything from body language to the words exchanged may suggest that the conflict is intensifying. The professor will then probably make it clear that he holds almost all the power by implying that it actually was a hastily slapped together and dreadful paper, reminding the student that there is still a final exam to grade, or hinting that the student is wasting his valuable time. The student will probably capitulate and leave.

The professor will decide that he's won. But, has he?

The student will probably leave angrier and less self-confident than he was when he gathered up the courage to confront the teacher. At the very least, he'll go away more frustrated, give the teacher a poor course evaluation, and complain about him to his friends back in the dorm. If he thinks the professor has been particularly arrogant and condescending, he may complain about the professor to the department chair.

What's more, each has had his negative expectations about the other confirmed. The professor and student are each likely to reinforce their prejudices not just about each other but all students and professors respectively.

In other words, the professor may have won in the short run. In the longer run, that victory looks anything but clear cut, in much the same way as the "victories" on the battlefield as we saw in Chapter 2.

We certainly do not fully understand these psychological dynamics or their behavioral implications. Nonetheless, whenever people confront each other and then resort to violence, they usually think in something like these terms. They do so because they think they have to. Fear of attack, of outsiders, of differences, or of the unknown easily leads to the assumption that when push comes to shove, when someone we think is fundamentally different from us threatens us, we have no choice but to try exert our power over them.

## MORE CONVENTIONAL EXAMPLES

So far, this chapter has not covered ground most political scientists and similar academics would be comfortable with. However, what we intuit from everyday life is echoed in the conventional, mainstream theories about conflict. As with so much of this book, there is too much to that literature to cover in half a chapter. Instead, we will focus on two of the areas in which mainstream analysts focus on these values and assumptions, though they rarely present their evidence and theories in quite these terms, the study of international relations and racism.

The following examples are particularly helpful in seeing the two contrasting aspects of our conventional way of thinking. First, those values and assumptions go a long way in helping us understand why people and the organizations they form act the way they do. Second, they also help us understand why we end up in destructive confrontations so often.

### Realism in International Relations

Of all the subfields in political science, international relations comes the closest to having a single, widely accepted theoretical model, realism (readers not familiar with that literature should see Nye 1993; Betts 1993; Viotti and Kauppi 1993). Traditionally, realists have focused on the nation state as the most important actor in international relations, although most now acknowledge that we need to consider other actors as well, such as the multinational corporations considered in Chapter 3. Realists start with premises which parallel those listed in the first two rows of Table 6.1. Actors are trying to maximize their self-interest (national interest in the case of the nation state) which realists typically measure in terms of power, territory, wealth, and other resources all of which are in short supply.

Most realists are convinced that, other things being equal, confrontation and conflict on the international stage are potentially more dangerous and destructive than at the interpersonal level because of what they call the "anarchic" world system. Within the nation state, there usually is a government that regulates the conflict between self-interested people and groups so that the conflict among them doesn't get out of hand. In the international arena, there is no such state, and supranational bodies like the League of Nations and the United Nations have not done much to alleviate the pressures in this largely Hobbesian vision of life.

The fact that there are these parallels with Hobbesian ideas is no coincidence. The state system they describe so well was created at the same time Hobbes and many of the other architects of "modern" thought were writing (Miller 1985; Brown 1992). The state system itself is widely seen as the product of the contemporaneous Treaty of Westphalia which brought the Thirty Years War, the bloodiest in history up to that point, to an end. The leaders who forged the treaty enshrined some of the key principles which have dominated realist thought ever since, especially the autonomy and sovereignty of the nation state.

Since then, most realists have argued that there is no way of achieving anything like what I'll call stable peace in the next chapter. Rather, the best they think we can do is a kind of tense standoff, which gets ever more tense as the stakes of the conflict rise.

The best way of achieving that standoff is through one of the realists' most famous concepts, the balance of power. The term is used to describe a set of formal arrangements reached following the end of the Napoleonic wars in 1815 which governed international relations among the major European powers for much of the next century.

The idea now has a more generic meaning to include any situation in which opposing states have roughly equal powers and resources. Realists argue that under those circumstances it makes no sense for either side to attack the other, because its leaders realize the odds of winning are low and the likely costs of fighting are quite high. In short, the system "works" when states act rationally by making what amount to cost-benefit analyses before they act.

Some realists even point to the Cold War in Europe as a success story. None would argue that the Cold War was a good or pleasant thing. Like John Mearsheimer (1990a, 1990b), though they do claim that the balance between East and West provided Europe with the longest period without a war at least since Westphalia and probably ever.

They do so, because they are convinced that deterrence worked exactly the way they think it is supposed to. The superpowers didn't go to war, because decision makers in Moscow and Washington "knew" that the risks were too great and because they kept their arsenals large and strong enough to make the threat of retaliation after a first strike credible.

While there are dozens of variations on the theme of deterrence, its basic principle is quite simple. Two sides deter each other by making credible threats against each other. If each knows that its attack will be met by an equally or devastating counterattack, no rational power will launch that first attack.

But deterrence also shows us the main problem with realism. Not all actors behave rationally.

Sometimes, people do not make those cost-benefit calculations. Sometimes, they simply won't act rationally, at least given the way the realists define the term, which some think was true of Saddam Hussein both before and after the invasion of Kuwait or for the Bosnian Serbs in their failure to accept any of the various peace proposals put forth since the fighting began. Sometimes, too, people misperceive the abilities or goals of their opponents, as certainly seems to have been the case for Saddam Hussein and his assumption that the United States couldn't or wouldn't fight.

A number of researchers who are in most other respects realists argue that perceptions and, especially, misperceptions on the part of key actors tend to make it difficult to make those calculations or, more importantly for our purposes, magnify the intensity of the conflict itself (Jervis 1968; Allison 1971;

Janis 1983; Frank and Melville 1988). In fact, decision makers really know very little about how their counterparts in other countries make up their minds.

There is always, in short, a lot of uncertainty even about what it means to pursue one's self or national interest. To illustrate that, analysts frequently use a "game" known as the Prisoner's Dilemma (Axelrod 1984). The two "players" have been arrested for a crime, in one recent version, the possession of illegal drugs (Nye 1993: 12–16). Prosecutors are convinced that they can get convictions for possession on the basis of the evidence they already have, but need corroboration from one of the accused to put them away for a more serious crime.

Cleverly, they put the accused men in a bind. They are held in separate cells and are not allowed to communicate with each other. The police then give the two a choice: cooperate with them and rat on the other guy or keep quiet. They make it clear what will happen under all circumstances as summarized in Table 6.2. If Prisoner A tells on Prisoner B while Prisoner B stays silent, B will get a maximum sentence of twenty-five years and A will go free. If B tells on A but A remains silent, B will go free while A goes to jail. If each tells on the other, both go to jail for ten years. If both stonewall, the prosecutors will have no choice but to proceed with the lesser possession charge, which will get them each a year in jail.

What does it mean to pursue your self-interest under such circumstances? Obviously, each prisoner would like to shut up and go free. But, shouldn't each assume the other would think the same way? In that event, it's very risky to keep quiet, since if your "buddy" rats on you, you can end up doing twenty-five years. Maybe your best bet is to assume your buddy will talk and do the same thing, because that way you at least avoid the worst possible outcome, a quarter century in jail.

Table 6.2
The Prisoner's Dilemma

|  |  | *Prisoner A* | |
|---|---|---|---|
|  |  | Keep quiet | Cooperate with the police |
| *Prisoner B* | Keep quiet | Each gets 1 year | B gets 25 years<br>A gets off |
|  | Cooperate with the police | B gets off<br>A gets 25 years | Each gets 10 years |

The dilemma doesn't get much easier if you let the two talk to each other. After all, drug dealers aren't the most savory characters in the world (sort of like nation states?). Why should they trust each other? If A says he'll keep his mouth shut, should B believe him or vice versa? It's hard to trust when the stakes are high and you question the motivations of the person or people on the other side. It's easy to misperceive what the other side is up to.

Most realists also talk about an even broader "security dilemma" which reflects the importance of zero-sum thinking in international as well as interpersonal relations. Basically, realists point out that actions one country takes to maximize its own security may reduce that of its opponents.

One obvious example here was the addition of new weapons systems during the Cold War or any other arms race. In the late 1970s, for instance, the Soviets deployed multiple warhead SS-20 missiles that could reach targets in Western Europe in nine or ten minutes. The Soviets saw their action as an obvious attempt to deter a NATO attack and was thus designed to enhance their own security. The United States and its allies, however, felt decidedly more insecure. They, of course, concluded that the only way the only thing they could do was add new missiles of their own, which in turn left the Soviets more vulnerable.

Given the uncertainties and stakes of most aspects of international relations, it isn't surprising that the image of the enemy plays an important role there as well. The same process of demonizing, enemy, or "we versus they" thinking enters into and hardens positions in international as well as in interpersonal relations.

The antipathy between George Bush and Saddam Hussein made a peaceful resolution of the Gulf crisis all but impossible. Calling someone the "next Hitler" and the like tends to drive wedges between people. Thinking in terms of enemies alone certainly did not lead to that or any other war, but it just as certainly makes peaceful resolution of the underlying conflict extremely difficult.

The psychoanalytic pioneer Carl Jung underscored all this when he applied his theories of the self to the Cold War shortly before his death.

We should give a great deal of consideration to what we are doing, for mankind is now threatened by self-created and deadly dangers that are growing beyond our control. Our world is, so to speak, dissociated like a neurotic, with the Iron Curtain marking the symbolic line of division. Western man, becoming aware of the aggressive will to power of the East, sees himself forced to take extraordinary measures of defense, at the same time as he prides himself on his virtue and good intentions.

What he fails to see is that it is his own vices, which he has covered up by good international manners, that are thrown back in this face by the communist world, shamelessly and methodically. What the West has tolerated, but secretly and with a slight sense of shame (the diplomatic lie, systematic deception, veiled threats) comes back into the open and in full measure from the East and ties us up in neurotic knots. It is the face of his own evil shadow that grins at Western man from the other side of the Iron Curtain.

But all attempts (to resolve the problem by moral and mental means) have proved singularly ineffective, and will do so as long as we try to convince ourselves and the world that it is only they (i.e., our opponents) who are wrong. It would be much more to the point for us to make a serious attempt to recognize our own shadow and its nefarious doings. If we could, we should be immune to any moral and mental infection and insinuation. (Jung 1964: 85, 168, 176)

In sum, as with interpersonal relations, the combination of all these factors make conflict a tinder keg. Not all conflict turns violent. Nonetheless, the same principles we saw in the last rows of Table 6.1 apply here as well. We may not want to resort to violence, but the realist assumes that at some point we will probably have to. Thus we should be always be prepared to do so, should deterrence, balance of power, and all the other rationality based mechanisms fail.

In closing, consider two statements from leading realist theorists. "Nations actively involved in international relations are continuously preparing for, actively involved in, or recovering from organized violence in the form of war" (Morgenthau 1978: 42). "Military force is important, if not central, in international politics. It brings some order out of chaos, and it helps to make and enforce the rules of the game" (Art and Waltz 1988: 1).

### Race and Ethnicity

Theories about racial or ethnic conflict are nowhere near as fully developed as those for international relations. Too many different conflicts with too many differing cultural factors have been involved for social scientists to boil things down into as simple and powerful a package as realism.

There is, however, a growing consensus about it in which the attitudes summed up in Table 6.1 play a major role. By definition, racism involves stereotypical thinking in which people lump all members of another group together and attribute terrible characteristics to them, much as in the image of the enemy.

Rather than rehash all the themes of Table 6.1, I will focus on one central notion, identity, which will play an increasingly important role in the rest of this book. Anthony Smith defined an ethnic community as "a named human population with a myth of common ancestry, shared memories, and cultural elements; a link with a historic territory or homeland; and a measure of solidarity" (1993: 28–29). An ethnic or racial identity, then, is one that sets me apart from you.

Such identifications need not lead to the catastrophic situations discussed in Chapter 5. Thus, the fact that I am a white Jewish-American really doesn't make much of a difference when I have to determine what I think of, say, Polish- or Italian-Americans. Indeed, many racial, ethnic, religious, and linguistic differences which used to spark intense conflict have been defused over the last half century or so, especially in the industrialized democracies.

But, if Smith is right, when an intense conflict arises over territory or some other resource, it can be the key psychological factor leading to the fear and hatred associated with stereotypical thinking and images of an enemy. In most parts of the world, it has become easier and easier for ethnic identification to crystallize into the kind of we versus they sentiment that makes such conflict so intense. The modern state imposes ever more extensive demands on its citizens, at least some of which can lead members of an ethnic or racial community to see themselves more clearly as different and discriminated against. The spread of the mass media have made it easier to sustain minority languages and spread the word about the need to organize around one's ethnic identification.

In this sense, racial or ethnic identification is but a form of nationalism which William Pfaff (1993) recently called the "wrath of nations." "Nationalism, of course, is intrinsically absurd. Why should the accident of birth as an American, Albanian, Scot, or Fiji Islander impose loyalties that dominate an individual life and structure a society so as to place it in formal conflict with others?" (17). But, as Pfaff and so many others who have written on nationalism go on to argue, it does. As Walter Russell Mead put it in his review of Pfaff's book, "Nationalism is bloody-minded and backward. It is also here to stay" (1993: 25).

Racial and ethnic identification can thus lead to the blind hatred that makes anything approaching the rationality of realism implausible, if not impossible. Take, for instance, a Kosovan (ethnic Albanian, living in Serbia) interviewed by Robert Kaplan over the din of a disco in the early 1990s:

You don't know what it is to kill with a hammer, with nails, with clubs, do you? Do you know why I don't like to drink plum brandy, why I drink beer always? Because the Chetniks used to do their killing after drinking plum brandy. Do you know what it is to throw a child in the air and catch it on a knife in front of its mother? To be tied to a burning log? To have your ass split with an ax so you beg the Serbs, beg them, to shoot you in the head and they don't?

And they go to church after. They go to their goddamn church. I have no words. There are things that are beyond evil, that you just can't speak about.

He went on shouting. Ismail was only twenty-six; he had no personal knowledge of the events he described. Rats infest his house, he told me. The Serbs were to blame. (Kaplan 1993: xvii)

Ismail's degree of anger and hatred are unusual. Still, it probably isn't all that uncommon among the skinheads of Germany or Los Angeles, the Brahmins who immolated themselves when the Singh government introduced its affirm-ative action policy, or, of course, the thousands of men and women who have been fighting in Ismail's own country.

Ethnic, racial, and religious identification, obviously, does not lead to this kind of attitude and violence among all of us. If it did, we'd truly be living in some sort of Hobbesian war of all against all. Nonetheless, it is a powerful enough force in enough individuals to produce the many examples of this one slice of the global crisis.

## AND THUS WE DRIFT

No one would argue that ways of thinking completely determine the way we act. Scholars writing about ethnicity thus also raise such issues as the size, geographical concentration, and resources of a group as key factors in deter-mining how it will assert its positions or whether it will do so at all.

No one would argue, either, that our thinking hasn't changed at all since Einstein wrote that famous sentence. If nothing else, we have learned to be far more cautious in contemplating the use of nuclear and other weapons of mass destruction.

But, most of our changes have occurred within the basic parameters of the way of thinking outlined in this chapter. As recent American political contro-versy has shown, most people still think the best way to deter (the use of this term here as well as in international relations is by no means coincidental) crime is to hire more police officers, build more prisons, and come down ever harder on the criminals. Similarly, Jonathan Clarke (1993) has recently decried what he called the "conceptual poverty" of U.S. foreign policy, because its architects, Republicans and Democrats alike, continue using in an all but unquestioned way the principles that guided our policy for the last fifty years into the drastically different post Cold War era.

What's more, the evidence is mounting that this way of thinking doesn't work. We have had remarkably little success reducing the crime rate in Washington, while in other troubled cities from Rio de Janeiro to Johannesburg to Moscow, it seems to be escalating all but out of control. And, despite the best efforts of the UN, the US and other governments, and individual negotiators such as Richard Holbrooke or Lord David Owen, we seem unable to resolve many of the wars taking place around the world. The most we seem to be able to accomplish is a costly armed standoff, of the type which all too often degenerates into violence as in the streets of Washington or Sarajevo.

If I'm right, the problem does not lie in the frequent leftist criticism of power-hungry or otherwise duplicitous leaders. Indeed, one cannot help but be struck by the good faith efforts being made by most political and other leaders around the world (even those one disagrees with) and the frustrations they so obviously feel when crises in Haiti or Somalia or Bosnia or Ireland bloodily drag on and on with no plausible solution in sight.

The problem lies far deeper than the misguided ideology or lack of talent in this or that set of politicians. Rather, its roots lie in the disconnect between problems characterized if not defined by interdependence and an approach to dealing with them based on independence. Out of that disconnect between a dramatically changed real world and a relatively constant way of dealing with it comes the gap depicted in Figures 1.1 and 1.2 and the difficulty politicians and average citizens alike are having solving the global crisis.

Under the best of circumstances, such a gap is cause for deep concern. It is all the more worrisome now when rapid and accelerating change is occurring in almost all areas of our lives. Such change is likely to lead to more rather than less conflict down the line (Toffler and Toffler 1990, 1993).

Business as usual by operating within the current paradigm has not led to much progress on any of these fronts, while the stakes involved in most of them have gotten higher. At such times, it makes sense to consider the messages implicit in the titles of two books whose themes will figure prominently in the chapters to come, "reinventing the future" (Kidder 1988) by speaking to each other "in a different voice" (Gilligan 1981).

By not reexamining our political and other paradigms, we have put much of human life and much of what we value in the human experience at risk, because, if the analysis presented here is on target, it is that paradigm that keeps us on the endless treadmill that leads from conflict to confrontation to exploitation to violence.

As Pfaff also suggests, humanity has faced other major turning points, but this time, the stakes are undoubtedly higher than they have ever been before. As Christopher Langton, one of the prime architects of the new, promising interdisciplinary study of complexity has put it, "By the middle of this century, mankind had acquired the power to extinguish life on earth. By the middle of the next century, he will be able to create it. Of the two, it is hard to say which places the larger burden of responsibility on our shoulders" (cited in Waldrop 1992: 283).

# REFERENCES

Allison, Graham (1971). *The Essence of Decision*. Boston: Little Brown.

Argyris, Chris (1985). *Strategy, Change, and Defensive Routines*. Boston: Pitman.

Art, Robert, and Kenneth Waltz (1988). *The Use of Force: Military Power and International Relations*. Lanham, Md.: University Press of America.

Betts, Richard K. (1993). *Conflict After the Cold War: Arguments on Causes of War and Peace*. New York: Macmillan.

Boehnke, Klaus et al. (1993). "Can the Threat of War be Conceptualized as Macro-Social Stress?" In Knud S. Larsen, ed., *Conflict and Social Psychology*. London: Sage, 3–14.

Brown, Seyom (1992). *International Relations in a Changing Global System*. Boulder, Colo.: Westview.

Clarke, Jonathan (1993). "The Conceptual Poverty of U.S. Foreign Policy." *The Atlantic*, September, 54–66.

Frank, Jerome (1985). "Image of the Enemy." Videotape. Palo Alto: Beyond War Foundation.

Frank, Jerome, and Andrei Melville (1988). "The Image of the Enemy and the Process of Change." In Anatoly Gromyko and Martin Hellman, eds., *Breakthrough: Emerging New Thinking: Soviet and Western Scholars Issue a Challenge to Build a World Beyond War*. New York and Moscow: Thomas Walker and Novosti, 199–208.

Gaddis, John Lewis (1987). *The Long Peace*. New York: Oxford University Press.

Gilligan, Carol (1981). *In a Different Voice*. Cambridge: Harvard University Press.

Janis, Irving (1983). *Groupthink*. Boston: Houghton-Mifflin.

Jervis, Robert (1968). "Hypotheses on Misperception." *World Politics* 20: 454–479.

Jung, Carl (1964). *Man and His Symbols*. New York: Doubleday.

Kaplan, Robert D. (1993). *Balkan Ghosts: A Journey Through History*. New York: St. Martin's.

Keegan, John (1993). *A History of Warfare*. New York: Knopf.

Keen, Sam (1986). *Faces of the Enemy: Reflections of the Hostile Imagination*. New York: Harper and Row.

Kennedy, Paul (1987). *The Rise and Fall of Great Powers*. New York: Random House.

Kidder, Rushworth (1988). *Reinventing the Future*. Cambridge: MIT Press.

Kuhn, Thomas (1969). *The Structure of Scientific Revolutions*. 2d ed. Chicago: University of Chicago Press.

Landau, Martin (1961). "On the Use of Metaphor in Political Analysis." *Social Research* 28: 331–363.

Macpherson, C. B. (1977). *The Life and Times of Liberal Democracy*. New York: Oxford University Press.

Mead, Walter Russell (1993). "This Land is My Land." *New York Times Book Review*, 7 November, 25.

Mearsheimer, John (1990a). "Back to the Future: Instability in Europe After the Cold War." *International Security* 15: 5–56.

———. (1990b). "Why We Will Soon Miss the Cold War." *The Atlantic Monthly* 266: 35–50.

Menzel, Peter (1994). *Material World.* San Francisco: Sierra Club.

Miller, Lynn (1985). *Global Order: Values and Power in International Politics.* Boulder, Colo.: Westview Press.

Morgenthau, Hans J. (1978). *Politics Among Nations,* 5th ed. New York: Knopf.

Nye, Joseph (1993). *Understanding International Conflicts.* New York: HarperCollins.

Pfaff, William (1993). *The Wrath of Nations: Civilization and the Furies of Nationalism.* New York: Simon and Schuster.

Schwartz, Barry (1986). *The Battle for Human Nature.* New York: W. W. Norton.

Selznick, Philip (1992). *The Moral Commonwealth: Social Theory and the Promise* of *Community.* Berkeley: University of California Press.

Slaton, Chirsta Daryl (1991). "Quantum Theory and Political Theory." In Edward L. Becker, ed., *Quantum Politics: Applying Quantum Theory to Political Phenomena.* New York: Praeger, 41–64.

Smith, Anthony (1993). "The Ethnic Sources of Nationalism." In Michael E. Brown, ed., *Ethnic Conflict and International Security.* Princeton: Princeton University Press, 27–42.

Toffler, Alvin, and Heidi (1990). *Power Shift: Knowledge, Wealth, and Violence at the Edge of the 21st Century.* New York: Bantam Books.

———. (1993). *War and Anti-War: Survival at the Dawn of the 21st Century.* Boston: Little Brown.

Viotti, Paul R., and Mark V. Kauppi (1993). *International Relations Theory: Realism, Pluralism, Globalism.* New York: Macmillan.

Waldrop, M. Mitchell (1992). *Complexity: The Emerging Science at the Edge of Order and Chaos.* New York: Simon and Schuster.

# 7

# INTERDEPENDENCE

The real voyage of discovery consists not in seeking new lands but in seeing
with new eyes.

—Marcel Proust

Chapter 1 promised an optimistic book that would cover both aspects
of a crisis as rendered in the Chinese ideogram. So far, there has been
a lot about the dangers, but little on the opportunities. That will now
change. If I'm right, the opportunity lies in forging cooperative solutions to
global problems. As should already be clear from Chapter 6, that will require
a dramatic switch from the conventional wisdom and business as usual to a
new way of thinking or, as Proust put it, "seeing with new eyes."

The reader has every reason to be doubtful, for there have been hundreds
of such proposals over the years. Most have been received as hopelessly idealistic
by academic experts, policy makers, and average citizens alike. Why that is the
case should be clear if we briefly consider two movies, one from near the
beginning, the other from near the end of the Cold War.

The first was the science fiction classic, *The Day the Earth Stood Still*. The
plot line was simple. A spaceship lands right in front of the Washington
Monument (what a coincidence) and out step a remarkably handsome (and
we later learn, brilliant) "man," Klatu, and his robot Gort. To make a long story
short, Klatu is a genius with superhuman powers who convinces a scientist
(who looks amazingly like Albert Einstein) of that fact by blocking all of the

world's energy and communications systems. The earth's very frightened leaders convene, listen to Klatu's warnings about violence, and proceed to achieve peace and harmony around the world.

The other, *Amazing Grace and Chuck*, was released in the mid-1980s. A star Little League pitcher, Chuck, is taken to visit a nuclear missile silo by a member of Congress, who happens to be a friend of his father (more coincidences). The boy is shocked and decides on a novel protest. He won't pitch again until the arms race is over. Then, Amazing Grace (real-life Denver Nuggets star Alex English; it says something about the film that English was its best actor) learns about Chuck and organizes an international boycott by professional athletes which is rather successful. A few months later, Amazing Grace is killed by the leaders of a nefarious international cabal reminiscent of the worst stereotypes about the Trilateral Commission. People around the world are outraged; everyone starts boycotting everything. At that point, the Soviet and American leaders have no choice but to agree on a sweeping program of arms reductions just in time, of course, for the opening day of Chuck's next Little League season, when they throw out the ceremonial first ball.

Such plots make for mediocre cinema and worse politics. They reinforce the skepticism that fundamental change in international relations and conflict resolution can occur. On the other hand, it would not make sense to write a book like this if proposals for a different and more peaceful world were, by definition, exercises in fantasy or futility. This chapter and the rest of this book lay out what I *believe* is a far more plausible scenario through which the ideas developed here *could* become reality.

The emphasis on the conditional is critical. There is no way of knowing for sure whether or not the kind of change described below is possible and, even if it is, no way of predicting how it would come about with any degree of precision. It is also far too early to anticipate what its institutions would be, including whether or not there would be a single global government.

There is some general agreement, however, about how such a world would work. Cooperation would replace confrontation and force as the major way of solving social and political problems. While we are a long way from creating such a world, it has become credible enough that Brown University's Center for Foreign Policy Development (Lindeman and Rose 1992), for instance, included it as one of four broad options Americans should consider over the next fifteen years or so.

We also know enough about how large scale political change takes place to at least sketch out a general strategy for making the shift to a more cooperative form of conflict resolution. Considerable evidence at the individual, organizational, national, and international levels suggest that at least some people,

including many powerful ones, have adopted some or all of what I will call
new thinking to give us some reason to believe that some version of this
sweeping change is possible.

This chapter lays out the first step in that argument. It suggests that unlike
the world for which realism was devised, today's reality is defined by interdependence, not independence. Those three letters in one word but not the other
make a world of difference. Viewing the crisis with a mental lens based on
interdependence undermines many of the assumptions and much of the power
of realist thought as well as its intellectual cousins in a number of other
disciplines (Capra 1984; Schwartz 1986).

Interdependence reflects the new reality driven home by the global crisis.
We are a single people, sharing a single, endangered planet. However much
our circumstances may differ, fundamentally we are alike. We breathe the same
air, drink the same water, share the same hopes for our children, and hunger
equally for the nourishment of food, knowledge, meaning, useful work,
dignity, and affection. We depend equally on this tiny, eight thousand mile
wide life support system floating in the infinite cold blackness of space.

Perhaps most important of all, the reality of interdependence opens the door
to a dramatically different way of understanding the world and, with it, a new
way of thinking and acting that *might* provide a way out of the global crisis.
In short, interdependence gives us those Proustean "new eyes" which will allow
us to better see the world we live in and the one we might want to create.

## THINKING ABOUT INTERDEPENDENCE

Paradigm shifts can occur only when disconcerting discoveries lead people
to question the "first principles" of the existing one. Then, people can become
open to adopting a new model that yields more fruitful insights about a wider
range of phenomena.

Interdependence can supply both the new principles and deeper insights
needed in a new paradigm today. With it comes not just new ways of understanding, but a wholly different prescription for ways of acting that could lead
to qualitatively different and (at least from my perspective) better outcomes.

Interdependence is not a new idea. It can be found in the ethical teachings
of most major spiritual traditions. But today, it has taken on new empirical
importance as well, because it has become our most accurate way of understanding the world we live in.

Concrete evidence that the world is interdependent is so familiar that it
almost does not bear repeating here (for general, readable overviews, see Attali
1991; Toffler 1990). Most international relations experts acknowledge that the

world is increasingly interdependent, but that has not qualitatively changed the way they analyze global trends (Nye 1993: ch. 7 and 8; Keohane and Nye 1989). The nation state remains the critical unit of analysis and power is still defined in terms of one actor's ability to force another to accede to its wishes.

At first glance, the events around the world seem to support this viewpoint which stresses continuity at least as much as change. Interdependence certainly has not ushered in a new era of peaceful relations. The current global system is as contentious as ever. International relations is still about power politics. The determinants of power are shifting away from the purely military vision of security to include economic, social, and environmental forces as well. But the conventional image is still of struggle between sovereign nations locked in conflict which leads to zero-sum outcomes. If that weren't the case, why would we be so worried about the Japanese?

Yet, the world is interdependent. That is "reality" every bit as much as the continued reliance on confrontation and the rest of our conventional way of thinking.

What we have here is a classic instance of the "gaps" outlined in Figures 1.1 and 1.2. "Reality" has changed fundamentally, but we continue to use "business as usual" in trying to figure out what to do about it. In other words, there are two world views at work here, one based on interdependence, the other on independence, and they lead to dramatically different empirical and normative conclusions about conflict resolution. The former keeps us on a collision course with the dangerous side of the crisis; the latter could point us to a new paradigm and the opportunities which are part of the crisis as well.

Very much like war, the former is obsolete. Obviously, we can still use it, because we still do use it. However, the question to ask is whether or not it is still doing an effective enough job in helping us solve the problems we face.

As is often the case, the intellectual background for this new paradigm lies in the natural, not the social sciences. Most of the natural sciences have already gone through a paradigm shift. In virtually every case, the key was the adoption of organizing principles analogous to the interdependence of human systems. Each is based on the unity of the field the scientists are studying in which everything is intertwined in a single, completely interdependent system.

Assumptions about the independence of actors have their roots in the now largely discredited Newtonian model. The new scientific paradigms are based on the premise, instead, that all actors are interdependent.

The most important and least easy to understand occurred in physics during the first third of this century (Becker 1991). Most physicists abandoned atomistic Newtonian models that stressed the autonomy of particles acting and reacting with one another and sharply differentiated between energy and mass because those models no longer provided accurate answers or persuasive interpretations for the questions they were studying.

Instead, physicists tend to see matter as a network of relationships that seem more like waves than particles. Everything is connected in a seamless web (the word "web" appears in almost all writing on interdependence). If one "piece" moves, everything else is affected by the wave it creates. The actor is, in turn, acted upon in a universe which is an interconnected whole.

More recently, ecologists have reached similar conclusions. That ecologists stress interdependence as well is hardly surprising, since the very word "ecology" literally means the study of the whole.

As most ecologists see it, the earth is a single "life support" system. If it is disrupted in one place, unpredictable and often undesirable impacts occur elsewhere. Some, like the British ecologist and astrophysicist James Lovelock (1979, 1988), go so far as to argue that the earth itself is for all intents and purposes a living organism, because it meets the key scientific criterion for the existence of life: the ability to sustain "oneself" by stemming entropy.

Even ecologists who don't go that far have shown the value of biological and social diversity. While traditional social scientists have looked upon diversity as a source of conflict and hence violence and instability, ecologists have demonstrated that diverse biological systems have more ways to respond to environmental stresses than do more homogeneous ones. Think here of the most commonly cited example of monoculture, the Irish potato famine of 1845–1850.

Consider one more contribution modern environmentalists have made, the importance of learning and adaptation. One of the common denominators in Chapters 2 through 5 is the accelerating rate of change in almost all areas of life. As a result, rather than the stability or equilibrium that most conventional social science models are based on, the key dependent variable today may well be understanding how people and the organizations they form adapt to that rapid change.

Here, modern evolutionary theory is instructive, because it has moved dramatically away from the simplistic interpretation of Darwinism as the "survival of the fittest." Now, most biologists look at evolution as favoring the species that can best respond to changing conditions. Thus, dinosaurs died out not because they were dumb or weak, but because they didn't have the genetic capacity to adapt to a sudden shift in the earth's climate.

Closer to the intellectual home of most readers are the organizational and management scientists who have been working with systems theory (Senge 1990; Argyris 1990). The basic principles of systems theory are familiar to many political scientists, because it enjoyed a flurry of popularity in the 1950s and 1960s. In political science, systems theorists explored how people and the organizations they formed made "inputs" which were translated into "outputs" by the state and other decision makers (Easton 1965; Deutsch 1963). Those outputs then helped shape what people did later on through what Easton inelegantly called "the overall intrasystemic feedback loop." The whole system was constrained as well by nonpolitical and international factors which made up its "environment."

The systems perspective is now widely used in most of the natural sciences. It was, for instance, the intellectual underpinning for the modeling of natural resource systems in the Club of Rome's *The Limits to Growth* (Meadows, et al. 1972) and has been used in most environmental research ever since. While much use of systems theory is rather abstruse and computer heavy, some educators have been able to design programs like LOGO (Papert 1980) to help younger students learn the logic of mathematics and computing or STELLA (High Performance Systems 1985) to help older ones explore dynamic, inter-connected systems even if they lack sophisticated programming and other computer skills.

Systems theory points us in three important and related directions which the more widely accepted social science models tend to underplay.

First, it emphasizes feedback. Today's actions affect how you and I and everyone else will behave tomorrow, which will shape the way we act the day after that and so on. In short, neither people nor their actions are ever independent of each other.

Second, feedback makes systems analysis dynamic. Traditional social science models tend to focus on actions at particular points in time and thus resemble an intellectual snapshot. Systems theory suggests we need to think in the long term and create the unbroken, social scientific equivalents of videotapes. To take but one example, traditional international relations theorists examining the Gulf war tend to concentrate on a series of all but immediate causes (the Iran-Iraq war, the cult of personality around Saddam Hussein) and conse-quences (the balance of power in the region after the war). Systems theorists would have us cast our net deeper into the past and consider the way Iraq was created in the first place during and after World War I and explore what its longer term consequences might be, for instance, in reinforcing anti-western sentiments or the widespread Iraqi cultural norm of what amounts to a garrison mentality.

Third, these theorists argue that there are three ways systems can evolve. Social scientists who use systems theory have spent the most time trying to understand stable or *homeostatic* systems which develop mechanisms for bal-ancing themselves akin to the way a building's thermostat keeps its temperature within a few degrees of the desired heat. They did so because they were worried about *dysfunctional* democracies which lacked those mechanisms and thus tended to collapse into authoritarianism (e.g., Weimar Germany). Those social scientists did not pay much attention to the third type, *eufunctional* systems. These systems have mechanisms which allow them to "learn" from changes going on around them and "grow" or improve their performance steadily and significantly over time. Such systems will be at the core of much of the rest of this book.

The last area of research worth mentioning here is the new science of complexity, which is an outgrowth of the more widely known chaos theory (Gleick 1987, Waldrop 1992). Interdisciplinary teams of scientists have been modeling scientific phenomena based on assumptions which are almost the exact opposite of those used in classical social scientific research. Instead of starting with the neoclassical economist's assumption of perfect rationality and then proceeding deductively, the complexity theorists start with the closer to real life assumption that actors are struggling to figure out what to do in a rapidly changing world filled with lots of and perhaps too many variables and choices. Then, they proceed inductively and watch how their actors behave and learn (or fail to as the case may be).

Their simulated discoveries have thrown much of classical economic and other social science theory into question. An initial set of conditions can lead to a wide variety of outcomes, only one of which is equilibrium, the most important dependent variable and normative goal in conventional economic thought. What look like minor decisions can have a major impact, increasingly determining the trajectory of the system as a whole by narrowing the range of possibilities open to it, a feature they refer to as "path dependency." Ultimately, as a result of those decisions, systems tend to "lock in" to a pattern, but there is no reason why the lock in will turn out be beneficial or end up anywhere near equilibrium. That only happens if the actors learn effectively by adapting their behavior to fit their changing environment. To see how path dependency can lock us into something less than optimal outcomes, simply consider the adoption of the QWERTY keyboard[1] or VHS rather than Beta as the standard VCR technology when early rational decisions resulted in extremely irrational results later on.

---

[1] QWERTY are the first six letters on the top row of an American keyboard and were originally arranged in that order because typewriter mechanics were very primitive, and most people would be able to type faster than the keys could move if arranged in the most ergodynamically efficient way. Today, no one could outtype an electronic computer however the keys were arranged.

As in systems theory, these new and still highly speculative complexity studies stress the twin notions of feedback and learning. In at least three respects, however, complexity scientists go even farther.

First, they are almost exclusively interested in the dynamics of adaptive systems through what the economist W. Brian Arthur (1990) calls "positive feedback loops." As in the related field of artificial intelligence, they are seeking the causes of successful adaptation, which leads them to discuss self-reproducing or co-evolving systems rather than the dysfunctional ones of conventional structural-functional analysis or the economist's "law" of diminishing returns.

Second, unlike their mainstream counterparts, these theoreticians work inductively rather than deductively. They are convinced that real world actors rarely decide what they are going to do on the basis of any set of a priori assumptions. Instead, they are more likely to act in largely ad hoc ways in response to real life conditions. General principles are important, as they obviously are in this book. However, their models suggest that the important patterns of learning and adaptation emerge from tangible experiences, not abstract reasoning (Axelrod 1984).

That insight is especially important given the rapidity of social, political, economic, and environmental change these days. A priori principles, again, do matter. But, if their experiments with everything from the prisoner's dilemma to the stock market and the origins of life are at all accurate, successful adaptation is in large part a function of the flexibility that allows an actor to see and respond to such change.

On the other hand, the factors that lead to lock in and then to diminishing returns tend to make systems less flexible and adaptive. In other words, one of the implications of this area of research is that we should assume that no one set of practices or institutions is likely to perform well for very long. Rather than trying to develop a detailed blueprint for the edifices of a new world order through a strengthened United Nations or some form of world government, we should probably be trying to develop our capacity to change and keep changing instead.

Third, and perhaps most importantly of all, these theoretical studies undermine one of the most central premises of all Newtonian science: the autonomy of the individual actor, be it the individual of microeconomic theory or the nation state in the realist view of international relations. Arthur and his colleagues do not deny that the individual has the *capacity* to act on his or her own. Rather, they suggest that individuals thinking they are pursuing their individual (or national as the case may be) interest need not reach the optimal outcomes anticipated by those theories. Mitchell Waldrop summed all this up well in discussing Arthur's early work on increasing returns.

But increasing returns cut to the heart of that myth. If small chance events can lock you in to any of several possible outcomes, then the outcome that's actually selected *may* not be the best. And that means that maximum individual freedom—and the free market—might *not* produce the best of all possible worlds. (Waldrop 1992: 48)


## THREE BIG LESSONS

At this point, it makes sense to ask why any of this scientific material is relevant to the study of politics and conflict. The answer is surprisingly simple. A paradigm based on interdependence leads to a new and more useful way of understanding human behavior and its implications. It puts most of the key normative and empirical principles underlying conventional modes of thinking into question. It stresses such notions as positive feedback, adaptation to rapidly changing environments, individual and organizational learning, and cooperative solutions that build on rather than work against our interdependence and diversity.

In sum, these new scientific models teach us at least three profound and interconnected lessons.

The first is to think in the long term by incorporating feedback. We now see the importance of asking how one actor's behavior at one point in time will affect the rest of the system and that actor itself down the line.

Second, in the traditional way of thinking and acting, one "wins" by imposing his or her power over an adversary. Such victories are pyrrhic at best, because "winning" in the short run almost always yields negative outcomes in the longer term.

Third, interdependence suggests that only positive-sum or win-win solutions that benefit all participants will work in the longer run. Only they actually resolve[2] conflict and enhance the performance of the system as a whole, as well as its component parts. The conflict itself begins to disappear. Meanwhile, the members of the system have adapted and learned, which leaves them better able to handle further conflict later on.

To see that in the simplest kind of two person system, let's return to the conflict over grades between a teacher and student discussed in Chapter 6. We saw there that the faculty member typically "wins" any such confrontation but that the victory can very well evaporate in the longer run. Both will bear emotional scars that will harm not just their relationship with each other

[2]Once again, etymology is instructive. The same word, resolve, has an intriguing musical meaning. A tonal piece ends with a chord which "resolves" the music. Like this kind of conflict resolution, it brings it into harmony.

but, to some degree, the way they deal with other students and teachers as well.

On the other hand, what if the faculty member and student acknowledged from the beginning that a conflict exists and agreed that their challenge was to settle it once and for all? The teacher might then reread the paper and take another stab at showing the student why it wasn't very good. More importantly, the teacher could provide concrete, constructive suggestions about how to improve it.

The faculty member may spend more time with that student than he or she would in a more confrontational scenario and, in that sense, might look upon the encounter as a net loss. However, in the longer term, the student will do better work, enjoy the class more, and, perhaps, let friends and other faculty members know how effective the teacher was. Meanwhile, the faculty member may have gotten some new insights into how to help students craft arguments that could be conveyed once to the whole class rather than in a string of long and unpleasant sessions in the office. That, in turn, would probably give the professor more time for scholarly research as well.

Once this happens, the social "learning" which organizational theorists discuss can occur. As the faculty member and student see that they get more out of cooperation than confrontation, they *may* realize that more and more of their efforts should go toward the former rather than the latter. And, while few of us are as well trained in cooperation as confrontation, the more we try it, the better we become at it.

On a global level, interdependence leads us to consider something akin to what Kenneth Boulding called "stable peace" (1978, 1988; see also Singer and Wildavsky 1993, Elias and Turpin 1994). In traditional realist analyses, peace is usually equated "simply" with the absence of war. Boulding went farther and suggested that lasting or stable peace occurs only when two countries erect a psychological barrier that makes going to war all but impossible. That happens only when countries develop conflict solving mechanisms that provide better outcomes than war, which is what has occurred in western Europe since World War II. As Boulding put it, "Stable peace can almost be measured by the amount of dust on the plans for invasion in the various war offices" (1988: 164).

In other words, cooperation is a process which could lead to positive-sum outcomes on that whole range of issues, which can be summed up in a simple but powerful phrase, "a world that works for everyone." It would have to include environmentally sustainable development, but also development that addresses the wrenching poverty and gross inequalities within and between nations. It would have to offer ways of overcoming racial and ethnic hostilities so that human diversity in all its forms becomes an asset, not a liability (King and Schneider 1991).

This leads to the third and perhaps more remarkable lesson in thinking interdependently. In realism, microeconomics, and other variants on the conventional way of thinking, self-interest is defined as my ability to get what I want here and now. Little attention is paid to the impact my behavior has on you or to the long-term implications of my self-interested behavior. The same would hold for national, class, or any other "interest" that groups or individuals might pursue.

Using interdependence as our "mental lens," something very different emerges. If one thinks about longer-term implications, one's short term self-interest may well not be in one's self-interest over time. If my gain (or my group's or my country's) comes at your expense, it is likely to come back to haunt me, unless, again, I can wipe you out and, in the process, end the relationship.

In other words, win-win conflict resolution means that my self-interest and yours tend to converge at least in the medium to long term. In the short run, they may seem quite different. The student wants a better grade; I want to get him or her out of my office to get back to my writing. In fact, I may lose some time from my writing in the short run. But, over time, we both have the same goal: doing our jobs better. Similarly, countries which are able to achieve stable peace are obviously able to reduce tensions between them while each can then free up scarce resources for, say, needed social programs.

Interdependence and the search for win-win solutions to which it leads open the door to removing the security dilemma that has frustrated realists for years. If the argument being made here is correct, any short term gain produced by actions reinforcing the security dilemma are likely to be detrimental to all parties *in the longer run*. Only actions that enhance the security of all parties are likely to work beyond the here and now.

No one has made that point more forcefully than former Soviet President Mikhail Gorbachev in his remarkable speech to the United Nations in December 1988 (Gorbachev 1988; see also 1987). In it, he argued that traditional antagonisms and ways of settling them had grown too costly and that the world could only survive if it found new and cooperative ways of settling those differences:

It would be naive to think that the problems plaguing mankind today can be solved with the means and methods which were applied or seemed to work in the past. Today we face a different world, for which we must seek a different road to the future [and] the emergence of a mutually interrelated and integral world. Today, further global progress is only possible through a quest for universal human consensus as we move towards a new world order. (1988: 11–13)

Anatoly Gromyko, one of Gorbachev's strongest supporters (and son of the former Foreign Minister) made the same kind of argument for the issues in the security dilemma:

In a world of nuclear overkill and growing interdependence, it is impossible to secure a unilateral advantage for oneself to the detriment of the other side without ultimately impairing one's own interests. Recognition of this basic fact provides the basis for establishing one of the main principles of the new way of thinking. The stark realities of the nuclear age demand a revision of such basic notions as strength, superiority, victory, and security. Genuine security in the present nuclear age must always mean universal international security. (Gromyko 1988: 113–114)

The realists and their intellectual cousins are probably right on one score. People and the organizations they form are likely to want to pursue their own interests. And, if they're right, that's pretty much what most of us do most of the time. After all, who would want to be poor or unhappy or weak?

Interdependence suggests that the realists are only off the mark in the way they would have us calculate what that self-interest is. Although we have been estimating our interests in short run terms for centuries, it now makes sense to factor in the long term implications of our actions for ourselves and everyone else in everything we do. In the traditional realist or microeconomic model, the rational actor was the one who did cost-benefit analyses and did whatever promised to be the most profitable. Given interdependence, today's rational actor is the one who makes such calculations for a longer period of time and for everyone who is part of the system and would be affected by those actions.

It is important to acknowledge two problems with this argument before moving on. First, as anyone who has had one of those conflicts with a student (or a similar one with any other person) will attest, it is by no means easy to reach that kind of agreement. Second, and even more important, it is even more difficult to envision how we could go from these two person systems to the far more complex and divisive problems discussed in Part One.

At this point, though, I simply want to make this as a first step in that larger argument and leave these and other criticisms for later chapters. All I want to claim at this point is that cooperation can lead to win-win outcomes which, in turn, mean that the conflict itself *can* be resolved because people work together to settle its root causes.

## THE PRISONER'S DILEMMA REVISITED

You can get a more intellectually refined glimpse at this argument by considering one of the few contributions to complexity theory by a political scientist, Robert Axelrod's *The Evolution of Cooperation* (1984). As we saw in Chapter 6, people who play the game once find themselves in an interpersonal version of the security dilemma. They tend to make what looks like the most rational choice by ratting on their "partner." As a result, they both end up losing. This outcome and those of more complicated versions of the game have been used to buttress realist and related "Newtonian" theories ever since Anatol Rapoport and his colleagues "invented" the game more than forty years ago.

Axelrod's spin on the prisoner's dilemma was to hold a tournament in which game theory experts and computers played the "game" over and over to see who got the highest score. The winner (who, by the way, was Rapoport) won each time the tournament was played with a strategy he labeled "tit-for-tat." The second player observed what the first player did in the previous round and did the same thing the next time. Pretty soon, the players "learned" from each other (even though they couldn't communicate) and consistently chose to cooperate with each other by not informing.

This did not yield an ideal outcome for either prisoner, since both spend time in jail. Nonetheless, it is very much like a win-win outcome, because both spend less time there by playing tit-for-tat than any of the other strategies in the other entries.

Thus, one of the classic examples used to teach about and justify the realist perspective in international relations produces very different outcomes if one starts thinking in the long term rather than the short.

One can actually take the argument an important step farther than Axelrod did. The "payoffs" in the various cells are utterly arbitrary numbers dreamed up by the game's inventors and others who have adapted it since.

In other words, the payoffs can change. As the players get "better" at cooperation, they not only can develop the kind of self-reinforcing behavior of increasing returns, they can change the rules, the payoffs, themselves. They can make both the benefits of cooperating and the costs of not doing so greater. The limited research on learning suggests that this is exactly what does happen in a system that works for all its members.

## A WORLD THAT WORKS FOR EVERYONE

Basing our analyses on interdependence, finally, puts the problems of the global crisis in a different perspective.

A model based on interdependence leads us to seek policies that reduce tensions not just for the problem we are most interested in but for all the others it overlaps with as well. As the German Greens have argued most persuasively

(Frankland and Schoonmaker 1993), creating a more peaceful world also means creating one in which everyone can lead a life of dignity free of discrimination or poverty and in a sustainable environment.

In short, a politics based on interdependence leads us to try to build a world that works for everyone. Though that obviously cannot happen overnight, any other strategy will sustain and deepen the tensions that led us to the global crisis in the first place.

As I have suggested at various points already, there is no shortage of proposals that would take us a long way toward that kind of world. What's missing is the political will to make those changes happen. If I'm right, that's largely the case, because we stick with the values and assumptions outlined in Chapter 6 which, by definition, cannot take us beyond incremental change of the status quo.

I began this chapter with my favorite quote from Marcel Proust, that the "real voyage of discovery" comes not from traveling to new places but in "seeing with new eyes." Interdependence gives us those new eyes.

And they are amazingly different eyes, because they call into question so much of what mainstream social scientists take for granted. Since the beginning of the behavioral revolution in the 1950s and 1960s, empirical political scientists, for instance, have advocated value free and objective research and teaching.

Given what we've seen here, all that seems far less certain. The objectivity they talk about is grounded in the values and assumptions of realist international relations, neoclassical microeconomics, and the like. As I've suggested, those models provide something less than optimal descriptions of human behavior once our frame of reference extends beyond the short run. What's more, their prescriptions are even more troublesome, again when we look beyond the here and now.

Models based on interdependence lead us to put values, emotions, and other issues ignored by mainstream social scientists on center stage, because they work on the assumption that everything people do matters. Interdependence also tends to blur the distinction between normative and empirical analysis typically drawn by social scientists. One cannot determine what actions are "realistic" actions without also having a clear sense of where one wants to go or of what one thinks things should be like.

Interdependence puts into question a way of thinking that goes back at least to the Enlightenment and the scientific revolution. In it, we tend to separate the scientific from the spiritual, the real from the ideal, fact from value, and, in the terms of today's pop psychologists, the left from the right brain. Interdependence, instead, leads us to look with new eyes so we can integrate all we know, because that now seems to provide us a far better picture of the way the world and we as individuals actually work.

## SCIENCE, MYTH, AND METAPHOR

Most people think of science as nitty-gritty research carried out in the lab or the field. Most people, too, think that scientists learn through the accumulation of ever more evidence which they then analyze systematically.

In fact, most creative scientists stress the speculative and inductive nature of their most important insights. In Brian Arthur's terms, science is about metaphors or symbolic representations designed to help us understand what cannot ultimately be understood. No one has ever actually seen an atom. No one has gone into a black hole. The terms are metaphors which help bring abstract and unknown phenomena to life.

In Newtonian science, the metaphor was the "well oiled" machine, working like "clockwork." Now, the research by Arthur and his colleagues in all the scientific disciplines mentioned earlier have exploded that particular metaphor. As he put it in an interview with Mitchell Waldrop, "Non-scientists think that science works by deduction. . . . But actually science works mainly by metaphor. And what's happening is that the kinds of metaphor people have in mind are changing" (1992: 327).

Those metaphors include interconnected webs and simple events having dramatic consequences. The most important of them probably is the picture of the earth as a whole taken from space. For someone like Joseph Campbell, the most important of them become the myths that help make sense of the world and organize our lives. As he put it in a remarkable series of interviews with Bill Moyers, new myths and with them new paradigms and operating principles emerge out of new insights about new realities. As he put it, "The only myth that's going to be worth thinking about in the immediate future is one that's talking about the planet, not this city, not these people, but the planet and everybody on it" (1988: 32).

In short, interdependence.

## REFERENCES

Argyris, Christopher (1990). *Overcoming Organizational Defenses*. Englewood Cliffs, N.J.: Prentice Hall.

Arthur, W. Brian (1990). "Positive Feedbacks in the Economy." *Scientific American,* February, 92–99.

Attali, Jacques (1991). *Millennium*. New York: Times Books.

Axelrod, Robert (1984). *The Evolution of Cooperation*. New York: Basic Books.

Becker, Edward, ed. (1991). *Quantum Politics: Applying Quantum Theory to Political Phenomena*. New York: Praeger.

Boulding, Kenneth (1978). *Stable Peace*. Austin: University of Texas Press.

————. (1988). "Moving from Unstable to Stable Peace." In Anatoly Gromyko and Martin Hellman, eds., *Breakthrough: Emerging New Thinking: Soviet and Western Scholars Issue a Challenge to Build a World Beyond War*. New York/Moscow: Thomas Walker/Novosti, 157–167.

Campbell, Joseph, with Bill Moyers (1988). *The Power of Myth*. New York: Doubleday.

Capra, Fritjof (1984). *The Turning Point*. New York: Bantam/New Age.

Deutsch, Karl (1963). *The Nerves of Government*. New York: Free Press.

Easton, David. (1965). *A Systems Analysis of Political Life*. New York: John Wylie and Sons.

Elias, Robert, and Jennifer Turpin (1994). *Rethinking Peace*. Boulder, Colo.: Lynne Rienner.

Frankland, E. Gene, and Donald Schoonmaker (1993). *Between Protest and Power: The Green Party in Germany*. Boulder, Colo.: Westview.

Gleick, James (1987). *Chaos: The Making of a New Science*. New York: Viking.

Gorbachev, Mikhail S. (1987). *Perestroika: New Thinking for Our Country and the World*. New York: Harper and Row.

————. (1988). "A Road to the Future." Speech to the United Nations, December 7, 1988. Available either in the FBIS Daily Report, *Soviet Union*. 8 December 1988 or *A Road to the Future*. Santa Fe: Ocean Tree Books.

Gromyko, Anatoly (1988). "Security for All in the Nuclear Age." In Anatoly Gromyko and Martin Hellman, eds., *Breakthrough: Emerging New Thinking: Soviet and Western Scholars Issue a Challenge to Build a World Beyond War*. New York/Moscow: Thomas Walker/Novosti, 111–120.

High Performance Systems (1985). *Stella: Software for Education*. Hanover, N.H.: High Performance Systems. Note: this is a piece of computer software, not a book or article.

Keohane, Robert, and Joseph Nye (1989). *Power and Interdependence*. New York: Scott Foresman.

King, Alexander, and Bertrand Schneider (1991). *The First Global Revolution: A Report by the Council of the Club of Rome*. New York: Pantheon.

Lindeman, Mark, and William Rose (1992). *The Role of the United States in a Changing World*. Guilford, Conn.: Dushkin.

Lovelock, James (1979). *Gaia*. New York: Oxford University Press.

————. (1988). *The Ages of Gaia*. New York: W. W. Norton.

Meadows, Donella, et al. (1972). *The Limits to Growth*. New York: Universe Books.

Nye, Joseph (1993). *Understanding International Conflict*. New York: HarperCollins.

Papert, Seymour (1980). *Mindstorms*. New York: Basic Books.

Schwartz, Barry (1986). *The Battle for Human Nature*. New York: W. W. Norton.

Senge, Peter (1990). *The Fifth Discipline: The Art and Practice of the Learning Organization*. New York: Doubleday.

Singer, Max, and Aaron Wildavsky (1993). *The Real World Order*. Chatham, N.J.: Chatham House.

Toffler, Alvin (1990). *Power Shift*. New York: Bantam.

Waldrop, M. Mitchell (1992). *Complexity: The Emerging Science at the Edge of Order and Chaos*. New York: Simon and Schuster.

# 8

# NEW THINKING

Peace is not an absence of war, it is a virtue, a state of mind, a disposition
for benevolence, confidence, justice.

—Baruch Spinoza

The new world order that is being born around us will not be calm. If anything, we are likely to face more intense conflict in the foreseeable future, not less. As the world "shrinks" and people of different races, cultures, religions, and ideologies increasingly come into contact with each other, there is every reason to believe that there will be a rapid succession of new issues and crises just as there has been in the first few years since the end of the cold war.

It behooves us then to develop new ways of handling those difficulties. This chapter will explore how everything we've seen so far opens the door to a more cooperative approach to conflict resolution through the new mode of thinking Einstein was alluding to in that telegram he sent about the arms race a half century ago.

## DIVORCE AND FOREIGN POLICY REVISITED

It is easiest to get a first glimpse at this approach to conflict resolution by returning to the foreign policy and divorce exercise used in Chapter 6 to introduce today's dominant mode of thinking and its role in determining how we try to resolve conflict. I normally continue it by asking the participants to figure out how the international conflict and, then, the interpersonal dispute could have been handled better for all concerned. They have a much harder time with this part of the exercise, especially after I rule out two naive possibilities. I do not let them make the objective differences that produced the conflict in the first place disappear nor do I do allow them to embrace and trust the other side immediately.

In almost every case, the group tries and then discards reluctant compromises that leave all participants disgruntled with the outcome, albeit relieved that the immediate crisis has passed. Eventually, someone stumbles onto the academic notion of the positive-sum or win-win outcome by suggesting that the sides build an agreement over time that all parties benefit from. Such outcomes satisfy everyone. The resolution eliminates the lingering antagonisms which are left in win-lose situations and frequently lead to more conflict down the line.

Like a good realist, though, I push the group further, by saying something like, "Gee, that's nice, but how are you going to make it happen? What about the real world?"

The group then grapples with the problem some more and begins exploring the ways such agreement can be worked out. They begin to see the conflict as something both sides share and which both will have to help resolve. Some of them talk about treating the other side with dignity and respect all the while maintaining their own beliefs. Most stress the importance of truly listening to the other side, working through the rhetoric, taking the other position seriously, and looking for places where even limited agreements can be built. The most perceptive see increased trust as an outgrowth of those initial small agreements, which in turn make later agreements easier.

Thus, when we discussed the Palestinian-Israeli conflict in the late 1980s and early 1990s, they typically decided on a settlement which would give Palestinians their homeland while providing firm guarantees for Israeli security, exactly what the Israeli and PLO emissaries arrived at during their fall 1993 negotiations. And, like those negotiators, they realized that any long-lasting and wide-reaching agreement would have to be built in stages over a period of time during which all parties could take some small steps toward stable peace and then build on them down the line.

They reach the same kinds of conclusions for domestic disputes. If I'm lucky, there's someone in the room who has been part of a shaky relationship which has gotten back on firm footing. That person won't allow pie in the sky discussions along the lines of if-you-just-try-it-will-all-work-out to last long. Instead, they force the group to look at the small and tentative steps that begin the process of overcoming a frayed relationship. They talk about the hard work of listening to a partner, overcoming old wounds, and working together to find new ways of dealing with each other.

In sum, just as the first version of this exercise gave the workshop participants and students a first glimpse at the traditional way of thinking, this one opens the door to an approach to conflict resolution that covers the whole range from superpower to interpersonal relations.

## IDENTITY

Embedded in those exercises are the key ingredients of a paradigm on conflict resolution based on interdependence. There are dozens of different versions of it in the growing number of scholarly and popular works on new thinking. Most, however, seem to include a series of values which represent a late-twentieth-century version of Spinoza's virtue, state of mind, disposition for benevolence, confidence, and justice.

The first is a basic transformation of the way people define themselves, much of which can be summed up in the difference between two little words, "me" and "we." In the simplest terms, basing our thoughts and actions on interdependence impels us to shift away from approaches to our problems which put "me" first and putting "we" first instead.

Each of us has a basic self-definition that determines how we think and act. For most people and for most of history, that identification has been limited to "me" and "mine." What is included in that "me" or "mine" does vary. Sometimes it is just one person, literally me. At others, it means my family, close friends, people from my racial, religious, or ethnic group, or those from my own country. But that kind of self-definition is always limited. There are always people outside "my" world.

That sense of limited identification is an integral part of the reasons why we end up in confrontation and violence so often. It is what leads us to view others as "outsiders" and then "enemies," draw sharp lines separating "us" from "them," and viewing "them" as a threat which must be met.

Thinking in terms of "we first" is very different indeed. At the most obvious level, it means making the earth as a whole the focus of our identity and loyalty. People have always been able to do so, and the type of global identification described here has been part of many spiritual traditions for thousands of years. But before this century, most people had little exposure to other nations and cultures. Therefore, it was hardly surprising that their primary loyalties were to nation or religion or clan or race or some other less than global unit.

There was also little need for such an identification, because the issues raised in Part One had yet to have anything approaching devastating worldwide implications. Now, with the global crisis, we all have to think globally, because that may be the only pathway to resolving problems which are themselves increasingly global.

Modern technology has given us a symbolic or metaphoric way of seeing the earth in an interdependent way. Unlike earlier generations, we can now see it whole from space. Only a few hundred men and women have left the earth's atmosphere and seen that image first hand. Most have been profoundly touched by that experience (Kelly 1988). None has put what it meant better than Russell Schweickart who piloted the Apollo 9 mission and now serves as co-president of the Association of Space Explorers, which brings together former astronauts and cosmonauts from around the world:

You go around every hour and a half, time after time after time. You go out across the Atlantic Ocean and back across Africa, and you do it again and again and again.

And you identify with Houston and then you identify with Los Angeles and Phoenix and New Orleans. And the next thing you recognize in yourself is that you're identifying with North Africa. When you go around the Earth in an hour and a half, you begin to recognize that your identity is with that whole thing. And that makes a change.

You look down there and you can't imagine how many borders and boundaries you cross, and you don't even see them. And from where you see it, the thing is a whole, and it's so beautiful.

There are no frames, there are no boundaries.

You look down and see the surface of that globe that you've lived on all this time, and you know all those people down there and they are like you, they are you. (Schweickart 1986: 10–11)

Few of us are ever likely to venture into space. Nonetheless, we can all learn to think interdependently, by putting our common concerns and the needs of the whole first. In so doing, our priorities change. We see that we will all benefit from meeting those basic human needs that have been ignored for centuries. We see that everyone gains when we protect the environment. And most of all, we see that there is something far better than confrontation and violence for settling disputes.

Practically, that means "expanding" the mental lens we use in order to take in the entire system and the long term implications of our actions. For international issues involving war and the environment, that means putting the needs of humanity and the earth as a whole first, which is essentially what Schweickart realized while outside his space capsule.

There is a tendency in the study of international relations to "reify" the nation state. Scholars (especially realists) tend to argue and, more important, to assume that the nation state is the natural unit of international affairs and/or is the largest unit people can or will identify with (for a somewhat critical analysis of this, see Bloom 1990).

That view is probably mistaken, because it misses some critical changes which have occurred over the course of human history. Until very recently, people did not identify with units anywhere near that large. In the Anglo-Saxon epic poem *Beowulf*, for example, the warring groups controlled no more than a few dozen square miles and held the loyalty of no more than a few hundred people (Tuso 1975). Since then, men and women have come to make larger and larger units the primary object of their self-definition and loyalty.

Indeed, the modern nation state is a relatively new invention, no more than three hundred years old. As recently as the beginning of the nineteenth century, most Americans probably identified more with their state than with the United States and most French men and women with their *pays* rather than a "France" which had relatively little importance in their daily lives.

Since then, however, most people, at least in the industrialized world, have become subjects of massive governments to which they owe their primary loyalty. The nation state has also become the main focus of their sociopolitical identities. Thus, two hundred forty million Americans share a common identity today. So do more than a billion Chinese.

The logic of interdependence suggests going beyond the nation state to make the earth and humanity as a whole the focus of our self-definition. On the political level, expanding one's identification means making the planet as a whole the object of our primary loyalty, the next step in that developmental process that has been taking place throughout recorded history.

There is no need to give up those older and limited self-definitions just as there was no need for Ohioans or Normans to give up those identities as they came to think of themselves as American or French. Americans, French, Christians, Muslims, whites, blacks, and all other groups have reason to be proud of who they are. Indeed, it is hard not to identify with those institutions and ideas that have played such a role in shaping who we are as individuals and as civilizations.

Thinking globally does not necessarily lead to some form of world government or the blending of world cultures. Identifying with the whole is probably compatible with a wide variety of governmental structures and can coexist with and even thrive on the diversity that imperils so many societies today in its present form.

New thinking is not just about seeing the earth as a whole. It applies to any system, whatever its size. Theorists define a system simply as a bounded and interdependent entity. In that sense, a class or a company or a country can *and should* also be viewed as a whole. In Schweickart's terms, it's important to see that there are no frames or boundaries in the complex web of relationships which constitute life as the twentieth century draws to a close.

As a teacher, expanding my identity means including the set of relationships I have with all my classes, the university administration, the admissions office, the support staff, and others I work with routinely. Part of my identity is still that of a professor, which remains a central piece of my self-definition. But my main identity, and hence my highest priority, goes to that community or system as a whole.

The importance of this shift to thinking about whole systems cannot be underestimated. It dramatically changes the mind set we use when approaching problems, be they at the interpersonal or the international level.

Thinking in terms of systems transforms what we mean by such key notions as self-interest. It is no longer the pursuit of my personal benefit if it comes at someone else's expense. Instead, at least in the long run, we all have the same self-interest, helping each other. If we work together, you will be happier and more inclined to help me out down the line even if it seems to cost me something now.

Many "debt for nature" and other sustainable development strategies involve short term sacrifices. Northern banks, governments, and other lending institutions, for instance, will not recoup all of the principal and interest laid out in the original terms of loans made to LDCs. However, the plan is that forgiving some of the overburdened countries' debt will free up resources to protect the environment and develop other resources which will make larger and more profitable markets available down the line.

The same kind of logic holds for the management revolution sweeping American businesses. Many of America's most dynamic corporations have used a variety of techniques to "reengineer" themselves. A smaller number have engaged in extensive training programs designed to help managers empower women and minorities so that their careers succeed and the company can take advantage of their diverse talents and perspectives. Such programs are very time consuming and reduce employee productivity in the short run. But, the still largely anecdotal evidence we will see in Chapter 11 suggests that they can have tremendous payoffs in the medium to long term.

## REDEFINING SECURITY

The evidence in Part One raised serious doubts about the assumptions and prescriptions made in conventional analyses of security, because it is becoming harder for any country or group to maintain its security in a zero-sum or win-lose manner. It may well be that this has always been the case. It may be that if we look at the long term history of a given conflict, whenever it occurred, that exerting "power over" the other side does not work. The fact is that until the global crisis began to loom, we probably could get away with making such shorter term calculations in determining what to do.

Now, that is no longer the case. As the world has shrunk and the stakes of conflict risen, we continue to define security in traditional terms at our peril.

A number of people, including some prominent and influential ones, are beginning to rethink what security means. There are literally dozens of examples of such attempts in recent years, including many of former president Gorbachev's ideas and the findings of UN-sponsored commissions headed by Willy Brandt, Olaf Palme, and Gro Brundtland.

As is often the case when new ideas are being developed, there is still a lot of confusion in these new attempts to think about what security means. Nonetheless, there is now a growing group of scholars and decision makers who advocate a shift to what Michael Klare and Daniel Thomas call "world security" (1994: 1–4; see also Brown 1992).

In all the ways and for all the reasons discussed in Chapters 2 through 6, using traditional power politics to "ensure" security tends only to make things worse at everything from the interpersonal to the international level. To be sure, political leaders and academic analysts have proposed lots of alternatives to traditional realism, some of which (e.g., collective security) have been relatively influential. Collective security and other ideas of its ilk, though, are still anchored in the long-held belief that the balance of power and other forms of armed standoffs are the best we can hope for given human nature, the anarchic international system, and the rest of the "real" world.

The idea of world security breaks with that tradition. It is very much a way of thinking in which peace and security are much more than "merely" the absence of war. Notions such as Gorbachev's new thinking or Klare and Thomas's world security go much further.

The emergence of economic, environmental, and other issues has forced us to dramatically broaden what we mean by security. No longer can it be restricted to the territorial issues of traditional national security studies. Now, these other problems threaten the security of the world's nations and their people in more complex ways.

Interdependence does not mean that conflict is going to disappear by any stretch of the imagination. It does mean that the options available to governments and other actors who continue to rely on traditional mechanisms will be reduced. There are no longer many, or perhaps any, effective forceful attempts to get around the security dilemma. The number of cooperative options may be declining as well. To see that, simply think of the inability of the Clinton administration, other national governments, and the United Nations to find solutions to the recent crises in Bosnia, Somalia, Rwanda, or Haiti.

Providing security requires more than just protection against attack. However, to protect the world's people from economic or environmental insecurity, we will have to go a lot further and develop ways of protecting their human rights and guaranteeing them lives with dignity in a sustainable environment. As Klare and Thomas put it, "When human rights and the environment are protected, people's lives and identities are likely to be secure; where they are not protected, people are not secure, regardless of the military capacity of the state under which they live" (1994: 4).

## DEALING WITH CONFLICT

Effectively dealing with the conflict which grows out of the global crisis will require policies which guarantee other peoples' and nations' security as well as our own. That, of course, is at odds with the way we have traditionally defined ourselves and our security and amounts to a redefinition of core values and assumptions that have guided conflict resolution for centuries.

Given the approach to settling differences discussed in Chapter 6, it is hardly surprising that most people think of conflict as dangerous and destructive. How can it be otherwise if we assume ending conflict means one side has to force the other to go along?

New thinking leads us in a very different direction. Differences of opinion are natural and can only be settled by open dialogue and cooperation, not through confrontations that often lead to violence. Through cooperation, solutions that benefit all participants can be reached, and the root causes of the conflict diminish and sometimes even disappear. The system as a whole adapts in a way that enables it to perform better in the future. In other words, conflict can be an opportunity for learning and growth: something to be valued, not feared.

To see that, consider Table 8.1 which adds a column on new thinking to the one initially presented in Table 6.1.

New thinking about conflict has the same basic starting point as the traditional approach discussed in Chapter 6. Even if new thinking becomes the normal way we resolve our differences, competition for limited resources will remain one of the main sources of conflict, and politics will still be the process for determining who gets what, where, when, why, and how.

In all other ways, the two modes of thinking diverge dramatically. Interdependence leads people to think about the long term and define self-interest as

Table 8.1
Contrasting Values and Ways of Thinking

| Area of Concern | Current Value | New Thinking |
|---|---|---|
| Availability of resources | Scarce | Scarce |
| Nature of relationships | *In*dependent | *Inter*dependent |
| Motivations | Self-interest | Good of whole |
| Time perspective | Short term | Long term |
| Nature of conflict | We vs. they | We with they |
| Nature of power | power over | Power with |
| Interpretation of conflict | Bad | Potentially good |

the good of the whole system. Adopting new thinking means rejecting solutions that harm others. As we have seen time and time again in this book, harming any part of a system only contributes to harming the whole over time.

New thinking stresses actually resolving conflict. Today, most conflict in daily or international life is not really resolved. Imposing one's viewpoint may allow one side to temporarily subdue an adversary, but that rarely resolves much of anything. At most, imposed solutions yield hollow, temporary victories. When people lose, the unresolved conflict festers below the surface, waiting to explode. The losers wait for an opportune time to reopen the conflict in the hope that they can then turn the tables and gain some measure of revenge.

New thinking leads people to seek creative and preventive solutions in which everyone wins. There is no agreement among the experts about exactly how one goes about doing that. Most methods, however, involve some version of all parties working together to find common ground and then a mutually beneficial solution. There is no way to find such a solution if participants cling to feelings of ill-will, mistrust, and blame. When we blame someone else for our problems, we see ourselves as victims and avoid taking responsibility for our actions. Blaming is the least creative and least effective way of solving any problem. We wait for our perceived enemy to take the first step rather than realizing that we only have control over one actor, ourselves, and that we could and should make the first, constructive move on our own.

On the other hand, a spirit of good will and respect for one's adversaries opens up the possibility of dialogue and, eventually, cooperation rather than erecting barriers that make communication and agreement difficult, if not impossible. Expressions like "a spirit of good will" often conjure up sappy images of religious faith or blind trust. Here and in the examples raised in the rest of this book, I will try to argue that good will is a practical and pragmatic way of dealing with deeply held differences which can help people get around the dead ends of either reliance on force or blind trust.

Not blaming my adversary does not mean ignoring the differences between us. They exist and, as we have repeatedly seen so far, can be terribly destructive. We cannot sit back and hope they somehow disappear.

On the contrary, new thinking entails facing them responsibly and directly. The difference between these approaches and more conventional ones is that violence and power exerted over the other side are both ruled out. Rather, to use another so far underused term from the book's title, the challenge is to transform the conflict by turning hateful adversaries into cooperating partners who also have sharply different views about something.

Power can thus be something one side exerts *with* the other, which can only happen if they cooperate. Working together to find cooperative solutions can reduce the underlying tensions that produced the conflict in the first place. As the history of the Middle East since the Camp David Accords shows, there is still plenty of conflict between Israel and the Arabs. Nonetheless, the objective differences that sparked that conflict can, without doubt, be lessened somewhat.

Cooperative problem solving and win-win outcomes can also contribute to building a reservoir of good will that can be used to deal with other issues that are bound to arise. As people get to know each other, it is easier to anticipate how they will act. Successful attempts at working out differences become the equivalent of what arms control experts call confidence building mechanisms that reduce underlying tensions and make further negotiations easier.

New thinking provides the philosophical underpinning for a number of conflict resolution techniques, which have been rather widely adopted in some settings (see also Chapter 10), most noticeably in the pathbreaking and highly popular work of Roger Fisher, William Ury, and their colleagues at Harvard's Negotiation Project (Fisher and Ury 1981; Fisher, Ury, and Patton 1991; Fisher and Brown 1988; Ury 1991). Fisher (an international lawyer and student of diplomacy) and Ury (an anthropologist) go farther than most and argue that a negotiated agreement can be found for just about any conflict.

There may not be a win-win outcome imaginable for every conflict (see, for instance, Donohue and Kolt 1992). It's hard to envision what one would be like for the abortion debate in the United States. Such instances, however, are few and far between, and it is more important to note that in some political conflicts which seemed among the most intractable (e.g., South Africa, the Palestinian-Israeli conflict), participants have recently taken major steps toward win-win solutions.

Fisher and Ury are but the best known of a growing body of experts who have worked on developing conflict resolution techniques that lead to win/win outcomes. Their main conclusions can be summed up in the following eight points.

**Admit that the conflict exists.** Deal with it as soon as possible so that it doesn't fester and tensions don't mount even further. At the same time, try to get the others involved to do the same and figure out together what the underlying issues are. Above all else, make it clear to the other side that you are committed to working things out on a win-win basis, even if your statements are greeted with skepticism or derision.

**Separate substantive issues from emotions.** Both are important, but emotions often get in the way of seeking or even seeing alternative outcomes. In particular, take responsibility for your own emotions. Be aware of the kinds of actions or tactics opponents use that are likely to lead to anger on your part. In the meantime, try to shed ill will toward the people on the other side and look for emotions or attributes they have that you can identify with that make it easier to work with them.

**Put yourself in the other person's shoes.** Figure out why someone would take a position so different from yours. Especially in dealing with people who seem unwilling to negotiate in a cooperative manner, agree with them whenever possible without giving in, acknowledge the emotions they are feeling, treat them as decent human beings, rephrase rather than reject outright a position you can't accept, and, generally, try to create a climate in which cooperative problem solving becomes easier. Make it as easy as possible for the other side to say "yes" rather than "no" by constantly seeking alternatives you both can live with in a manner that allows both sides to maintain their dignity and self-respect.

**Don't obsess about specific demands.** Focus on your broader interests instead because, when you do, it becomes easier to come up with alternatives to your specific demands that would make you just as happy and would pose fewer obstacles for the other side. Always be willing to reframe the debate in a way that increases the options available to everyone involved. That makes it easier for you to stay open to assessing initiatives from the other side.

**It is your job to try to find options that will benefit all parties, even if the other side doesn't seem willing to cooperate.** It may not always work (see the discussion of criticisms of this approach at the end of this chapter), but often the other side will come around if you do come up with what looks like a win-win outcome. As William Ury puts it, try to bring the other side to its senses, not its knees, and try to give it every opportunity to make the agreement, especially by coming up with face saving measures.

**Be willing to bring in a third party to help out.** This could be a professional mediator, a service now used in many divorce cases, or the "good offices" of a diplomat, such as the role played by Johan Holst the Norwegian foreign minister in brokering the agreement between Israel and the PLO in 1993.

**Make certain any solution you are thinking of accepting really is satisfactory both substantively and emotionally.** Be sure, too, that the agreement is likely to be a lasting one. And, especially if this is a new and especially bitter conflict, take former President Reagan's one-liner about arms control seriously, "trust, but verify." Make certain there are clear criteria for evaluating compliance with the agreement and the outcome as a whole.

Noticeably missing from all these suggestions is the assumption of trust. Peace activists and others who advocate this type of nonviolent conflict resolution are often mistakenly accused of being too willing to trust other people or groups or countries. That is a misreading, at least of what is being proposed here. If it ever exists, trust is the outcome of successful problem solving. Moreover, it is not required to produce successful conflict resolution if the parties follow the steps outlined here or others much like them.

**Assume it will take time.** Given how strongly ingrained the traditional way of thinking is in most of us, it would be naive at best to assume we can quickly and easily solve all of our major problems this way. Rather, improvement is likely to start with a series of small, painfully negotiated steps. With each new round of success, negotiation should become easier as each side becomes more predictable and trustworthy. Still, as each of the examples we will consider in Part Three will show, successful conflict resolution today still starts slowly and with what the limited steps the arms controllers call "confidence building measures."

## TWO SURPRISING EXPERTS

I could have cited dozens of conflict resolution specialists or peace movement activists who have explored both new thinking and its implications, but doing so would not convince a skeptical reader that we should, let alone could, find an alternative to confrontation and violence. The work of two more conventional students of violence might.

The first is John Keegan, the military historian whose work figured heavily in Chapters 2 and 6. There, we saw that Keegan is convinced we must stop using war in a Clausewitzean way. Now, it's important to see that he thinks we can.

As he sees it, war and violence are the exception, not the rule, in our lives:

It is the spirit of cooperativeness, not confrontation, that makes the world go round. Most people pass most of their days in a spirit of fellowship and seek by almost every means to avoid discord and to diffuse disagreement. Despite a potentiality for violence, we also have an ability to limit its effects even when no superior force stands ready to spare us from the worst of which we are capable. (1993: 386)

In a sense, his argument seems to contradict the one being made here, because he thinks that war is deeply embedded in our culture and that a tendency toward violence is a part of our very psychological make up.

But he is also convinced that those parts of the human condition can be overcome. Countries may already be less willing to go to war now than they were a century or two ago; if nothing else, we certainly have shown restraint in using nuclear weapons since those two fateful days in August 1945. As he put it, "Once man moved beyond the primitive, the proportion of those who preferred, to fighting, something else—tilling the soil, making or selling things, building, teaching, thinking or communing with the other world—increased as fast as the resources of the economy would stand" (1993: 227).

Warfare has been a part of human history, because people and the political units they formed needed it or at least thought they did. Now, if Keegan is right, that is no longer the case. As a military historian who has spent much of his adult life around soldiers, Keegan is not one to underestimate how difficult it will be to find alternatives to war. But, and this is the important point, he is convinced it can be done.

Throughout history, people have shed behaviors they didn't like, controlled their worst instincts, and improved the way they lived in the process. In Keegan's eyes, the world does still need warriors, but tomorrow's soldier will not be an aggressor but a peacekeeper whose job they will be to protect civilization against racists or power hungry potential despots.

The second and even more compelling case has been made by the political scientist, James Q. Wilson (1993). Like Keegan, Wilson has spent much of his career studying violence. He wrote a major book on crime and policing and received a lot of publicity for his proposal to allow the police to frisk people they think are likely to be carrying weapons in American inner cities. He is also widely known in academic circles for stressing the importance of short term self-interest as the key incentive leading activists into sustained political activity (1973).

Like Keegan, Wilson began work on this book after realizing from his earlier research that most people are not violent or criminal, and that it is worth trying to figure out why most people act decently most of the time. Wilson is convinced that all people have a moral sense (though its impact on behavior does vary from individual to individual) that is in some ill understood way a combination of our innate selves and the way we are brought up, especially in the first few years of our lives. If he is right, it is this moral sense that leads virtually every civilization to condemn certain kinds of behavior (e.g., murder) and the people who violate the moral codes we have created. Obviously, people do not always act according to those codes; if they did, there would be no need for this book.

He is convinced, too, that people are by nature social animals and that the ability to live together cooperatively is as much a part of the "primitive" part of our brain as the capacity for violence (1993: 135). We have a natural tendency to bond with each other, especially in families and other small groups. What's more, our tendency toward cooperation is reinforced and even rewarded by the way we are "trained" as we grow up.

If Wilson is right, when those moral values shape our behavior, we tend to act in ways consistent with new thinking and end up solving problems roughly along win-win lines. In the words Wilson uses to end his book:

Mankind's moral sense is not a strong beacon light, radiating outward to illuminate in sharp outline all that it touches. It is, rather, a small candle flame, casting vague and multiple shadows, flickering and sputtering in the strong winds of power and passion, greed and ideology. But brought close to the heart and cupped in one's hands, it dispels the darkness and warms the soul. (1993: 251)

## SOME SERIOUS CRITICISM

It would be nonsense to claim that I have made an open and shut case for new thinking. There are too many powerful criticisms of it, at least some of which are on target and, therefore, should be addressed before moving on.

Some of the criticisms do not make much sense. For instance, many realists argue that new thinking is simply a 1990s version of Wilsonian (Woodrow, not James Q.) idealism or is pure normative theory with no real empirical base underlying it. I hope to have shown already that these kinds of knee jerk reactions do not reflect what this argument is all about.

The fact that what I've called traditional ways of thinking are so deeply ingrained is not a terribly telling criticism either. If what the authors of the Seville Statement and others who have been studying human nature are saying is true, most of the values and assumptions discussed in this book are changeable, though doing so will be no mean feat.

That said, observers from the realist tradition have leveled a number of criticisms which cannot as easily be overcome.

First, even the most ardent advocates of nonviolent conflict resolution acknowledge that their approach is easiest to follow on the micro level. Wilson, for instance, presents compelling evidence that our moral side is most likely to come out when we are dealing with people we are close to, likening it to the force of gravity which declines at a rate equal to the square of the distance between two objects. It is harder to generate the empathy and sympathy that make cooperation easier between, say, George Bush and Saddam Hussein, than it is between two people who have grown up together and share lots of interests, values, and habits.

The issues involved in the global crisis are far more complex than those most people deal with at work or at home. In other words, it may be easy intellectually to envision what a win-win outcome would be like even in the most intractable international conflict. But as the bloody attacks on both sides since the Israeli-PLO accords were signed show us, getting there is another story altogether.

Second, it is by no means clear how effective new thinking can be if the other side refuses to "play the game" this way. William Ury (1991), among others, has offered a wide variety of techniques one can use to get that recalcitrant party to come around. And, as I suggested with the example of the prisoner's dilemma in Chapter 7, one can work to create an environment in which the benefits of cooperating and the costs of not doing so both rise.

Still, one only has to look back to the Gulf war to see that those techniques do not always work. There is still a lot of controversy over the relative responsibility of the Iraqis and the allies in the failure to resolve the conflict short of war. However one comes down on that debate, there can be little doubt that the Iraqi government was not terribly interested either in negotiating or in withdrawing from Kuwait (Denoeux 1994).

The third, related criticism involves what one does when conflict gets "out of hand" as it has in so many areas. In the last decade or so, new thinkers, like everyone else, have had to address some very serious and violent conflicts, including the Gulf War, the Contra rebellion against the Sandinistas, and the struggle against apartheid in South Africa, to name but a few.

When the conflict gets as intense as it did in those cases, new thinkers don't have much to offer. Their conflict resolution techniques are far less likely to work once the level of hatred and violence escalates that far. The same holds, of course, for a mediator who steps in to try and help a couple put a marriage which has been on the rocks for years back together.

Quite frankly, there is little likelihood of a nonviolent outcome of any sort under these circumstances. The two sides who have let a situation deteriorate that much are not going to find it easy to shed the blame and ill will or to listen to constructive suggestions from the other side or a neutral third party.

Most new thinkers opposed Operation Desert Storm if not Desert Shield, few believed the United States should aid the Contras, and most endorsed strict sanctions against South Africa. But, most found themselves unable to develop constructive *and effective* alternatives to the fighting and confrontation at the height of any of these crises.

From my own experience, I would add a fourth critique. Most people who become new thinkers make a major effort to apply these ideas about conflict resolution to their everyday lives. They find that it is very hard to really *be* a new thinker. What I earlier called the shift from "me" to "we" may seem simple, but it is no easy task for individuals, let alone their governments, to do.

It involves rejecting an old set of values and assumptions that are so deeply ingrained that we rarely think about them before we act. Despite our best intentions, I've seen my colleagues and, more revealingly, myself lapse back into enemy-thinking, aggressiveness, short-term self-interest if not greed, and occasionally violence.

There really are only two responses to those criticisms. Neither is very satisfying, but at the same time, neither undermines the basic argument being made in this book.

To begin with, these valid criticisms actually underscore the first point in the list of suggestions earlier in this chapter. The longer a conflict festers and the deeper the antagonisms grow, the harder it becomes to resolve it, *cooperatively or otherwise.*

Furthermore, while new thinkers may have little to offer in these situations, the other options are even less attractive. Violence may help bring the conflict to an immediate end, as it did in the years preceding the election of President Violetta Chamorro in Nicaragua. More often, violent, interventionist policies only worsen the situation in the longer run. Even when they do seem to "work" in the short run, they only lay the seeds for further violence "down the line."

## MORE THAN THE ABSENCE OF WAR

This presents us with a daunting challenge. For most realists, peace is simply the absence of war. If the case being made here is correct, that peace isn't very peaceful, because plenty of unresolved conflict still lurks just below the surface, "waiting" to erupt.

For good or ill, most people most of the time have assumed that this is the best we can do, especially when the stakes of a given conflict get high. All I hope I have shown so far is that we have to do better and that, at least in principle, we can.

So far, I have only tried to show that such a capacity exists. Now, it is time to move on to the last piece of the argument and tangible examples of new thinking in action, which suggest that it could possibly become the way we deal with most, if not all, conflict and address the issues of the global crisis.

## REFERENCES

Bloom, William (1990). *Personal Identity, National Identity, and International Relations.* Cambridge Studies in International Relations 9. Cambridge: Cambridge University Press.

Boulding, Kenneth (1988). "Moving from Unstable to Stable Peace." In Anatoly Gromyko and Martin Hellman, eds., *Breakthrough: Emerging New Thinking: Soviet and Western Scholars Issue a Challenge to Build a World Beyond War.* New York/Moscow: Thomas Walker/Novosti, 157–167.

————. (1978). *Stable Peace.* Austin: University of Texas Press.

Brown, Seyom (1992). *International Relations in a Changing World System: Toward a Theory of the World Polity.* Boulder, Colo.: Westview.

Denoeux, Guilain (1994). "Iraq." In Charles Hauss, *Comparative Politics: Domestic Responses to Global Challenges.* St. Paul: West Educational Publishers.

Donohue, William A., with Robert Kolt (1993). *Managing Interpersonal Conflict.* Newbury Park, Calif.: Sage.

Fisher, Roger, and William Ury (1981). *Getting to Yes.* New York: Penguin.

Fisher, Roger, William Ury, and Bruce Patton (1991). *Getting to Yes*, 2d ed. New York: Penguin.

Fisher, Roger, and Scott Brown (1988). *Getting Together: Building Relationships As We Negotiate.* New York: W. W. Norton.

Hauss, Charles (1989). "A Rational Basis for Hope." In Linda Renney Forcey, ed., *Peace: Meanings, Politics, Strategies.* New York: Praeger, 203–218.

————. (1994). *Comparative Politics: Domestic Responses to Global Challenges.* St. Paul: West Educational Publishers.

High Performance Systems (1985). *Stella: Software for Education.* Hanover, N.H.: High Performance Systems. Note: this is a piece of computer software, not a book or article.

Keegan, John (1993). *A History of Warfare.* New York: Knopf.

Kelly, Kevin G., ed. (1988). *The Home Planet.* Reading, Mass./Moscow: Addison Wesley/Mir.

Klare, Michael T. and Daniel C. Thomas, eds. (1994). *World Security: Challenges for a New Century.* New York: St. Martin's.

Nye, Joseph (1993). *Understanding International Conflict.* New York: HarperCollins.

Schweickart, Russell (1986). "No Frames, No Boundaries." In Pamela Peck, ed., *Island in Space: Prospectus for a New Idea.* Vancouver, B.C.: Agency Press. This is also available on videotape from either the Foundation for Global Community in Palo Alto or Varied Directions Videos in Camden, Maine.

Senge, Peter (1990). *The Fifth Discipline*. New York: Doubleday.

Tuso, Joseph F., ed. (1975). *Beowulf: The Donaldson Translation, Backgrounds and Sources, Criticism*. New York: W. W. Norton.

Ury, William (1991). *Getting Past No: Negotiating with Difficult People*. New York: Bantam Books.

Waldrop, M. Mitchell (1992). *Complexity: The Emerging Science at the Edge of Order and Chaos*. New York: Simon and Schuster.

Wilson, James Q. (1973). *Political Organizations*. New York: Basic Books.

————. (1993). *The Moral Sense*. New York: Basic Books.

# PART THREE

# CHANGE

# 9

# CHANGE

To everything there is a season and a time to every purpose under heaven.
                                                               —Ecclesiastes

At the height of the Vietnam war, John Gardner (1971) rewrote the epic saga *Beowulf* from the monster's perspective. *Grendel* is a wonderfully witty novel, which one would expect given its premise of a highly introspective and insecure monster.

It's hard not to read *Grendel* as a statement about how little humanity had changed in the thousand years or so since *Beowulf* was written. People may now identify with massive nation states and use all kinds of sophisticated new technologies, but in the end we still resort to violence and war to settle our disputes. And, Gardner suggests, the results remain just as tragic and futile.

He thus ends the first paragraph of the book with Grendel's lament, "And so begins the twelfth year of my idiotic war" (1). Later Grendel tries to explain life and people to her mother. "I tried to tell her all that had happened, all that I'd come to understand: the meaningless objectness of the world, the universal bruteness" (21–22). She then describes human civilization from a depressingly monstrous perspective:

Now and then some trivial argument would break out, and one of them would kill another one, and all the others would detach themselves from the killer as neatly as blood clotting. Normally, the men would howl out their caring, and the evening would get merrier, louder and louder, the king praising this one, criticizing that one, no one getting hurt except maybe some female who was asking for it, and eventually they'd all fall asleep on each other like lizards, and I'd steal a cow. (27)

It's easy to get caught up in the depression Gardner had Grendel feel and be pessimistic about the prospects for change. On the other hand, I will try to show in this last part that we can escape that depression by making new thinking the way most of us handle most conflict most of the time. If I'm right, we are on our way to doing so, though we are admittedly at the earliest stages of what will at best prove to be a long, complicated, and difficult journey.

Before turning to the way such change could occur, it is important to keep a couple of reservations in mind. If it happens, this kind of change will not, first, come about quickly or, second, easily. An intellectual understanding that new thinking is better is not enough. As the research on win-win conflict resolution shows, acting on the basis of new thinking requires a lot of practice and patience, especially in dealing with opponents who operate adversarially. Moreover, while individuals may decide to become new thinkers rather quickly, institutions, including governments, learn far more slowly.

In other words, do not treat what follows here and in the next three chapters as a blueprint or road map for getting to a society which has changed its way of thinking. There is too much uncertainty and unpredictability in political life ever to be that specific in anticipating the future.

## WHAT CHANGE CAN'T BE LIKE

Sweeping political change has typically occurred as a result of revolution or some other type of protest movements which involved significant violence on the part of both those demanding and those resisting change. The amount of violence on the part of people advocating change has, of course, varied tremendously. There was relatively little in the US civil rights movement or the "events" of May and June 1968 in France. There was a lot, however, in the toppling of first the Somoza and then the Sandinista regime in Nicaragua.

It should almost go without saying here that violence cannot be a part of any movement whose aim is to get us beyond confrontation. As the last three chapters have tried to show, violence lays the foundation for further violence, even when it is used for a "good" cause. Coercive governmental programs to clean up the environment or to limit population would have to be ruled out, too, no matter how attractive their goals and proposals might seem at first glance (see, for instance, Hardin 1993). Instead, any change toward new thinking will have to be based on a nonviolent strategy that concentrates on changing the way people deal with conflict, each other, and all the issues considered so far in this book.

While there are far more instances of violent than non-violent change, there are plenty of examples of entire communities, even entire societies, changing the way they think and act. When that happens, they are able to make sweeping changes in the way things are done. It is at those moments that the most important progress in history has been made in science, politics, and everything else.

## PARADIGM SHIFTS

Such change occurs through the paradigm shifts which I've mentioned before but not explored very much (Kuhn 1969; Gilman 1988). There are times when a community can get away with incremental reforms which tinker with the status quo. There are other times when there is so wide a gap between what can be done with business as usual and what has to be accomplished that incremental approaches just won't work (see Figure 1.2 on p. 11).

Paradigm shifts do not occur through the accumulation of facts or the analysis of data but when the community shifts to a new mind set that yields a far more accurate view of the part of the world the scientists are interested in. Such change is anything but incremental.

It is also rare enough that it is worth our time exploring how it tends to happen here. As noted earlier, the analysis of paradigm shifts began with the study of scientific revolutions. From that perspective, a paradigm is the "mental lens" scientists use to make sense of the phenomena they are studying. Without one, they have no way of interpreting the data they collect.

Paradigms are also powerful theories that explain and/or predict events for an entire scientific discipline. Like the chemical periodic table of elements or Einstein's general theory of relativity, a paradigm is also remarkably simple, including only a few variables and constants.

But paradigms aren't always so wonderful, something Gareth Porter and Janet Welsh Brown note in defining the term in their recent overview of global environmental politics: "a set of assumptions about reality that define *and often limit* the scope of inquiry in any field of knowledge" (1991: 191, emphasis added). Scientists have a tendency to cling to paradigms even after they have outlived their usefulness, at which point scientific and political change begin to look remarkably alike.

To see that, consider one classic example of a scientific revolution. For nearly two thousand years until the sixteenth century, just about everyone in the West assumed that the Ptolemeic view of the universe was correct. The earth was at the center, and the sun and planets and stars revolved around it. Given the available evidence at the time, that made perfect sense. After all, everyone could see the sun and moon circle around, rising in the east and setting in the west. This mind set allowed people to predict where all the heavenly bodies would be on any particular day, and they could use those patterns to structure their calendars and determine when they should plant crops. Anyone who questioned what everyone "knew" was considered either misinformed or crazy.

But in the sixteenth century, the newly invented telescope showed that the movements of heavenly bodies was much more complex than had been supposed. The new evidence did not fit the Ptolemeic model's predictions (the equivalent of the gap in Figure 1.2). Nonetheless, the scientists still tried to make the evidence fit the orthodox model of the universe. They went to remarkable lengths to do so, for instance, by positing that planetary orbits included curlicue-like epicycles so that the new observations would still mesh with what everyone "knew" to be true.

Eventually, astronomers like Kepler and Copernicus asserted a revolutionary idea. The earth is just another one of the planets revolving around the sun. In spite of its apparent betrayal of common sense, the Copernican view was far more consistent with the evidence that kept pouring in.

Those who considered the idea with an open mind changed their view of the universe. The problem was that relatively few people were that open minded. Recall that they wrote during the time of the Inquisition, when the Church resisted Copernican ideas. Thousands of people were imprisoned and killed for publicly espousing heretical ideas such as this heliocentric model of the solar system.

In time, however, the Copernican model won out and, in modified form, is still used by astronomers today. The new paradigm was a dramatic restructuring of the way scientists thought the universe operated. With it, they equally dramatically changed the way they taught and did research in ways that has opened the door to tremendous progress ever since.

This one example also shows us why paradigm shifts are so rare. Paradigm shifts are possible only when people have to confront a lot of new evidence which is sharply at odds with the conventional wisdom. Even then, however, scientists usually start by refusing to admit that they have a problem with their theory, much like the substance abuser who denies his or her addiction. Then, because they "know" their models are correct, they warp the data to try to make them fit the current paradigm. Only after quite a while does an innovative scientist or group of scientists come up with a qualitatively different theory. That, in turn, opens the door to a protracted struggle between advocates of the two paradigms.

The fact that a paradigm shift *can* occur does not mean that one *will*. If one does, however, the scientific community ends up making a great leap forward in what it "knows," which can guide its work for years to come.

What I will try to show in the rest of this chapter is that much the same applies to the rest of history, including politics.


## PARADIGMS AND HISTORY[1]

Changes akin to paradigm shifts have been a frequent and powerful theme throughout history. Dramatic adaptations to dramatically changed circumstances have marked most of the major turning points in the evolution of the planet itself and the species which inhabit it.

Physicists have traced time back to a stupendous first event that began the universe something like twenty billion years ago (Hawking 1987). Some kind of great light probably exploded outward from a single point, which ultimately produced all the energy and matter there is in the cosmos today. As that energy and matter spread outward, some of it began to condense into sub-atomic particles and hydrogen atoms, which in turn coalesced into the first stars. Fifteen billion years passed before enough of that material came together to form our own solar system.

The new earth was very different from what it is today. There was no air or water. Volcanoes released gases and water vapor from below the earth's surface that began creating the atmosphere. The earth had to be just the right size and distance from the sun for this to happen. If it had been larger, gravity would have held the gases too close to the surface. If it had been smaller, the gases would have escaped altogether. But, the balance held, and the atmosphere and oceans were formed.

About four billion years ago, organic molecules somehow came together to form amino acids in the seas. These evolved into an organism that could duplicate itself. Life had begun.

It took another two billion years for cells to develop nuclei and form colonies which became the first multicelled organisms. During that period, there were only plants, and they gave off so much oxygen as waste that they put the survival of all life in jeopardy, because there was now not enough of the carbon dioxide they needed for fuel in the atmosphere. Somehow, a new type of cell evolved that could use that oxygen as its fuel and produce carbon dioxide as waste. Animal life emerged and, with it, the atmospheric balance was restored.

---

[1] This very nonacademic section is based heavily on a number of presentations by Don Fitton of the Foundation for Global Community. A fuller version can be found in Roney (1988).

Later some of these creatures faced yet another challenge. With the formation of land masses, great bodies of water dried up. In order to survive, many aquatic animals had to move onto the land by replacing gills with lungs and fins with legs.

Hundreds of millions of years later, the dinosaurs came to dominate the land. Then, some great climatic change we don't fully understand happened. The dinosaurs could not respond, and they disappeared very quickly. Evolution favored smaller, more nimble creatures that resembled today's tree shrew. These animals developed an opposed thumb and binocular vision, both helpful for grabbing branches. Their descendants, the various apes, came down from the trees and began to inhabit the open plains, where the need to look for danger over the tops of tall grasses favored those which were able to learn to walk upright.

About fifty thousand years ago, one of the most important turning points in history occurred. *Homo sapiens* evolved from one of those species of upright apes. By somehow gaining consciousness, humans could think for themselves. No longer were survival and evolution tied solely to natural processes. People could gather evidence, discover cause and effect relationships, and begin shaping the future. That new curiosity, of course, has been a mixed blessing. It allowed people to make tremendous progress but also gave them the ability to cause equally tremendous harm, as we saw in Part One.

Some ten to fifteen thousand years ago, scattered groups of people learned to farm. They no longer had to rely on hunting and gathering but could settle in fixed locations. But, agriculture also brought a rapid expansion of the human population, notions of land ownership, boundaries, and, probably, soldiering.

History since then is filled with examples of people using their minds to make major advances, and to get themselves into serious trouble. Beginning about forty-five hundred years ago, a series of wise men left their mark on our religious and ethical values, from Abraham and early beliefs of a single god to Socrates, Jesus, Buddha, Confucius, and Muhammad, which remain powerful to this day.

Two thousand years later, Copernicus, Kepler, and their colleagues not only changed scientific theory, but legitimized scientific discovery as something independent of religion, a change that has helped the generations that followed understand and master more and more of the natural processes which had hitherto dominated human life. They also developed the new idea that the universe is made up of a vast number of independent actors and, with it, the mode of thinking developed in Chapter 6.

Barely two hundred years ago, a group of brilliant men and women took those scientific ideas one step farther by arguing that people were independent actors, too. In this country, Thomas Jefferson proclaimed the then radical notion that all men are created equal and opened the door to humanity's most optimistic experiment with political and religious freedom as well as the further expansion of what we mean by "men" and "equality," to be discussed in the next section (Barber 1984).

But even that step forward had its costs. In the United States, it brought with it slavery and the deaths of thousands upon thousands of Native Americans and the devastating subordination of those who survived. Everywhere, capitalism and the industrial revolution brought massive pollution, the effects of which we are just now beginning to take seriously.

The most recent of these great intellectual leaps forward came just over a century ago and, as has often happened in the past, started in the sciences. Darwin, for instance, proposed a theory of evolution which linked humanity with all forms of life both now and all the way back into the past. Freud and other pioneering psychologists explored our minds. Einstein and other path-breaking physicists went the farthest, arguing that the Newtonian models which stressed the independence of physical phenomena. Instead, they showed that time, space, light, energy, matter, and gravity were all part of a single seamless web and part of an interconnected *uni*verse. On the other hand, ironically, Einstein and his colleagues brought us the most devastating threat this planet has ever seen by showing how some forms of matter could be turned into the unprecedented energy of nuclear weapons.

Embedded in this history and other themes in the evolution of life which we could have considered, such as the development of iron based technologies or modern national identity, are three lessons which parallel what the historians of science have written about their paradigm shifts.

First, history is filled with them. None happened overnight, but once they did occur and as a new life form or a new idea came to dominate, dramatic, non-incremental change did come about.

Second, paradigm shifts were made possible and, perhaps also necessary, because something like the gap in Figure 1.2 developed. As noted earlier, the existence of such a gap does not necessarily mean that a paradigm shift will occur, only that it can. Even more important, since the dawn of consciousness, those paradigm shifts have been deliberately brought about by people. In other words, paradigm shifts in human civilization have occurred because we are the one species which is capable of shaping its own evolution, not by growing a sixth finger or developing better muscles, but by using the one asset we alone have, our creative and conscious minds.

Third, evolutionary success, and that's what paradigm shifts really are all about, do not necessarily fit the Darwinian stereotype of the fittest: the roughest and toughest. Rather, at least at times when there are such massive "gaps," survival goes to those people or species with the greatest flexibility and the ability to adapt to those changing circumstances.

## POLITICAL PARADIGM SHIFTS

We can see the political importance of paradigm shifts by considering three well known historical examples. They are particularly useful for our purposes here, because they were mostly nonviolent and illustrate a point that is critical for the type of paradigm shift being offered in this book. Successful ones occur when large communities of people reach new agreements about fundamental principles.

### The United States Constitution

In 1787, the founders of the United States were in a position much like the one we are in now. For six years, they had struggled to govern the new nation under the Articles of Confederation. It wasn't working. There was fighting in many states. Commercial and other problems were raising tensions between the states as well. The new country, the world's first experiment with democracy, was in danger of collapse.

That summer, the states convened a convention in Philadelphia to amend the Articles. Quickly, however, the delegates realized that there was no way to revise the old system and concluded they had to write a new constitution that broke away from the conventional notions that democratic governments had to be weak and decentralized. The Constitution concentrated power far more in the hands of the national government, while protecting against abuses of power by establishing a system of separation of powers known today more colloquially as checks and balances.

Lots of other interests and issues were involved. Since the time of Charles Beard in the 1920s, many scholars have been convinced that the framers were at least as interested in protecting their economic interests as in providing political stability. Whatever their real motives were, that should not keep us from seeing that the new order they proposed was qualitatively different than the one they started out with that summer in Philadelphia.

It also shouldn't keep us from seeing that it was by no means certain that the Constitution would be adopted, let alone work. A nationwide debate on whether it should be ratified began in which Anti-Federalists advocated keeping the status quo and the Federalists claimed that only the new constitution could solve the nation's woes. The Federalists won out in large part because their arguments about such things as "curing the evils of faction" convinced the overwhelming majority of the state legislators who were to vote on the draft constitution over the next two years (Hamilton, Madison, and Jay 1961). Even then, the struggle wasn't over. It was another fifteen years or so before substantial support for anti-federalism disappeared, and almost all politically active Americans accepted the regime laid out by the Framers that summer in Philadelphia.

### Civil Rights

The importance of changing paradigms is also clear in the way Americans have expanded what they meant by the famous statement, "All men are created equal." When that statement was included in the Declaration of Independence in 1776, it meant only white, property owning males. Women and most poor men could not vote. Almost all African-Americans were slaves who would be counted as three-fifths of a person when the new constitution was written a decade later.

The first of these shifts in its meaning came with the abolition of slavery. Altogether, more than fifteen million blacks had been forced to come to the Western Hemisphere as slaves. Until the late eighteenth century their enslavement was taken for granted. Most people did not think a world without slavery was possible given the seemingly insurmountable economic, political, and social problems that would have to be overcome.

It took nearly two hundred years to end slavery. The abolitionist movement began with but a few individuals who believed the institution was morally wrong, a radical idea at that time. Gradually, however, a growing number of people began to see that slavery was incompatible with the increasingly popular principles of democracy. By the early nineteenth century, the political and social institution of slavery was coming under increasing attack not just in the United States but around the globe. The fact that it took a civil war to end slavery in the United States should not keep us from seeing that it was the energy of reform-minded individuals and not just the war that built the abolitionist movement and enabled political leaders to make the decisions that ended slavery. Blacks were by no means regarded as the equal of whites, but they had been freed, which was anything but an incremental step.

Next, people came to see that "all men are created equal" must include women as well as blacks. In the early nineteenth century, women could neither vote nor hold political office. Married women had no legal identity apart from their husbands.

Given the democratic principles gaining strength in the United States and Europe, it was only a matter of time until the legal inferiority of women also gave way. Just like abolitionism, the women's suffrage movement began small. A tiny group of people attended the first Women's Rights Convention in Seneca Falls, New York, in 1848, where Elizabeth Cady Stanton and Lucretia Mott made explicit use of Jefferson's ideal by stating outright that all men *and women* were created equal.

Granting women even a modicum of legal equality only occurred after a struggle that lasted almost a century and included 296 campaigns at the national level and 527 more in individual states. Suffrage amendments were introduced every year from 1868 to 1896 with little success. As late as 1910, the women's suffrage movement was able to claim victory in only four western states.

But the stage was set. The pioneer feminists had built a rapidly expanding base of support. Membership in the National American Woman Suffrage Association grew quickly from seventy-five thousand in 1910 to two million by 1917. In 1916 both major parties announced their support. Finally, the Nineteenth Amendment to the Constitution passed the Congress, won the approval of two thirds of the state legislatures, and went into effect in 1918.

As with the emancipation of the slaves, women were by no means treated as the equals of men, and their struggle continues to this day. Still, women had won the vote, which next to no one had dreamed possible a century before.

A final example of how paradigm shifts turn the seemingly impossible into reality is the civil rights movement which removed most legal barriers to equality along racial lines.

After regaining control over their own affairs after Reconstruction, the southern states passed a variety of "Jim Crow" laws that legitimized "separate but equal" institutions and generally segregated blacks and whites. In 1905, the National Association for the Advancement of Colored People (NAACP) was formed to end those practices and seek equal treatment for African-Americans through the legal system. The Urban League was founded the next year to obtain equality in employment, housing, and welfare services.

But progress came so slowly that it wasn't until the outbreak of World War II that any significant change occurred. Because of the demands of wartime production, millions of African-Americans entered the armed forces and the industrial labor force. Having proved themselves on the battlefield and in the workplace, African-Americans felt the injustice of second-class citizenship ever more keenly.

Slowly, the government began to respond. In 1948 President Truman issued an executive order prohibiting racial discrimination in the armed forces. By

1954 mainstream thought had shifted enough for the Supreme Court to throw out the "separate but equal" doctrine that sustained segregated schools.

A year later the modern phase of the civil rights movement began when a single individual, Rosa Parks, was arrested for refusing to give up her seat at the front of a segregated bus to a white man. Her act of courage galvanized Martin Luther King, Jr., and other community leaders into organizing a bus boycott, beginning a nonviolent movement that would confront the national conscience. Still, there was little response from the government. The two most powerful senators, Democrat Lyndon Johnson and Republican Everett Dirksen, led the forces that kept meaningful civil rights legislation from passing.

Again and again in the next decade, Americans watched on television as African-Americans and their allies peacefully suffered the abuses of white mobs in pursuit of their rights as Americans. Public opinion began to shift in almost all areas of the country, culminating in the August 1963 March on Washington. Seeing that base of support grow, the politicians also began to change. A year later the Civil Rights Act was passed in large part because those same two men, then President Johnson and Senate Minority Leader Dirksen, had come around.

As with the other two examples, the passage of the civil rights, voting rights, and other laws of the 1960s did not come close to ending this country's most difficult, divisive, and, frankly, embarrassing problem. But, it did mark major changes in the way people deal with each other in this country.

### Gorbachev's Soviet Union

To see that paradigm shifts do not always occur, even when much of the groundwork for them has been laid, quickly consider one more familiar example: the reform efforts before the Soviet Union collapsed in 1991.

There were growing signs of economic trouble in the Soviet Union from the 1960s on (see the discussion of "thumbs" and "fingers" in Lindblom 1977 or the many memoirs of Soviet leaders such as Arbatov 1992). The Brezhnev era leadership, however, blithely ignored those difficulties and, in so doing, only made things worse.

A flurry of reform began under Brezhnev's successor, Yuri Andropov, but little was accomplished in part because Andropov's health failed and in part because the reforms faced too much resistance from the party hierarchy. When Gorbachev took over as General Secretary of the Communist Party in 1985, economic reform was on his agenda. However, his early policies which, among other things, called for more discipline and restricted the availability of vodka were clearly conceived within the party-state paradigm which had existed since Stalin's days.

Within a couple of years, however, Gorbachev and his colleagues came to the conclusion that the system itself was the problem and proposed what amounted to a new paradigm based on a more open (*glasnost*) and democratic (*demokratizatsiya*) society, a market-oriented economy (*perestroika*), and a new cooperative approach to foreign policy which Gorbachev himself called new thinking (Gorbachev 1987, 1988). Though Gorbachev and his colleagues never spelled out all the details of their proposed reforms, they clearly anticipated dramatic changes, including the end of the Communist Party's monopoly over economic and political power.

Almost immediately, the protracted political struggle that led to the collapse of the Soviet Union began. The entire Soviet political spectrum moved to the left (if that is the proper way to describe these reforms), but nothing like a consensus on the scope or pace of reform developed. Groups demanding more rapid reform sprang up on Gorbachev's left, while more conservative colleagues in the party thought things were moving too far too fast. In particular, proposed economic reforms, such as the Shatalin plan to remake the economy in five hundred days, never got off the ground. Gorbachev and his dwindling group of supporters grew less and less decisive as they faced problems on more and more fronts. Finally, the system collapsed around them, and the successor states are still struggling without much success to find a political, social, and economic paradigm that might work.

## HOW POLITICAL PARADIGM SHIFTS OCCUR

There is a common pattern to all these examples which is every bit as fully illustrated by the failure of the Gorbachev reforms as by those successes in American political history. Paradigm shifts occur only after protracted periods of struggle during which the community involved reaches a consensus about some new and important principles.

Not everyone has to agree for profound change to take place. There are still people, for instance, who cling to the notion that blacks are inferior to whites or women to men. But, once most Americans agreed to new definitions of what that famous assertion of equality in the Declaration of Independence really meant, change occurred. The few who rejected that consensus found themselves in a minority with little or no social or political influence.

Daniel Yankelovich (1985; Yankelovich and Immerwahr 1994), one of the leading pollsters in the United States, argues that these new agreements about new principles occur at unusually charged moments in a community's history.

He distinguishes between raw opinion and public judgment. Opinion can be very fleeting, since most people neither know much about nor pay much attention to public affairs. When truly important issues touch people's lives *and* challenge their basic values, that can change. People can reach profound new judgments or overall assessments of the issues involved. Yankelovich argues that such individual realizations take place in people's homes or at work through "a dialogue that is so active and effective and highly charged that it leaves none of the participants untouched and unchanged. At the conclusion of such a dialogue, no person is quite the same person he or she was before the dialogue began." In short, people teach each other and help each other see that change is needed and possible.

What's more, Everett Rogers (1983) and others have uncovered remarkable similarities in the way new ideas get adopted in everything from the marketing of new products to fundamental value shifts. Essentially, Rogers and his colleagues are convinced that openness to a new idea is distributed along a normal curve and that as you move along it, adoption of a new idea speeds up.

At first, a new idea develops support very slowly, because it is the province of a tiny proportion of visionaries way out on the "tail" of the distribution. As we learn in introductory statistics courses, no more than one half of one percent of the total population is even three standard deviations to the "left" of the mean in any normal distribution. That's the case here, because relatively few people have the capacity to generate new ideas in the first place, and those who do are usually "ahead of the times" and often unable to get their point of view across to their more prosaic fellow citizens.

That helps explain why forty years passed before the NAACP and the Urban League saw any tangible progress in Washington. During those years, there were very few people demanding equality for all citizens regardless of race.

But by the early 1950s, things had begun to change, because the idea had begun to "move" into the next standard deviation of people.[2] If Rogers is right, these people, whom he calls "early adopters," are risk takers, much like the innovators who came up with the idea in the first place. However, they tend to be opinion leaders with considerable influence in their communities.

In the case of the civil rights movement, more and more religious and educational leaders, black and white alike, put their weight behind the demand for change. There were thousands of people like the young Martin Luther King, Jr., Bob Moses, or Joan Baez. All were largely unknown then, but they already

---

[2] I've drawn heavily on Taylor Branch's remarkable *Parting the Waters* (1988) here, which confirms the more anecdotal version of the history I've presented.

could make the idea of equality come alive in their speeches, organizing, or singing.

At that point, support for a new idea can begin to grow faster, as we saw in the streets during the late 1950s and early 1960s. Rogers is convinced that this is one of the most important phases in the adoption of any new idea, since he finds that once it has the support of about 5 percent of the population, it is "embedded" and highly unlikely to disappear.

With the backing of early adopters, support can spread a lot more quickly in the rest of society. When a new idea has the support of community leaders who are widely known and respected, most of the rest of us are willing to get on board. Because respected community leaders like Dr. King did join in, the civil rights movement in Montgomery and elsewhere mushroomed. Around the country, people who agreed with King and the other visible civil rights activists drew courage from their example, especially as they watched them stand up to the violence being meted out by southern officials and vigilantes. They began educating their friends and neighbors. They began learning to influence other leaders in their communities and, ultimately, in the centers of state and federal power.

From then on, support for civil rights among whites as well as African-Americans grew even faster. My family's experience is probably fairly typical of this phase of the movement. I was a high school student, living in a small industrial city in New England. My family was rather liberal, but civil rights and politics in general were rarely discussed at the dinner table until 1961 or 1962. All of a sudden, it was something we talked about all the time. My parents' views evolved. Similarly, my teammates began to ask each other and then our coaches why they were next to no African-American athletes on our football, basketball, and baseball teams, even though they make up about twenty percent of the student body.

Once dialogues like that begin to happen on a widespread basis and middle of the road people like my parents or friends change, Rogers is convinced that the idea is "unstoppable." At that point, the majority of community leaders have come to see the need for change and become active supporters of the innovative idea. Since most of the rest follow in their footsteps, the idea can then become the commonly accepted one fairly quickly. In the case of civil rights, in less than a decade, the legal equality of blacks and whites ceased being the "unrealistic" demand of a small minority and became something that the vast majority of Americans took for granted.

It is at that point, too, that politicians who fear being too far ahead of their constituents become more supportive. Elected officials do not normally take a lot of risks by adopting positions that are dramatically out of line with what they think their voters want. After all, their careers depend on our votes, and it is thus only on issues they feel most passionately about that elected officials are willing to endorse positions that only a minority of us hold.

Lukewarm support turned into stronger statements by such prominent members of the administration as Attorney General Robert Kennedy. The federal government began enforcing existing laws more rigorously. By the time President Kennedy was assassinated, civil rights legislation was squarely on the administration's agenda.

In short, the political elite did not respond much if at all early in the life of the civil rights or any such movement. The politicians were not willing to commit political suicide, whatever their personal viewpoints may have been.

But everything changes once that base of support begins to grow. Decision makers can no longer avoid dealing with the issue. They get too many letters and too many visits from constituents. The people they trust and rely on are talking about the new issue, too. In their trips back home, they see the newly aroused public in the informal sessions they hold with their voters.

Decision makers have become part of a national dialogue. It may be because of a cynical pursuit of power. It may be because they, too, have put their morality and values into question. Whatever the reason, once that base gets built, enough new leaders emerge and enough current leaders change for the decisions they make to change, too.

This section has been written using almost exclusively American examples, and one could argue that such an approach to change can only work in a reasonably open, democratic society. While there is no doubt that it is easier to do the kind of organizing that makes this kind of value change possible in an open society, there is compelling, if anecdotal, evidence that the same thing happens to authoritarian governments before they collapse.

It is easy to focus on the violence of the white "securocrats" and the violent response of the black "comrades" in South Africa (Sparks 1990). However, if one looks back over the development of the anti-apartheid movement after the Sharpeville massacre of 1960, the development of a new, assertive consciousness, especially among young black people, seems far more important. The African National Congress, the Black Consciousness movement headed by the late Steve Biko, the United Democratic Front, and other organizations did a remarkable job of educating a large portion of the African population, showing them that there were alternatives to apartheid.

Similarly, changing social and political values were a necessary precondition for the all but completely nonviolent revolutions which swept communist regimes from power throughout Eastern Europe in 1989 (Garton Ash 1990; Mason 1992: 105–112; Dawisha and Parott 1994). People were better educated and knew more about politics and culture in the West than they had a generation before. By the mid-1980s, for instance, most East Germans could watch West German television, while travel and other forms of contact with the west were easier than ever. Groups like Solidarity in Poland and individuals such as Vaclav Havel in Czechoslovakia had built considerable support for change. Then, of course, the limited reforms of glasnost (which were not taken as far as in the former Soviet Union) made political education and organization easier. Without the organization and education that had taken place over a period of years, the millions of people who protested with such power and dignity would never have turned out nor would their movement have spread so quickly.

## TOWARD A GLOBAL PARADIGM SHIFT?

As I have tried to point out on several other occasions, there is no way of predicting exactly how a global shift toward new thinking would happen. Nonetheless, one can extrapolate from the model laid out so far in this chapter and see the broad outline of how it might occur. If nothing else, we can anticipate who the global equivalents of the opinion leaders and early adopters Rogers discussed might be.

Change would probably come most quickly among individuals and small groups. For simple reasons of scale it is easiest for them to change in any direction. It's probably also easiest for people with the most resources, however one defines that term, to change. People who have more time or money, for instance, have more opportunities to experiment with new ideas and practices than others who are struggling to survive. Moreover, as we'll see in the next chapter, there is some reason to believe that people who are highly educated are disproportionately likely already to have adopted some parts of new thinking.

We'll also probably see two types of transnational non-governmental organizations playing a growing role. Not surprisingly, NGOs working on such issues as the environment will almost certainly continue their dramatic growth of recent years, which has seen them play major roles at both the 1992 Rio Summit on the environment and development (see Chapter 12) and the 1993 one on human rights. More surprising for some will be the increased influence of multinational corporations. To use the language of the 1960s, MNCs have more often been part of the problem than the solution up to now. However, as we'll see in Chapter 11, many highly successful businesses have undergone a managerial revolution which parallels new thinking in many ways. In particular, they've found that cooperative relationships with their own workers, their customers, and the environment they work in all tend to enhance profit.

As these ideas spread, it is likely that the affluent and democratic countries will be able to or have to take the lead for the reasons already noted. They have the most resources to devote, for instance, to aid programs that would help LDCs develop, protect the environment, and begin creating new markets for northern products. By the same token, the industrialized democracies are going to have the most leverage over countries which fail to cooperate with emerging global norms. If, for instance, there is a new and more transparent nonproliferation regime which calls for the imposition of stiff sanctions on countries that violate it, the richest countries will have the greatest impact because they have the most influence in global trade and the economy as a whole.

There is also likely to be considerable social "learning" if individuals, groups, and countries experiment with these ideas. As noted in Chapter 8, we have far more experience with confrontation than cooperation. If these ideas are adopted by a significant number of people, that added experience is likely to produce new insights into how to work together better. That has already happened to some extent, as we can see in the work of the Harvard Negotiation Project. The initial edition of Fisher and Ury's *Getting to Yes* (1981) was filled with useful tactics that people seeking win-win conflict resolution could try. A decade later, the authors themselves had a lot more experience working with these principles and could include practical responses to questions and problems people had raised about their techniques (Fisher, Ury, and Patton 1991) and write a wholly new book in which Ury explored techniques to try with opponents who didn't want to cooperate (Ury 1991).

There will be rough moments and maybe even some horrible future crises like the Gulf war, the collapse of Yugoslavia, or the bloodbath in Rwanda. But, *if* these ideas spread and we become better at putting them into practice, we should be able find ways to raise the benefits of cooperation and the costs of confrontation.

At the end of any paradigm shift, there are always people who refuse to go along. After all, there are still people who believe the earth is flat. But, those people on the "far" end of Rogers' normal curve are in such a numeric and cultural minority that they end up having next to no influence. In this case, there will still be people who advocate confrontation or resort to violence. But, we will have learned how to deal with conflict well enough and early enough that they are not likely to rise to positions of political, social, or economic prominence.

There is a final reason to believe that such a change is plausible.

To some degree, it is already happening, which is what we'll be exploring in the next three chapters.

## REFERENCES

Arbatov, Giorgi (1992). *The System: An Insider's Life in Soviet Politics*. New York: Times Books.

Barber, Benjamin (1984). *Strong Democracy: Participatory Politics for a New Age*. Berkeley: University of California Press.

Branch, Taylor (1988). *Parting the Waters: America in the King Years: 1954–1963*. New York: Simon and Schuster.

Dawisha, Karen, and Bruce Parott (1994). *The New States of Eurasia*. New York: Oxford University Press.

Fisher, Roger, and William Ury (1981). *Getting to Yes*. New York: Penguin.

Fisher, Roger, William Ury, and Bruce Patton (1991). *Getting to Yes*. 2d ed. New York: Penguin.

Gandhi, Mohandas K. (1951). *Non-Violent Resistance (Satyagraha)*. New York: Schocken Books.

Gardner, John (1971). *Grendel*. New York: Vintage.

Garton Ash, Timothy (1990). *The Magic Lantern: The Revolution of '89 Witnessed in Warsaw, Budapest, Berlin, and Prague*. New York: Random House.

Gilman, Roger (1988). "The Process of Change." *In Context*, December, 5–9.

Gorbachev, Mikhail S. (1987). *Perestroika: New Thinking for Our Country and the World*. New York: Harper and Row.

————. (1988). "A Road to the Future." Speech to the United Nations, 7 December 1988. Available either in the FBIS Daily Report, *Soviet Union*, 8 December 1988 or *A Road to the Future*. Santa Fe: Ocean Tree Books.

Hamilton, Alexander, John Jay, and James Madison (1961). *The Federalist Papers*. New York: New American Library.

Hardin, Garrett (1993). *Living within Limits: Ecology, Economics, and Population Taboos*. New York: Oxford University Press.

Hawking, Steven W. (1988). *A Brief History of Time: From the Big Bang to Black Holes*. New York: Bantam Books.

Kuhn, Thomas S. (1969). *The Structure of Scientific Revolutions*. Chicago: University of Chicago Press.

Lindblom, Charles (1977). *Politics and Markets: The World's Political-Economic Systems*. New York: Basic Books.

Mason, David S. (1992). *Revolution in East-Central Europe: The Rise and Fall of Communism and the Cold War*. Boulder, Colo.: Westview.

Porter, Gareth and Janet Welsh Brown (1991). *Global Environmental Politics*. Boulder, Colo.: Westview.

Rogers, Everett (1983). *The Diffusion of Innovation*. New York: Free Press.

Roney, Richard (1988). "Beyond War: A New Way of Thinking." In Anatoly Gromyko and Martin Hellman, eds., *Breakthrough: Emerging New Thinking: Soviet and Western Scholars Issue a Challenge to Build a World Beyond War*. New York: Walker/Moscow: Novosti.

Sparks, Allister (1990). *The Mind of South Africa*. New York: Ballantine Books.

Ury, William, (1991). *Getting Past No: Negotiating with Difficult People.* New York: Bantam Books.

Yankelovich, Daniel (1985). "How the Public Learns the Public's Business." *The Kettering Review.* Winter.

Yankelovich, Daniel, and John Immerwahr (1994). "The Rules of Public Engagement." In Daniel Yankelovich and I. M. Destler, eds., *Beyond the Beltway: Engaging the Public in US Foreign Policy.* New York: W. W. Norton, 43–77.

# 10

# THE GRASS ROOTS

Her full nature spent itself in channels which had no great name on the earth. But the effect of her being on those around her was incalculably diffusive, for the growing good of the world is partly dependent on unhistoric act.

—George Eliot

It took most of 1993 and 1994 to write this book. Those were not good years for the argument being made here. They began with the deteriorating situation in Somalia and the first signs of trouble for the Clinton administration and ended with the electoral debacle in November and the Russian invasion of Chechnya.

Yet, I remain convinced that we have taken some important, if limited, steps toward the paradigm shift defined in general and abstract terms over the last three chapters. This chapter is the first of three which document some of what is already taking place and focuses on the grass roots and growth in support for the ideas and principles of new thinking.

I do not want to overstate the case here or in the two chapters which follow. Whatever progress has been made, we are still a long way from seeing the kind of support Everett Rogers and his colleagues believe is needed before a new idea becomes a major contender in the political arena.

Nonetheless, it is clear that a growing number of people are coming to see the importance of something akin to new thinking and are becoming empowered to act in the process. Some have gained a degree of notoriety, like the Norwegian speed skater Johan Olaf Koss, who donated his ample bonuses from the Lillehammer Olympics to aid besieged Sarajevo. Most, however, live their lives and practice their politics in relative obscurity in their neighborhoods, schools, and workplaces. The importance of average citizens in sparking profound change is something George Eliot understood more than a century ago in ending her epic saga *Middlemarch* (1964). She was discussing the most likable character, Dorothea, who, like the groups and individuals to be described here, labored quietly but had plenty of influence on the men and women around her.

They may not be prominently featured in the news today, but that doesn't mean such individuals and groups are powerless. There is substantial evidence, for instance, that American and Soviet activists played a major role in ending the Cold War by convincing their fellow citizens and then their leaders that the costs of the conflict were too great (Warner 1991). Most West German communities had "citizens' initiatives" in the 1970s which launched everything from local recycling efforts to the creation of cooperatively run child care centers, something one also found in small-town America a decade later. In fact, much of the change in environmental policies around the world can be attributed to pressures from citizen activists who base their efforts on something like new thinking (Stoel 1994).

Because these efforts have been so scattered and so non-newsworthy, they have not received much in the way of systematic attention from journalists or scholars. As a result, there is no way I can estimate how many new thinkers there are, how fast their ranks are growing, or how much impact they have had. All I can suggest is that they represent a small but growing group as far as both their numbers and impact are concerned (Lappé and DuBois 1994).

## ORGANIZATIONS

The groups discussed here are neither the largest nor the most influential organizations in the peace, environmental, or social justice movements. They warrant our attention here, because each has achieved considerable success and does so by explicitly focusing on new thinking in one form or another.

### Beyond War

Of the hundreds of groups that have made up the United States peace movement over the last decade or so, Beyond War was the most influential one to define its mission as developing support for new thinking.

Initially, Beyond War was to be a limited project of another organization, Creative Initiative. Creative Initiative was an unusual group with explicitly spiritual roots but which also took on a number of social and political issues in an attempt to get people to do just what its name suggested, take creative initiatives in their lives.

In the late 1970s, Creative Initiative had attracted a few hundred members, mostly in the San Francisco Bay, Denver, and Portland areas. Its influence was quite limited, but, intriguingly, it had been able to attract a significant number of wealthy and often politically conservative members, largely because it was nonpartisan and, in some respects, even apolitical.

Then, in 1982, a number of Creative Initiative activists saw the moving documentary on nuclear weapons, *The Last Epidemic*. They realized that the threat of nuclear war gave them a new opportunity to educate people about interdependence as they had already done in their other projects, which ranged from raising environmental consciousness in northern California to sending groups of high school graduates to work for a year in the Third World.

Within a year, they had developed a curriculum for a three-evening seminar which used the nuclear threat to help people see the personal and political implications of living in an interdependent world. By 1984, they had launched Beyond War as a separate organization. That summer, about eighty members of the core group who were able to take at least two years off from full time paid work (there are benefits to recruiting among people who have made a lot of money) moved to fourteen states to begin organizing broader support for the movement.

Beyond War's efforts were concentrated on the grass roots educational efforts for which the seminar, dubbed an orientation to a world beyond war, was the most important activity. But it did a lot more. There were intensive seminars which dealt with interdependence in more depth. Volunteers often spoke before Rotary Clubs, PTAs, and other local groups. They tried to get aspects of new thinking included in elementary school curricula. Some volunteers chose to work on other issues and use that involvement to talk about constructive forms of conflict resolution.

Because it never had a regular system of membership and local groups were pretty much self-organizing, there are no firm statistics on Beyond War's impact. In all likelihood, around fifteen thousand people volunteered at least an evening a week from 1985 until it became clear that the Cold War and the immediate threat of nuclear war had ebbed in late 1988 or early 1989.

Somewhere between two hundred and five hundred thousand people went through the orientation. Many never continued with the movement, but the curriculum was set up in such a way that even people who never dealt with

Beyond War again could still spread new thinking. In fact, the most important goal of the series was to help people see that they made a difference in their daily lives and that trying to solve the conflict in it along the lines discussed in this book was a necessary first step in building a world beyond war. Typical was the following statement from a physician who was chief of staff at a large, urban hospital.

I found that my thinking about relations with nurses, other administrators, and patients had changed because of the work I had done on conflict resolution on the one-to-one level. Then I began to work with the problem of the Medicare bureaucracy denying hospitalizations for the elderly. It seemed to me to be an opportunity to apply those techniques of conflict resolution at the next higher level.

I formed a coalition of physicians, hospital administrators, other caregivers, and the elderly themselves. We spent the first few meetings defining the problems of caring for the elderly from each group's perspective. For me, it was a real eye opener, because I learned about challenges in the home care and social service areas I had not thought of before. The other group members also learned about problems from the perspective of the physician and the hospital.

After still more meetings, we began to brainstorm the methods we might use to improve the present system. We ended up deciding to focus on only a couple of them. By this time enough trust had been generated that no one got upset when their issue wasn't picked. People had enough investment in the larger goals of the group to allow themselves to detach themselves from their own special interests (personal communication).

Needless to say, this doctor and his colleagues have not solved the country's health care crisis. They did, however, create a better work environment for themselves, dealt with conflict in the hospital better, and put more pressure on their elected representatives to change the way health care is provided for seniors. Most Beyond War "veterans" have such stories to tell about how its ideas helped reshape their personal and/or professional lives (Rice and Mary 1989).

Beyond War was also able to put on some rather splashy events that gave it more publicity and credibility in large part because it was able to raise far more money than most other peace groups. The most impressive of these was the annual Beyond War Award initiated in 1984. The award was granted to individuals and groups who had done the most to move the world beyond war in the preceding year or so. Beyond War used two of the first awards to stage elaborate televised satellite "space bridges" long before such events were commonplace. The first went to the International Physicians for the Prevention of Nuclear War and was given out simultaneously in San Francisco and Moscow in late 1984. The next year, the award went to the heads of state of Mexico,

Argentina, India, Tanzania, Sweden, and Greece for their work in developing the Delhi Declaration through which non-nuclear and non-aligned states weighed in against the nuclear arms race. This time the space bridge linked San Francisco with the national capitals of each of the signatories, the first time five continents had ever been linked together and the first time anything had ever been televised in Tanzania. Such events gave Beyond War considerable exposure outside the United States and led to the creation of small groups in India, Japan, Canada, and what was then West Germany.

The movement also embarked on a number of less spectacular, but still significant, projects. For instance, it built on its contacts in the Soviet Union to put together a team of Soviet and American scholars who wrote a book on new thinking which was simultaneously published in the USA and the USSR, the first time that had ever happened on a political topic (Hellman and Gromyko 1988). Beyond War brought the Soviet authors to the United States for a publicity tour with well over a hundred public sessions with at least one American and one Soviet contributor followed by a week of lobbying Congress.

Despite these accomplishments, Beyond War's influence was always rather limited. Because its efforts revolved around the orientation, its work initially had to be concentrated in the regions its emissaries first moved to. Although it spread to larger areas in those and other states, it was all but unknown in many parts of the country, including Washington, DC.

Like the peace movement as a whole, Beyond War had little success building support outside of the white middle class. However, because of its origins, Beyond War was able to reach out beyond those circles of mostly middle class people who had been politicized in the 1960s and early 1970s. As noted earlier, Beyond War drew a surprising number of business executives, many of whom had been experimenting with introducing teamwork and other cooperative approaches in restructuring their companies. Most volunteers were professionals, though few were intellectuals. There were a lot of teachers, but almost all taught at the elementary and secondary levels. Most numerous of all, perhaps, were social workers and therapists, many of whom had had prior exposure to the new approaches to conflict resolution discussed here in Chapters 7 and 8.

Relatively few active workers had been politically active in the Vietnam and other protest movements of the 1960s. Instead, most had been drawn to Beyond War because it refused to do the "we versus they" politics of the traditional left or right and/or because some change in their lives, such as the birth of a child, had made them take a step back, look at nuclear weapons or some other global issue, and realize that they had to get involved somehow (Oskamp et al., 1992).

Beyond War also had trouble dealing with the rest of the peace movement. Many other activists and organizations were troubled by a group which had so many business executives and even former CIA officers among its leaders, rejected any form of confrontation, and was as willing to talk to conservatives as to leftists (Faludi 1987; Lofland 1993).

For all its success, Beyond War "suffered" from the end of the Cold War. Despite the broader message about the global crisis, involvement in Beyond War began to decline, as it did in most peace movement organizations. Beyond War spent the next two years figuring out what to do next. In 1991, it transformed itself into the Foundation for Global Community with the mission of working on issues growing out of interdependence in general, but it has yet to find the focus and energy that the campaign around nuclear weapons provided for most of the 1980s (Montminy 1989).

## RESULTS

RESULTS[1] started as the handiwork of a single man, Sam Harris, who seemed an unlikely candidate to head an international political organization. As Harris tells the story, he was an alienated junior high school music teacher of thirty-one when he saw an ad in the New York subways for a Harry Chapin concert to benefit starving people in the Third World (Harris 1994). He began to notice other hunger related events, like Dick Gregory's cross country run later that year. He was only spurred into action when his yoga teacher called off class one night so she (and the rest of the class) could attend a presentation on world hunger. But then, he was hooked.

In 1980, he founded RESULTS, which he initially ran after school and on weekends. RESULTS quickly developed what turned out to be a highly successful model for citizen lobbying and empowerment.

Over the years, RESULTS has initiated or supported a number of bills pending before the House and Senate, like one to designate several million dollars for Oral Rehydration Therapy (ORT), which uses a ten cent mixture of sugar, water, and salt to overcome the dehydration which kills about five million children annually.

While Harris and the two other full time staffers in Washington lobby Congress, the real key to the success of RESULTS lies at the grass roots. As of late 1993, there were more than a hundred RESULTS chapters in the United States and another forty or so abroad. The most important work of these chapters is to train average people with little or no political experience

[1] Responsibility Ending Starvation Using Legislation, Trimtabbing, and Support.

(RESULTS members have the same basic socioeconomic profile as Beyond War) to become effective lobbyists. The organization provides techniques to help people master the basic issues and learn how to make presentations and write op-ed pieces.

A group typically spends part of its monthly meeting discussing and summarizing an article on something like ORT. Groups then work together to develop two or three minute "laser talks" on the subject. Armed with their laser talks and organization-supplied videotapes, RESULTS members establish contact with their members of Congress and editorial writers at local newspapers. Within a matter of months, most have been able to get their opinions reflected on the op-ed pages and develop an ongoing working relationship with legislators and their staffs. If nothing else, hunger and health related issues are on both the community and Congressional agendas.

While it is hard to determine just how much impact any lobbying organization has on the legislative history of any bill, representatives on both sides of the aisle agree that RESULTS has been a major force in trying to block cuts in foreign aid spending since the Reagan-Bush years. The *Washington Post*'s Colman McCarthy, for instance, wrote: "There is not a rich lobby in Washington that wouldn't trade its limos for the group's achievements" (Reynolds 1991, Hendrix 1990, Klein 1989).

Just as important for our purposes is what RESULTS has done at the grass roots level that extends far beyond its impact on any piece of legislation. That's evident in the title Harris gave his book, *Reclaiming Our Democracy, Healing the Break between People and Government*.

Like many Americans, Harris and his colleagues began RESULTS sharing the frustration and cynicism that is such a part of political life these days. At first, Harris thought giving people laser talks, videotapes, and other tools would help them get past their frustrations with politics as well as their fear of talking in public.

He soon realized that the sense of powerlessness lies much deeper. The feeling that politicians don't care and that the system does not respond to the people actually ends up paralyzing us, much like the image of the enemy first discussed in Chapter 6. What RESULTS has tried to do is to help people see that they can take initiatives, and that if they just keep at it, they will begin to have an impact. No organization with just a hundred chapters is going to have the leverage of, say, the World Bank, but Harris and his colleagues have been able to help their members see that average people can make a difference. And, as in Beyond War and other such organizations, a fair amount of RESULTS' organizational development time is spent on precisely the kinds of efforts that will help people feel good about themselves and their chances for political success while not overcommitting themselves and running the risk of burnout.

As with Beyond War, one should not read too much into RESULTS. It remains a small organization that has had relatively little impact on the policy making process, even though it has probably fared better than most progressive organizations on that score in recent years. What's important to see in its story is the importance of new thinking or similar ideas in its operations, the base it has been able to build, and the potential for further growth.

### The Institute for Global Ethics

The Institute for Global Ethics is a different type of organization. It was created by Rushworth Kidder, who began his professional career as an English professor. He spent a sabbatical on the staff of the *Christian Science Monitor* and ended up staying there for more than a decade.

While with the *Monitor*, Kidder wrote general features, including a number of works on global and scientific issues. That culminated in the publication of two books in the late 1980s. The first, *An Agenda for the Twenty First Century* (1987), brought together interviews about issues in the global crisis with over thirty political, educational, and intellectual leaders from around the world. The second, *Reinventing the Future* (1989), reported on a conference at which the participants considered what our response to global issues should be. As the title suggests, most of the participants (including Kidder himself) came to the conclusion that dramatic, non-incremental change would be needed to meet the political, economic, and environmental challenges of the future.

As these kinds of projects took up more and more of his time, Kidder found his own priorities changing toward a focus on ethical issues. Like James Q. Wilson (1993) on whose work I drew heavily in Chapter 8, Kidder is convinced that people have a moral side and that there are ethical positions which are common to all societies and cultures, such as an equivalent of the Judeo-Christian Golden Rule. Moreover, Kidder argues that when we fail to follow ethical principles in our actions, we get ourselves in trouble much as we do when we pursue win-lose conflict resolution. On the other hand, acting ethically tends to lead to better outcomes, in much the same way that seeking win-win outcomes does in the long run.

By 1990, Kidder had decided that he wanted to become a more active participant in efforts to make ethical concerns a more important factor in the way global decisions are made. He left the *Monitor* to establish and run a new Institute for Global Ethics in Camden, Maine.

Unlike Beyond War or RESULTS, the Institute is not primarily an activist organization. Instead, it relies more on its staff to "promote the discussion of ethics in a global context, because we will not survive the 21st century with the 20th century's ethics."

The Institute has grown rapidly. Funding comes from several thousand individual members plus major foundations and corporations.

Not surprisingly given Kidder's background, the Institute devotes a lot of time to publications. Kidder has published a book based on interviews with global leaders about ethical issues and a broader work on the ways people make tough choices in this shrinking world (1994, 1995). The Institute also puts out a monthly newsletter on ethical concerns; recent issues have included articles on international arms sales, the views of Dutch theologian Hans Küng, abortion, free trade, Bosnia, the legacy of war in Vietnam, affirmative action, banking, and terrorism.

Just as important are the Institute's educational outreach efforts. Kidder himself is a popular speaker who has made presentations to hundreds of colleges, community organizations, and companies. With Varied Directions, Inc. (the company which produced the successful PBS series, *Making Sense of the Sixties*), it has prepared the first of a series of half hour videos, *Personal Ethics and the Future of the World*.

The Institute has also begun two educational programs. First, it has developed curricula for K-12 teachers to use in incorporating values, ethics, and critical thinking in the classroom, which have been tested in school systems in Ohio as well as Maine. Second, the Institute has developed training programs to expand the importance of ethical considerations in the corporate world. So far, those seminars have been held with teachers and workers in the food service, financial, and bio-technology industries.

### Greens

Despite what this chapter might seem to suggest so far, the most successful organizations espousing some variant of new thinking are not American. Rather, they are the various Green parties in Europe.[2] The German Greens burst on the political scene in 1983, when they won 5.6 percent of the vote and twenty-seven seats in the Bundestag, making them the first new party to win parliamentary representation since the formation of the Federal Republic in 1949 (Frankland and Schoonmaker 1992).

[2]There is a small network of Green organizations in the United States. They have not (yet) developed either the size or breadth of support of their European counterparts.

At first, "respected" observers did not take them seriously. The day the new parliamentary session opened, for instance, the *New York Times* ran a front page photo showing mainstream members of parliament wearing suits looking skeptically at one of their new colleagues who had long hair and a shaggy beard and wore a sweater and jeans. The pundits, too, had trouble with some of the Greens' policies which, among other things, called on all office holders to step down halfway through their terms so that no one would get "intoxicated" with power.

Soon, however, it became hard not to take the Greens seriously. They have become a fixture in German politics, consistently winning 5 percent or more in national and local elections despite taking highly unpopular positions during the debate on German unification and the shocking deaths of their two most prominent early leaders, Petra Kelly and retired general Gerd Bastien (Parkin 1995).

Green parties have been formed virtually everywhere else in Europe. Green tickets contested the 1989 and 1994 European Parliament elections in most European Community countries and won over twenty seats both times. In national elections held in Italy and regional elections in France and Germany in the spring of 1992, various Green groups also did well, suggesting that there is potentially significant electoral support for pro-environmental forces (Rüdig 1992). In France's 1993 legislative elections, two separate parties of Greens and Ecologists shared 7.5 percent of the vote, which was actually a disappointing showing, given earlier polling data (Boy 1994). Greens remain most influential in Germany where there is now serious discussion about their joining governing coalitions at both the state and national levels, though that idea is controversial indeed both among the Greens and mainstream politicians.

Greens are more than just the environmentalists or peace activists their critics often portray them to be. In one form or another, the Green parties subscribe to the theory of "deep ecology" which sees the world's problems as interconnected and calls for radical, non-violent change. While few voters of any party fully understand or share its views, there is some polling data to suggest that Green voters are more sophisticated and more likely to share their party's views than most. And, there is considerable evidence to suggest that Green influence in the Bundestag and in a number of state governments is a main reason why Germany has the most extensive recycling and other environmental regulations in the world. Finally, as we will see in the section on public opinion later in this chapter, support for Green-like positions is much larger than for the parties themselves, so it may well be that these parties or mainstream ones that adopt or even coopt Green positions will do even better in the near future.

### The Right Livelihood Award I: Sarvodaya Shramadana

We know a lot less about support for new thinking outside of the industrialized world. In part, that reflects the fact that far less attention has been paid to movements there, especially by political scientists and pollsters. In part, it reflects the fact that devastating poverty leaves many people facing a struggle for survival which leaves them without the time or resources to worry much about such things as new thinking.

Still, there are plenty of examples of movements working for this kind of social change in the less developed world. Paul Ekins (1992) recently published a book outlining the activities and accomplishments of the forty-four individuals and organizations which were awarded the Right Livelihood Award between 1980 and 1990. The award, which its founder and chair Jakob von Uexkull has dubbed the "alternative Nobel Prize," "has helped bring into the open some of those grassroots expressions of humanity's irrepressible, instinctive urge for mutual aid" (Ekins 1992: ix-x). Among the honorees are two groups working on alternative models of development, which should provide a sense of the diversity and strength of movements supporting new thinking in the LDCs.

The first is the Sarvodaya Shramadana Movement (SSM) of Sri Lanka (Ekins 1992: 100–112). It was formed in 1958 by a twenty-six year-old teacher who wanted people to share their resources to help develop the country. SSM is trying to foster what it calls "balanced" development, including a clean environment, access to safe water, adequate food, clothing, shelter, health care, and educational facilities, along with meeting people's cultural and spiritual needs. The movement is inspired in large part by Buddhist and Gandhian beliefs that stress compassion for others and self-reliance.

To accomplish that, SSM had organized a core of about thirty thousand young volunteers in eight thousand of Sri Lanka's twenty-three thousand villages by the mid-1980s. People wishing to "awaken" their village together identify its most pressing need. At that point, SSM organizers help establish what amounts to a work camp to meet that need as well as an ongoing village organization to continue work there and reach out to other communities.

It has enjoyed remarkable success. By the end of the 1980s, SSM employed ten thousand people and had an annual operating budget of over $400 million. Its spiritual inspiration and avoidance of partisan politics has made it one of the few organizations that appeals to all ethnic groups in this deeply divided country. Indeed, it has been the only one that tries to step in and begin healing the wounds after a region has been touched by sectarian violence which observers believe it can accomplish only because of the successes it has had in its developmental efforts at the village level. A. T. Ariyaratne put it this way:

Our first loyalty is to the common man. Whoever gets injured or whoever is deprived of food and shelter and other basic amenities has to be helped. We have to help without finding out to which caste, race, religion, or political party they belong. We do not consider anyone as our enemy; nor should anyone look on us as his enemy. (Ekins 1992: 110)

The SSM has certainly not ended Sri Lanka's poverty or violence. But, the fact remains that it has gained such widespread respect in large part because of its steadfast commitment to values which parallel new thinking.

### The Right Livelihood Award II: The Grameen Bank

The second example, the Grameen Bank, is one of a number of organizations which provide funding for grass roots development efforts. For most of their existence, the major international financing institutions have given or lent LDCs money for large scale, industrial projects. Over the last decade or two, those efforts and the strings that come attached to them have been widely criticized, because they have largely failed to produce much real improvement in the lives of more than a handful of people or much in the way of self-sustained growth.

As a result, some people in the LDCs themselves have established their own, of necessity, small scale, financial institutions which enable them to determine and implement more of their own development policies (Ekins 1992: 112–138). In one form or another, each tries to mobilize local people to control their own resources which, in turn, can then be used to help finance others.

The best known of these is Bangladesh's Grameen Bank, which has been the subject of a report on "60 Minutes" and served as the inspiration for similar funding systems in underdeveloped regions of the United States, Costa Rica, and other countries. The Bank was founded in 1976 by Muhammad Yunus, then an economics professor at Chittagong University. Unlike the western experts, Yunus was convinced that average Bangladeshi peasants needed and could effectively use banking services to create businesses they could run, and profit from, themselves.

Yunus began with a single village and a lending program administered by one of the country's major national banks. By 1980, the Bank was ready to go off on its own. By 1990, it had branches in a quarter of Bangladesh's villages, eight hundred thousand borrowers, and an average of $5.6 million a month in new loans. It plans to have a thousand branches and serve a million people by the end of the 1990s. Almost all loans go to poor, landless women. Borrowers are also shareholders, owning three quarters of the bank's stock, a figure Yunus would like to increase to 95 percent in the near future.

Like the SSM, the Grameen Bank has been remarkably successful. Ninety-eight percent of its loans are repaid on time. That's the case in large part because the Bank provides extensive training to its staff, who run the village-based lending program by treating the borrowers with the same dignity and respect corporate clients would expect, say, from Citibank. Its profits have been used not only to make more loans, but to help start schools, build clinics, and improve the infrastructure of these villages in which almost everyone lives in abject poverty.

## PUBLIC OPINION

In and of itself, the fact that such groups exist means very little. After all, the world is filled with organizations with impressive ideas but which are politically impotent because they have no mass following or influence of any sort. In this case, however, there is considerable evidence, albeit indirect, that some of the tenets of new thinking are taking root, at least in the advanced industrialized democracies, the only countries in which any substantial research along these lines has been conducted.

### Ending the Cold War

Average voters rarely pay as much attention to foreign as domestic policy. Furthermore, it is always hard to document whether public opinion affects actual foreign policy making.

Nonetheless, the available polling data suggest that shifts in public opinion on nuclear weapons and Soviet-American relations during the 1980s had an effect in bringing the Cold War to an end (Hauss 1990; Yankelovich and Doble 1984, Yankelovich and Smoke 1988, and Yankelovich and Harmon 1988). Early in the decade, researchers found that most Americans supported the new weapons programs and the hard line toward the Soviets begun during the Carter and continued under the Reagan administration (Sandman and Valenti 1986; Loeb 1988; Greenwald and Zeitlin 1988).

In part through the efforts of the peace movement and in part as a result of powerful films such as *The Day After*, Americans began to change, a change that accelerated after Gorbachev and his colleagues initiated their reform policies in the Soviet Union. In particular, Yankelovich and his colleagues showed that Americans were more aware of the risks of nuclear war and less willing to run them. Americans were still suspicious of the Soviets, but came to support improved relations between the two countries through enforceable arms control agreements, cultural exchanges, and the like. Similar trends were discovered in polls conducted in western Europe and in the few systematic studies done of public opinion in the Soviet Union before communism began to collapse in 1989.

Some argue that such trends were undermined by support for the Gulf war in 1991. Even that support suggests that the American (and European) publics had come closer to a Yankelovich-like public judgment about the declining utility of war. One has to remember that the Bush administration had a hard time building popular support for the war and, indeed, failed in its attempts to do so until it raised fears about the possibility of Iraqi development of nuclear weapons and then linked support for the troops with support for the war. Even at the height of the war, popular support for it was thin and probably would not have survived a protracted conflict in which thousands of American or European soldiers died.

The evidence since then is sketchier. Nonetheless, there has been one clear trend. Americans are more reluctant to risk the lives of many or any of their soldiers through interventions in countries like Bosnia, Somalia, Rwanda, or Haiti. Whether that reflects a new isolationism or support for anything that resembles new thinking remains to be seen. The fact remains that Americans, and probably Europeans as well, are less willing to endorse the use of war than at just about any time since the end of World War Two.

### Environmental Concern

Even more revealing for our purposes is more recent evidence about support for environmentalism for two reasons. First, environmentalism actually requires people to change and sacrifice more than opposition to wars which, in the end, touch relatively few American or European lives. Second, as we will see in the next section, support for environmentalism reveals some interesting demographic trends in support for new thinking (and in opposition to it).

As of 1990, there were at least 450 national organizations working on environmental issues plus many more at the local level in the United States. The leading ones took in over $400 million in donations from 4 million contributors which is ten times what the Democrats and Republicans together raised that year (Bailey 1993:16).

That organizational strength reflects broader trends in public opinion (Dunlap 1991; Dunlap and Scarce 1991). Riley Dunlap and his colleagues found a dramatic and consistent increase in interest in environmental issues in response to the policies of the Reagan administration which were widely viewed as anti-environmental. Events such as the Chernobyl and Exxon Valdez accidents, the celebration of the twentieth Earth Day in 1990, and the oil well fires in Kuwait also heightened environmental concern. Now, a clear majority of Americans are convinced that environmental problems are serious and that neither business nor government is doing enough to stop environmental destruction. A similar proportion of the American population also claims to be willing to sacrifice some economic growth if that will help protect the environment (Ottman 1993: 55-56).

It's not just an American phenomenon. Polls conducted by the Roper organization and its global affiliates show that environmental concerns rank at or near the top of the list when people are asked about which issues are most important.

In 1992, its analysts broke the American population into five groups on the basis of their opinions about the environment (Ottman 1993: 30–37). Twenty percent of Americans are what they call "true blues," people who have changed their lives to help save the environment. They recycle, use biodegradable plastic bags, buy natural products, contribute to environmental organizations, and so on. Another 5 percent are "greenback greens" who are not personally very active, but do contribute to environmental causes. Yet another 31 percent, the "sprouts," would like to see more pro-environmental policies but tend to think they can't do much to make that happen. Under 45 percent are either "grousers" or "basic browns" who are indifferent or hostile to environmentalism.

There is also some limited evidence that people are taking environmental and other social responsibilities seriously, though most polls show that peoples' words speak louder than their actions (Dunlap 1991). Sales of natural products doubled between the late 1980s and the early 1990s. Less reliable evidence suggests that that the average consumer is willing to spend roughly 4 to 5 percent more for environmentally safer products. In late December 1993, National Public Radio reported that more than half of all Americans take a company's environmental record or reputation into account before deciding which products to buy, which is now easier to do given press coverage of environmental issues and the widespread sales of books such as the Council on Economic Priorities' *Shopping for a Better World*.

The same Roper study cited above showed that there has been a profound change in behavior over a very short period, 1989–1991, though it should be pointed out that most of the activities covered in Table 10.1 are not very taxing and may well not have much of an impact.

Shareholder initiatives and other efforts to add to corporate responsibility continue to grow throughout the industrialized world. In the 1992–1993 "proxy season," United States pension funds represented by the Global Proxy Services raised environmental, social, and other concerns at nearly twenty-five hundred shareholders' meetings outside the United States, roughly half of which were in Japan alone (Wayne 1993).

Table 10.1
**What Consumers Are Doing About Solid Waste Management**

|                                     | 1989 | 1990 | 1991 |
|-------------------------------------|------|------|------|
| Doing Something                     | 61   | 78   | 85   |
| Recycling                           | 54   | 70   | 78   |
| Buy products with less packaging    | 2    | 10   | 11   |
| Composting                          | 4    | 9    | 12   |

*Source: Consumer Solid Waste: Awareness, Attitude and Behavior Study III*, Gerstman and My-ers, July 1991 in Ottman (1993: 77).

### Making Sense of These Changes

On their own, these data, too, may not mean much. Public opinion is notoriously fickle. Few people understand political issues very well or have anything approaching a coherent or consistent set of beliefs. As far as the environment is concerned, other issues have knocked the environment off the list of issues most respondents cite when asked about their pressing concerns in most of Europe and North America.

Nonetheless, there is a body of indirect evidence about an intriguing and enduring pattern underlying the ebbs and flows in what the pollsters find, most notably in the work of Ronald Inglehart and his colleagues (1977, 1989, 1990; Inglehart and Abramson 1994). Both Inglehart's research methods and his findings are highly controversial. Nonetheless, he has gathered such consistent results for such an extended period of time that he must be on to something important.

Inglehart argues that the extended post-war economic boom ushered in a new era in which the traditional division between left and right began to evaporate. Instead, he has been charting a new dividing line which, he believes, increasingly structures the way average citizens interpret political life.

On one side are what Inglehart labels materialists; on the other, not surprisingly, are post-materialists. He measures people's positions by asking them to prioritize issues of national, personal, and economic security on the one hand and personal development, free speech, and the environment on the other. Materialists emphasize the former, post-materialists the latter.

Materialists share social characteristics and political views of both the traditional left and right. They are typically older, poorer, and less well educated than the average voter. They are the most worried about their personal economic situation and continue to think social service programs are important. They also worry about crime and other issues they fear threaten their personal security. Materialists are found disproportionately among the Reagan Democrats and demographic groups that have shifted toward the right to support Margaret Thatcher's brand of conservatism in Great Britain or the National Front in France. They are concentrated, as well, among the "angry white males" who became the subject of so much analysis in the aftermath of the Republican landslide in the 1994 off-year elections.

More interesting for our purposes are the post-materialists. Unlike the materialists, they are disproportionately young and tend to come from affluent families, many of which have lived comfortably for two generations or more. Inglehart hypothesizes that these younger voters who came of political age after the mid-1960s take economic and personal security for granted. As a result, they "can" be more concerned about what he calls "higher order" values, such as finding a meaningful job, working for the environment, improving the status of women, and the like. And, they are as likely to come from traditionally right as traditionally left wing families.

While we should take Inglehart's terms and methods with a grain of salt, he does find that the number of post-materialists is growing despite the rightward shift in most countries. In the seven European countries he has studied throughout his career, he found that there were 13 percent more post-materialists in 1990 than in 1973, ranging from a low of 4 percent in Belgium to a high of 28 percent in West Germany (1994: 339). In the European Union as a whole, there are about 50 percent more post-materialists than materialists among those born after 1956. In the next older cohort, the balance is just about even.

Even more remarkable are the different ways the two groups think and act politically. Post-materialists are far more likely to support the peace movement and vote for the left, especially in countries in which it has adopted some of the "new issues" of the last generation. Most striking of all is the difference between the two reflected in the way they view the environment. In the 1986 Eurobarometre poll of a sample of voters in the then twelve European Community countries, Inglehart asked the respondents if they might join an environmental movement. Only 15 percent of the materialists but 45 percent of the post-materialists said yes. In Germany, 23 percent of the postmaterialists but only 1 percent of the materialists reported voting for the Greens (Inglehart 1990: 56).

It must be repeated that the evidence here is entirely too sketchy to warrant drawing any kind of sweeping conclusions. Nonetheless, the signs in Inglehart's research are echoed in another body of admittedly personal and anecdotal evidence.

I have spent the last decade working in that wing of the peace and environmental movements that most stresses the need to shift to a new way of thinking. Almost to a person, my colleagues reflect the profiles outlined by Inglehart.

Perhaps even more striking and encouraging is what my colleagues and I are seeing on many college campuses around the country (Hauss 1990). Few have much in common with my generation of politicized students from the late 1960s. That said, more and more of our students are involved in environmental projects and have participated in programs such as Outward Bound or the National Outdoor Leadership School (NOLS). They have no trouble seeing the importance of either interdependence or of combining the personal and the political. Most take recycling for granted. Most, too, carry plastic mugs around with them wherever they go so that they never have to use Styrofoam products or waste the energy that would be required to clean cups and glasses in the cafeteria. On both fronts, they do a lot better than my academic colleagues, including those who were radical activists during the 1960s.

In recent years, this political trend was accompanied by an academic fashion statement, the new-found popularity of the Birkenstock sandal. On the campuses I know about, almost everyone who wears Birkenstocks seems to be a new thinker and post-materialist. On the other hand, there is almost no correlation between Birkenstock wearing and a student's political background. Students from conservative backgrounds are as likely to wear them as those from liberal democratic families. Or, as one of them put it at the end of a rather heated class discussion about these trends when she found herself agreeing with me for the first time, "Hey, even Republicans can wear Birkenstocks."

## WHAT DOES GEORGE ELIOT HAVE TO DO WITH IT?

Starting a chapter on contemporary change with a quote about a fictional character who "lived" more than a century ago might seem odd. Yet, there are at least three reasons why the way Eliot describes Dorothea is telling given what we have seen so far.

First, lots can happen in times of tremendous change and confusion. *Middlemarch* is set in rural England during just such a time, the years before the Great Reform Act of 1832. During such times, many people are threatened by the changes swirling around them, but many others are open to reconsidering their basic values and assumptions. If anything, the social and economic change is more rapid and the potential for political and "value" change greater today. The pundits who have written about such times have likened them to "sea changes" and shifts in tectonic plates. Research by Inglehart and others has shown us that there are millions of people who are open to "thinking new," a far larger number than those who have been explicitly introduced to it.

Second, Dorothea shows us that the activist does not have to be a saint. Like everyone I know who is working for new thinking, Dorothea stumbled and made mistakes. Still, she had a tremendous impact. She had it, moreover, not because she actively preached her values to anyone who listened, but because the people around her saw those values mirrored in the way she led her life. They responded accordingly, and the impact of her actions rippled out from her to her town of Lydgate and beyond.

Finally, that "ripple" can expand very quickly. Consider the two scenarios outlined in Table 10.2. The first assumes that between now and next year, I reach two people who adopt and agree to try to get others to do the same. At that point, there would be three of us. If we each do the same thing the next year, there would be nine of us (the original three plus the six we reach) at the end of the second. Again, assuming we all do the same thing for three more years, the numbers mount quickly to nearly 250 after five.

Now, raise the ante to a figure most of us should be able to reach: convincing ten people a year. The basic math is the same, but because the increase is by a factor of ten rather than two a year, the numbers mount even more dramatically to over one hundred fifty thousand after the same five years.

These figures, of course, rest on the unrealistic assumption that each person I reach will be as active and stay as active as I am. Even factoring in a substantial amount of burnout (including possibly one's own), an individual can have a tremendous impact in a relatively brief period of time.

Reaching those kinds of numbers may not be all that difficult. At least in their early years, Beyond War and RESULTS both grew at dramatic rates.

Even more important, organizations can grow quickly if new thinkers learn one of the most important lessons of the 1994 elections and the recent upsurge

Table 10.2
Building Support Over Time

| Number reached | Participants reach 2 people per year | Participants reach 10 people per year |
|---|---|---|
| After 1 year | 3 | 11 |
| After 2 years | 9 | 121 |
| After 3 years | 27 | 1,331 |
| After 4 years | 81 | 14,641 |
| After 5 years | 243 | 161,051 |

in support for the right wing in general. Use the new communications technologies.

The far right started by using direct mail advertising, which, among other things netted millions of small contributions for Oliver North's unsuccessful 1994 senatorial bid. More importantly, the conservatives have dominated talk radio, which one fourth of all Americans routinely listen to. It even controls a cable network, National Empowerment Television.

There is no reason why the far right has to be the only political force to effectively use these technologies. Consider the following two possibilities.

Ted Becker (who is also the editor of this series) and others have championed the development of Electronic Town Meetings (ETMs) for more than a decade (Becker and Slaton 1991; Becker 1993, 1994; Slaton 1992). ETMs can take place in a number of ways, all of which share a common premise. If you use modern technologies (e.g., local-access cable television) to inform people and help them participate in a debate and discussion and then make it relatively easy for them to take part in the decision-making process, they do. Analyses of ETMs held in Hawaii, the Pacific Northwest, and New Zealand indicate that *when done well*, people participate more and their participation is grounded in a more reasoned understanding of the issues than one normally finds in the electoral process. The emphasis on those three words in the last sentence is important. All too often, candidates and others have taken on the mantle of an ETM to hold one-sided and even manipulative forums. Still, the limited research on full blown ETMs suggest that they are an ideal way to educate people and increase informed participation.

The cost of holding such sessions will only decrease. In my area, for instance, we have half a dozen local-access cable stations, most of which provide production facilities for a minimal fee and then allow whoever made the program to circulate a tape of the broadcast to other outlets. The spread of interactive television and other similar technologies that increasingly integrate television, computer, and telephone should make such enterprises easier rather than harder.

Similarly, the Internet and the broader telecommunications super highway offer opportunities for supporters of new thinking (or anyone else as we learn more about the right wing "militias") to communicate with each and enhance their support. Here, the technology isn't new, since Beyond War and other organizations have used the Institute for Global Communications' PeaceNet for years, first for e-mail and now for broader purposes including distribution of material and discussion groups.

As with ETM-based approaches, people's ability to use these systems will only grow as technologies become cheaper and easier to use. One does not need a fancy Pentium or PowerPC computer to use the core features of the Internet. One friend gets along fine with an all but worthless Mac Plus, 1200 baud modem, and an $8 a month limited access account. In 1995, the Labour Party announced an agreement with British Telecom to connect every school, library, and hospital to the Internet, assuming, of course, it won the next election. Meanwhile, the price of sophisticated computers is declining dramatically, and the introduction of programs like Mosaic and Netscape make navigating the net ever easier.

In short, if you add the potential for networking shown in Table 10.2 to the broader grass roots changes described here, there certainly seems to be reason to believe that support for new thinking and the demand for political change which comes with it could grow and grow dramatically in the next few years.

## REFERENCES

Bailey, Ronald (1993). *Eco-Scam: The False Prophets of Environmental Apocalypse.* New York: St. Martin's.

Becker, Ted (1994). "Electrifying Democracy." *Demos* 1: 34–35.

———. (1993). "Teledemocracy: Gathering Momentum in State and Local Governance." *Spectrum*, Spring, 14–21.

Becker, Ted, and Christa Slaton (1981). "Hawaii Televote: Measuring Public Opinion on Complex Issues." *Political Science* 33: 52–75.

Boy, Daniel, (1993). "Écologistes: Retour sur terre." In Habert, Philippe, Pascal Perrineau, and Colette Ysmal, *Le vote sanction: Les élections législatives des 21 et 28 mars 1993.* Paris: Département d'études politiques du Figaro and Presses de la Fondation nationale des sciences politiques, 163–184.

Dunlap, Riley E. (1991). "Public Opinion in the 1980s: Clear Consensus, Ambiguous Commitment." *Environment* 33: 9–15, 32–37.

Dunlap, Riley E. and Rik Scarce (1991). "Environmental Problems and Protection." *Public Opinion Quarterly* 55 (Winter): 651–672.

Ekins, Paul (1992). *A New World Order: Grassroots Movements for Global Change.* London: Routledge.

Eliot, George (1964). *Middlemarch.* New York: Signet Classic.

Faludi, Susan (1987). "Inner Peaceniks: Can We Move Beyond War with the Power of Positive Thinking?" *Mother Jones*, April, 20–25, 51–53.

Frankland, E. Gene, and Donald Schoonmaker (1992). *Between Protest and Power: The Green Party in Germany.* Boulder, Colo.: Westview.

Gore, Albert (1993). *Earth in the Balance.* New York: Plume.

Greenwald, David S., and Stephen J. Zeitlin (1988). *No Reason to Talk about It: Families Confront the Nuclear Taboo.* New York: W. W. Norton.

Harris, Sam (1994). *Reclaiming Our Democracy: Healing the Break between People and Government.* Philadelphia: Camino Books.

Hauss, Charles (1990). "The End of the Cold War: Challenges for Peace Education." *Peace and Change* 15: 223–239.

Hellman, Martin, and Anatoly Gromyko, eds. (1988). *Breakthrough: Emerging New Thinking Soviet and Western Scholars Issue a Challenge to Build a World Beyond War.* New York: Walker/Moscow: Novosti.

Hendrix, Kathleen (1990). "A Passion for Results," *Los Angeles Times*, July 5, E1.

Inglehart, Ronald (1990), "Values, Ideology, and Cognitive Mobilization in New Social Movements." In Russell J. Dalton and Manfred Kuechler, *Challenging the Political Order: New Social and Political Movements in Western Democracies.* New York: Oxford University Press.

———. (1989). *Culture Shift.* Princeton: Princeton University Press.

———. (1977). *The Silent Revolution.* Princeton: Princeton University Press.

Inglehart, Ronald, and Paul R. Abramson (1994). "Economic Security and Value Change." *American Political Science Review* 88: 336–353.

Kidder, Rushworth (1987). *An Agenda for the Twenty First Century.* Cambridge: MIT Press.

———. (1988). *Reinventing the Future.* Cambridge: MIT Press.

———. (1994). *Shared Values for a Troubled World.* San Francisco: Jossey-Bass.

———. (1995). *How Good People Make Tough Choices.* New York: Morrow.

Klein, Edward (1989). "They Defy the Odds." *Washington Post*, July 23, 12.

Lappé, Frances Moore, and Paul Martin DuBois (1994). *The Quickening of America: Rebuilding Our Nation, Remaking Our Lives.* San Francisco: Jossey-Bass.

Loeb, Paul (1988). "Willful Unconcern." *Psychology Today*, June, 58–62.

Lofland, John (1993). *Polite Protesters: The American Peace Movement of the 1980s.* Syracuse: Syracuse University Press.

Montminy, Judith (1989). "Beyond War Group Widens Its Focus." *Boston Globe*, July 2, Section 6, p. 1.

Oskamp, Stuart, Jeffrey Bordin, and Todd Edwards (1992). "Background Experiences and Attitudes of Peace Activists." *Journal of Psychology* 128: 49–61.

Ottman, Jacquelyn (1993). *Green Marketing: Challenges and Opportunities for the New Marketing Age.* Lincolnwood, Ill.: NTC Business Books.

Parkin, Sara (1995). *The Life and Times of Petra Kelly.* New York: HarperCollins/Pandora.

Reynolds, Barbara (1991). "Keep Promises to the Children." *USA Today*, September 29, A11.

Rice, Susan, and Nancy L. Mary (1989). "Beyond War: A New Perspective for Social Work." *Social Work* 34: 175–179.

Rüdig, Wolfgang (1992). "Green Politic," *Environment* 33: 6–9, 25–31.

Sandman, Peter, and JoAnn Valenti (1986). "Scared Stiff—or Scared into Action?" *Bulletin of the Atomic Scientists*, January, 12–16.

Scott, Mary, and Howard Rothman (1993). *Companies With a Conscience.* Secaucus, N.J.: Carol Publishing Group.

Slaton, Christa (1992). *Tele-Vote*. Westport, CT: Praeger.

Stoel, Thomas B. (1994). "Public Engagement in International Environmental Policy." In Daniel Yankelovich and I. M. Destler, eds., *Beyond the Beltway: Engaging the Public in US Foreign Policy*. New York: W. W. Norton, 253–274.

Warner, Gale (1991). *The Invisible Threads: Independent Soviets Working for Global Awareness and Social Transformation*. Washington: Seven Locks Press.

Wayne, Leslie (1993). "Exporting Shareholder Activism." *New York Times*, July 16: D1–2.

Wilson, James Q. (1993). *The Moral Sense*. New York: Free Press.

Yankelovich, Daniel and John Doble (1984). "The Public Mood: Nuclear Weapons and the USSR." *Foreign Affairs* 62: 33–46.

Yankelovich, Daniel and Richard Smoke (1988). "America's 'New Thinking.'" *Foreign Affairs* 66: 1–17.

Yankelovich, Daniel and Willis Harmon (1988). *Starting with the People*. Boston: Houghton-Mifflin.

# 11

# PRIVATE AND PUBLIC

Astonishing as it may seem in 1994, ideas such as "management by wandering around" and "the customer is king" amounted to radical thinking in 1979 when Bob Waterman and I did our research for *In Search of Excellence.*

—Tom Peters

It might seem odd for a book which focuses on global issues and conflict resolution to have a chapter on management in the public or private sector. However, it is probably there that we can find the clearest evidence about what new thinking can lead to.

A decade ago, most American industrial corporations were in trouble. Productivity, profits, market share, and more were all in decline as the result of competition from more dynamic and efficient foreign firms. The owner of Yakima Products put the plight of one of those companies quite graphically in addressing his employees:

This article in today's *Wall Street Journal* reports that General Motors lost $4.5 billion last year. Let's assume the company runs 365 days a year, twenty-four hours per day. That means GM lost $12.3 million dollars per day, a half a million dollars per hour, $8,500 per minute, and more than $140 per second. (cited in Scott and Rothman 1992: 151)

Since the mid-1980s, there has been something approaching a paradigm shift in the American private sector. Hundreds of companies have adopted some form of what Tom Peters (1992) calls "liberation management." Some are new, small, high tech companies in which change came pretty easily. Others are older, larger operations with a predominantly blue-collar work force. Even the big three auto makers, once seen as the archetype of the American corporate malaise, have made tremendous strides, making better cars that can compete in a very tight market. And if recent press reports are accurate, American workers and their companies are once again the most productive in the world.

The new approaches to management have also found an audience in parts of the public sector. In their path breaking book, *Reinventing Government*, David Osborne and Ted Gaebler (1992) based their analyses and prescriptions on W. Edwards Deming's principles of TQM (Total Quality Management). Then, when Vice President Gore's commission (Osborne was a key advisor) issued its report (Gore 1993), none other than Tom Peters, who had become one of the best known private sector management gurus, wrote the Foreword.

Not everything is fine with American industry or the economy as a whole. Reengineered corporations, for instance, provide fewer people with highly paid or secure jobs, especially in manufacturing.

That should not keep us from seeing three key points about the management revolution. First, it is based on the same basic principles as new thinking. Second, precisely because these ideas have been most widely applied in the business community, we can use it to get a pretty good glimpse of the kinds of changes they can lead to. Finally, as we saw in Chapter 10, the adoption of these ideas and practices cuts across the traditional division between left and right. To be sure, there are plenty of sixties radicals like Anita Roddick or Ben and Jerry (Cohen and Greenfield respectively) who stumbled into the business world. Just as important are the pleas and models for change put forth by Tom Peters who started his career with McKinsey and Company and Amway cofounder Richard DeVos (1993), neither of which have ever been thought of as left wing companies.

One caveat has to be made at the outset. Most of the books and articles on new thinking in business have been written by practitioners for practitioners and rely heavily on individual cases. Recent issues of the *Harvard Business Review*, for instance, have included articles on managing sausage factories to the San Francisco FortyNiners. There is, alas, little systematic research in which the impact of these new approaches has been assessed in a representative sample of corporations or government agencies, especially those in which the management revolution has failed. In other words, though there is an impressive array of case studies in the trade journals or the volumes in your bookstore's business section, what follows has to be read with a degree of caution if not skepticism.

## NEW THINKING AND ORGANIZATIONAL THEORY

A surprising number of those works begin with the same story: the parable of the frog. Drop a frog into a pot of boiling water, and it will do everything it can to get out. On the other hand, if you put a frog into a pot of lukewarm water, it will happily (to the degree that we can judge a frog's emotions) swim around. Gradually heat up the water, and the frog will keep swimming until the temperature approaches boiling, at which point the frog gets groggy, can't hop out, and dies.

In short, these theorists are arguing that all too many corporations were like the frog being slowly boiled alive. In developing cures for boiling frog disease, they ground their work on three assumptions about the "changing water" those companies operate in which parallel the themes about the global crisis.

The first is the rapidity of change in what Peters (1992) calls the "nanosecond nineties." Companies have to be prepared to change their operations all the time in order to keep up with the lightning quick transmission of information, shifts in customer tastes, and the like. Among other things, that means that companies can no longer afford the time it takes for ideas and commands to work their way up and down massive bureaucratic structures. If the rest of his subtitle is right, they have to be flexible enough not just to change but also to go through a succession of "necessary *dis*organizations" (emphasis added).

Second, companies operate as part of a complex web in which they have to deal with a host of suppliers, workers, and customers, all of which are themselves changing rapidly. To take but one example, manufacturers want the inventory of goods that go into their products to arrive "just in time." As a result, they have to pay a lot more attention to the impact of their behavior on that web of other actors than was the case thirty years ago.

Third, companies can best deal with these challenges by relying on strategies grounded in systems theory because of its stress on feedback and the longer term. As Peter Senge puts it, systems theory

is the discipline that integrates the disciplines, fusing them into a coherent body of theory and practice. It keeps them from being separate gimmicks or the latest organizational change fad. Without a systematic orientation, there is no motivation to look at how the disciplines interrelated. By enhancing each of the other disciplines, it continually reminds us that the whole can be greater than the sum of its parts. (1990: 12)

These theorists' prescriptions can be summed up in four points which bear a remarkable resemblance to the ones on conflict resolution which we saw in Chapters 7 and 8.

**Learn and Change.** Tastes and technologies, markets and manpower change practically overnight. One can't hope for stability or resist change and hope to survive. In the computer world, Digital Equipment Corporation and Wang all but collapsed largely because their managers assumed they could run huge profits indefinitely selling mainframe based systems. The same almost happened to Apple until it realized it had to provide the same computing power and software at a lower price than consumers paid for MS-DOS and Windows machines.

Companies have to become "learning organizations" that can adapt quickly. The most successful ones strive to anticipate future trends and be ready for them when they materialize. Organizations have to innovate and take risks, which also means they have to be prepared to fail some of the time. They also sometimes have to be willing to forego short term profit to maximize their ability to compete and work effectively in the longer run.

Another way of saying all this is that companies can no longer afford the rigid kind of all but permanent organizational structure typical of General Motors or the United States government. As Peter Drucker put it,

Every organization of today has to build into its very structure *the management of change*. It has to build in organized abandonment of everything it does. *The ability to create the new* has also to be built into the organization. In the post-capitalist society, it is safe to assume that everyone with any knowledge will have to acquire *new* knowledge every four or five years, or else become obsolete. (Drucker 1993: 58–59. Emphasis in the original.)

**New structures.** Systems theorists believe that the structure of a system determines much of what goes on in it. Put talented, dedicated people in a dysfunctional system, and they are not likely to do very well.

In the 1990s, that means abandoning large, hierarchical organizations and flattening the hierarchy to the point that it has as few layers as possible. In discussing successful organizational structures, these theorists typically use a circle or web rather than a pyramid as a geometric metaphor. That's the case, because circles and webs incorporate feedback and, with it, the conclusion of earlier chapters, that, over the long haul, I can only be successful if you are (Hamel et al. 1989).

They also stress the importance of organizing work around cooperative teams. There's nothing magical to teams, and, in fact, they often don't work. When they don't, it's usually because team members come to them with their own goals and egos out of control. Teams that work consist of people who realize that they will succeed as individuals only if the team as a whole does.

These authors thus stress the importance of group dynamics very much along the lines discussed in Chapters 7 and 8. They call for ongoing dialogue in which people in a team really listen and non-judgmentally evaluate what others are saying, using those discussions as an opportunity to reassess their own thinking. Like the innovative conflict resolution theorists, the management gurus talk about suspending assumptions and avoiding blame, name calling, and defensiveness, while stressing brainstorming and other techniques which tend to elicit creative alternatives.

Whatever their differences, these theorists all advocate creating organizations which make it easier for people to work cooperatively. That, in turn, involves more than just concentrating on the job at hand, but treating colleagues and competitors with dignity and respect.

To cite a personal example, I spent 1988 working on a number of teams while on sabbatical, one of which was charged with writing a first version of this book. It wasn't going well. My mentor for the year, a management trainer at Hewlett-Packard, saw my frustration one day and said:

I know you're working hard, have good ideas, and write a lot better than I do. But, you're missing one of the key ingredients of good teamwork. You're putting the task ahead of the relationships you have with the other people. Flip it. Put the relationships first. It may take a longer time to get off the ground. But, because you build good working relationships first, it will become easier to write later.

He was right.

These new kinds of organizations also need new kinds of leaders. Skeptics are quick to point out that simply calling a worker an "associate" or having the CEO eat in the same cafeteria as the line workers is often no more than trendy window dressing for a company that has made no profound changes. That's not true of the companies to be described in the case studies later in this chapter. Their executives have discovered they need to be "close" to their staff members, which is what Peters has in mind when he advocates managing by wandering around, because they set the tone for the entire organization. Instead of issuing commands, they have become facilitators, motivators, and guides who listen and respond to what their "associates" are saying and doing.

That sense of closeness extends beyond the organization itself to everyone in the web it interacts with. Organizations have always needed information about their markets or suppliers. But in these days of rapid change, niche marketing, outsourcing, and just in time inventory control that's more important than ever. Peters, for instance, suggests that it makes sense for companies to have some of their own people working at the site of regular suppliers or sub-contractors.

Today, they also have to include the environment. Again, this is a direct outgrowth of thinking in terms of interdependent systems. No longer can a company ignore its impact on its physical environment. Even a company like Tom's of Maine, which only uses natural ingredients in making its personal care products, has an impact on the environment around its Kennebunk factory.

But the environment here is more than the trees and the air and the water supply. It means the entire environment as seen in terms of systems theory and therefore includes the community the company is located in, its employees' families, the government whose regulations it has to comply with, and so on.

The bottom line here is quite simple. Other things being equal, a company must be an open, flexible, and dynamic system if it is to consistently provide high quality products or services.

**You can have your cake and eat it too, but not all at once.** A remarkable number of these companies have entered a "virtuous circle" that tends to undermine the traditional belief that capitalism and compassion are incompatible. Some of these men and women went into business planning to use their companies to help reach explicit social, political, or environmental goals. Most did not. Most are committed to making money, if for no other reason than the survival of their business depends on it.

Beyond that, they have discovered that compassionate capitalism can work. From a systems perspective, treating your employees and others you interact with professionally well increases performance and enhances trust and confidence in you which tends to lead to even more business down the line. Most of these companies also treat their employees well. Typically, they offer higher than union-scale wages and benefits, stock ownership plans, child care and athletic facilities, and the like. It's good for the company, too. Donating money to socially useful causes or giving employees paid time off to work for them also can open the door to new customers and positive publicity which makes more people aware of your company and what it does.

If the case studies presented below are at all representative, many of today's entrepreneurs are open to the kind of long term socially responsible management and risk taking innovation these theorists stress. Every single one of these authors and consultants works on the assumption that people go to work and go into business to make money. They have also discovered that, however important self-interest in the traditional sense may be, it is not the sole motivation people have at work or anywhere else. Most want something more out of their jobs and seem a lot like Inglehart's post-materialists.

**It doesn't come easily.** Like learning to play the cello, hit a top spin backhand, or solve conflict along the lines discussed in Chapter 8, running an organization along these lines takes practice. Most managers don't have much experience in implementing these principles, and most workers are used to taking orders from some supervisor. After all, employee and employer alike were raised in the same society as the rest of us and have the traditional way of thinking ingrained in them just like the rest of us.

The first person accounts from these "new age" business leaders are filled with instances in which they themselves lapsed back into the traditional "command mode" or flew off the handle at an employee who made an honest mistake. But, like good systems theorists, they realized that they could use those incidents as helpful examples of negative feedback and learn how not to repeat their mistakes.

## NEW COMPANIES

There are a number of companies whose very creation was inspired by some variation on the theme of new thinking. Most are fairly small enterprises on the fringes of the economy. Many have flamboyant and unusual leaders and have often drawn the label "new age business" even though most were inspired more by 1960s radicalism than any quest for spirituality.

Whatever that inspiration, they clearly are not part of the economic mainstream. Of the twelve covered in one recent account (Scott and Rothman 1992), nine were aimed at relatively upscale, non-conventional markets in food (Celestial Seasonings, Ben and Jerry's, Alfalfa Markets), high tech personal equipment (Quickie Designs, Yakima), and clothing (Birkenstock, Patagonia, Esprit). However small and quirky most of them are, they deserve our attention because they have explicitly drawn on philosophies and techniques which mirror new thinking.

### Tom's of Maine

Tom's of Maine makes all natural toothpastes, shampoos, and other personal care products. The company has chosen to limit its rate of growth so it could concentrate on living up to its principles. As a result, its products are not available everywhere, though they are now found in most supermarkets, drug stores, and natural food outlets on both coasts and in other locations scattered around the country.

After graduating from college, Tom Chappell took a job as an insurance salesman. After a few years, he realized he wasn't cut out for the corporate world. So, in 1968, Tom and his wife Kate moved to Kennebunk, Maine, where her father had a small company that made commercial soaps.

In 1971, they introduced Clearlake, the country's first non-polluting laundry detergent. It came with a postage paid return carton so consumers could send the bottle back to be refilled. With a $5,000 loan, the Chappells launched Tom's Natural Soaps which became Tom's of Maine when the product line expanded.

By the early 1980s, Tom's had grown to well over $1 million in sales. At the same time, Tom Chappell was suffering from burn out. With the support of his family, employees, and board of directors, he cut back to half time and enrolled in the Harvard Divinity School. Exposure to the faculty, his fellow students, and the works of theologians like Jonathan Edwards and Martin Buber led Chappell to rethink his company's mission, especially its relationships. Early in his studies, he used his reflections on such ideas as Buber's I-and-thou to sketch out some ideas about restructuring his company.

Chappell brought the ideas and energy he had gained at Harvard back to Kennebunk. He even had his board of directors read Buber and meet with some of his professors! He also realized that just producing natural products wasn't enough. The company had to be run differently, starting with the owner and boss, which is to say, himself.

Until then, Tom's had been run pretty much like a conventional business. Chappell admits he was a traditional CEO, often acting haughtily and sometimes even abusively toward his employees.

On his return, Tom tried to impose his new ideas about management on the company. Quickly, he realized that wouldn't work. He began meeting with groups of employees and discovered all sorts of problems, ranging from potholes in the driveway which were ruining employees' cars to workers who felt they weren't treated with respect. Over the next few months, Tom's staff wrote and adopted a mission statement for a company they would all enjoy working in. The statement itself is quite long, but Chappell summed it and the company's priorities up as follows:

Most people want to come to work and to do a good job. They want to contribute to the growth and development of a company whose values they believe in. If the company has no principles other than maximizing profit, or if its values are unstated, workers will limit themselves to the least creative principle in business. Please the boss. A company will thrive when its managers and their employees are in sync. Common values, a shared sense of purpose, can turn a company into a community where daily work takes on a deeper meaning and satisfaction. Don't get me wrong—I'm in business to make money. But that's not my only goal. I believe that the conventional, sole focus of maximizing gains for shareholders strips away that part of ourselves that needs to thrive. Something in us wants to endure beyond retained earnings, and that something is our soul. (xv)

Under the Chappells' leadership, the company began putting its principles into practice. It gives 10 percent of its pretax profits to socially responsible causes, which the workers help choose. Workers can take paid time off to work on community projects. Tom's products all come with minimal packaging but with a statement which tells consumers what the product and company are all about.

And, the company has done better than ever. In 1992, sales topped $20 million even though the company faced new competition from larger companies like Arm and Hammer, which introduced its own line of natural products. New product lines are in the pipeline, and the company looks forward to continued, steady growth in large part because it redefined itself in these ways.

### The Body Shop

Like Tom and Kate Chappell, Anita and Gordon Roddick were products of the sixties who entered the business world only because they had to find a way to support themselves and their children. They first tried a residential hotel and a restaurant. Both kept the family afloat, but the Roddicks realized they needed more cash flow and more leisure time, especially since Gordon wanted to take two years off to ride a horse from the tip of South America to California.

In 1976, they decided Anita should open up a small cosmetics shop that would cater to the politicized, "alternative" young women who preferred not patronizing conventional stores. The Roddicks had next to no money, which meant that they had to do everything on the cheap, including buying in bulk and bottling the products themselves in reusable plastic bottles and jars. Another company threatened to sue over the use of the name, "body shop," and Anita launched a letter writing and public relations campaign that not only quashed the suit but established the company's principle of using media coverage rather than buying advertising.

The company began to grow pretty quickly, especially after Anita realized that it would sell even more products if she and her handful of employees were solicitous of customers, never pressured them, and tried to offer what they wanted to buy: high quality natural products, marketed without all the frills and added expenses of the mainstream industry. Soon, other people wanted to open Body Shops of their own. After some glitches, a system was established which required franchisees to run their stores in the same way.

The Body Shop takes what it sees as its social responsibility seriously. It carries no products tested on animals. Recyclable packaging is used whenever possible. Unlike most of the cosmetics industry, the Body Shop avoids anything that could even vaguely be construed as sexist in its public relations.

Far more than Tom's of Maine, the Roddicks have used the Body Shop to promote political causes. They also encourage employees to take a paid half-day off a week to work for a cause of their own choosing.

The company's "campaigns" are more than public relations stunts. They reflect the Roddicks' commitment to a model of sustainable development in which they use their company to conduct environmentally responsible business with impoverished people from the LDCs, whose natural products can be alternatives to the chemically manufactured ones of the mainstream cosmetics industry. The Body Shop has thus adapted some of the natural creams and lotions they found from India to Brazil for sale in its stores which are located in Europe and North America.

Not all those efforts have succeeded for either the company or the people it works with in Asia, Africa, and South America, but the ground rules for this "trading" as Anita Roddick calls it are clear and interesting, especially when contrasted with more conventional developmental projects. They only begin working with a group if it asks them to, the project does not endanger either the environment or the local culture, and it would provide real benefits for all involved. As Roddick herself put it, "Our job now is to show that there is an alternative and it's so incredibly simple. It is just a basic exchange of resources carried out in the traditional manner—as a token of friendship and respect" (1991: 213).

The company has been very successful. By 1995, it had topped a thousand retail outlets in more than forty countries, including over two hundred in the US. Its skyrocketing sales even sparked changes in mainstream companies, some of which are developing natural cosmetic lines of their own. Roddick herself had gotten a good deal of exposure, including her own ad for American Express, which is somewhat ironic since the Body Shop itself has never advertised outside the US.

Like Tom's of Maine, the Body Shop has thrived in large part because the Roddicks and their colleagues have built a learning, flexible, and adaptive organization using principles very much like those developed in Part Two here. Again, Anita Roddick's words tell it all:

You have to look at leadership through the eyes of the followers and you have to live the message. What I have learned is that people become motivated when you guide them to the source of their own power and when you make heroes out of employees who personify what you want to see in the organization. I think the leadership of a company should encourage the next generation not just to follow, but to overtake. No one—not even our most cynical critics—can deny that we are passionate in everything we do. (1991: 214, 218, 226)

Like Tom's of Maine and other "green" companies, while the Body Shop has carved out a strong niche for itself in a very large market, it is not about to displace any of the major cosmetic companies. On the other hand, it has been one of the few standout companies in a Britain which has endured tough economic times for several decades. It has won the prestigious Queen's Award for Exports and, even more remarkably, was named "Company of the Year" by the stodgy and conservative Confederation of British Industries, which is roughly equivalent to the National Association of Manufacturers in the United States.

### The Green Guy

Every Wednesday, the Green Guy, Joel Makower, appears on Robert Aubrey Davis's whimsical "PM Program" on one of Washington's public radio stations. After the strains of the New Christy Minstrels' "Green, Green" die down, the two men start to discuss some environmental issue in the week's news.

Makower never talks about companies like Tom's of Maine or the Body Shop. Instead, he focuses on the environmental record of more conventional companies.

One week he'll talk about new companies which have agreed to follow the CERES principles, an environmental equivalent of the Sullivan principles which led many American companies, universities, and pension funds to divest from South Africa. Another week will bring word of a major company offering environmentally friendly products, like California's Fetzer vineyard, which makes about seventy-five thousand cases of organic wine a year.

This show is but a small part of Makower's overall effort to spread the word on what mainstream companies are doing environmentally and, then, to get others to do more yet (Makower 1993; also see Moore and Miller 1994). For these companies, the impetus typically comes from the marketplace, not from some ideological conversion on the part of the CEO. Poll after poll shows an American public willing to hold companies accountable for their economic performance in the aftermath of the Exxon Valdez accident and all the other environmental disasters of recent years. The same polls show that the public has at best a fuzzy notion of who the "good guys" and "bad guys" are on this score. The public still ranks McDonald's among the worst despite the fact that it eliminated Styrofoam products and has done a lot to reduce its overall waste production.

Makower and people like him use market pressure as leverage in raising more general arguments that acting environmentally now can mean larger profits down the line. It is now widely understood that profit and economic growth figures do not fully incorporate the environmental costs of production (Makower 1993: ch. 2; Myers 1993; Hawken 1993). Even given that, these analysts help companies see that they can operate more efficiently economically by operating more efficiently environmentally. Reducing its consumption or waste of natural resources can be as important to a company's bottom line as any other factor in production.

Together, the pull of profit and the push of the market have produced a shift in the way some companies operate. None is more dramatic than the alliance forged between McDonald's and the Natural Resources Defense Fund. The Fund agreed to do an audit of McDonald's environmental practices. After months of suspicion followed by hemming and hawing, the company went along and then adopted most of the Fund's recommendations. Overnight, it went from being one of the "worst" to one of the "best" companies from an environmentalist's point of view.

Also typical of the companies Makower likes is 3M. In 1975, it instituted its 3Ps (Pollution Prevention Pays) program (Ottman 1992:60–1). Employees were encouraged to submit suggestions which could earn them bonuses if adopted. Since then, the company has followed enough of these suggestions to save over $500 million and reduce its waste generation by half. It has introduced new products, such as a paint stripper that for all intents and purposes eliminates methylene chloride which is suspected of causing cancer, a version of Scotchguard without CFCs, and Post-its on recycled paper.

3M is not alone. The International Chamber of Commerce has established a "Business Charter for Sustainable Development" which the Global Environmental Management Initiative (GEMI) is urging companies to adopt. As noted above, another grass roots group, CERES (Coalition for Environmentally Responsible Economies) is pushing a similar charter of its own which goes one step further by requiring signatory companies to open their books to full public disclosure. Even the Chemical Manufacturers Association has a program of Responsible Care which companies will soon have to adopt to remain members.

Most companies now have some sort of environmental program. About half have a senior vice president for environmental matters. Some even have given a member of the board of directors responsibility for environmental matters.

While example could be piled on top of example, it's more important to see the bottom line. To be sure, American business is by no means "green" yet. If it were, people like Makower would be out of a job, and there would be little reason to write a book like this.

Plenty of problems and plenty of pollution remain. There are loopholes to the ICC and CERES charters, just as there were to the Sullivan principles for South Africa. Many of the efforts have turned out to be little more than window dressing or publicity gimmicks. Whatever companies are doing, the over-whelming majority of them could be doing more. Nonetheless, there is a lot going on in the business community.

Perhaps even more important, the still sketchy research suggests that green-ing one's business is often good for the bottom line. One study found that companies that employed sound environmental practices outperformed those that didn't by at least 2 percent in sales and asset growth, return on assets, equity, and investments, and operating income.

## LIBERATING MANAGEMENT

Tom's of Maine and the Body Shop are two of many companies on the leading edge of implementing new thinking in the business community. While few mainstream companies have moved anywhere near as far on such issues as employee activism, there are signs that these kinds of ideas are finding their way into the management and growth strategies of companies that are as far from these two as one could imagine.

What makes these companies so interesting here is that they have not turned to new-thinking-like practices out of any sense of ideological commitment. Instead, they got there because they discovered that doing business responsibly can be highly profitable.

Here, the evidence is even more impressive if still anecdotal, since an even larger number of companies have dramatically changed the way they operate and a similarly larger number of scholars and consultants have written about them. As with the environment, one of those consultant-authors will be enough for our purposes here.

Tom Peters has now written five main books (1995, 1992, 1987; Peters and Austin 1985; Peters and Waterman 1982). Each book is longer than its predecessor (*Liberation Management* runs to more than seven hundred pages), because there are more stories to be told. Each book digs deeper and comes closer to what I've called new thinking.

You can see that in the titles Peters chooses. The first two were about the search and passion for "excellence." That made sense in the late 1970s and early 1980s, when we were becoming painfully aware of how shoddy so many American goods were. The third was called *Thriving on Chaos* and showed managers that they had to learn to live in a world that was changing in dramatic and unpredictable ways. The most recent one evokes radical theology in its main title, while its subtitle, *Necessary Disorganization for the Nanosecond Nineties*, clearly takes us a long way from "mere" excellence.

Peters is not alone. When he started as a fresh MBA with McKinsey and Co., he quickly learned he was far ahead of most of his colleagues on most management issues. Today, McKinsey and all the other major consulting groups have thriving practices on liberation management or whatever one chooses to call it.

The basic principles Peters and the like try to get businesses to adopt should be familiar by now. Decentralize the company into small, autonomous profit centers. Get as close to suppliers and customers as possible. Empower your workers. Organize them in flexible teams that come together for specific tasks and then are disbanded. Manage by walking around so that you know what's really going on. Minimize the complexity of your organizational structure so you can maximize your ability to change with changing circumstances. Information management is the most vital organizational task in a business environment in which knowledge is typically the most valuable commodity. Above all, think in terms of networks that fit market niches.

## ABB

More than most of the management gurus, Peters shows that such methods work outside of small high-tech companies and have spread beyond Japan and the United States to Europe as well (*Economist* 1994a). Consider the case of ABB (Asea Brown Boveri) (Peters 1992: 44–55).

ABB is a huge company with nearly $30 billion in sales in 1991. It's not a household name, because it makes things like power plants and other components for generating and transmitting electricity.

ABB is based in Sweden and Switzerland but has manufacturing operations all over Europe. In fact, it was the challenge posed by European integration which led the company to radically restructure itself in the 1980s.

The company as a whole has two hundred fifteen thousand employees divided into eight business sectors. At its heart are five thousand autonomous profit centers with about two hundred employees each, which, in turn, are broken down into high performance teams of ten or so. The company is so decentralized that there are really only three levels of management, the executive committee based in Zurich, roughly two hundred fifty senior executives, and the leadership teams at each profit center. Moreover, next to none of those senior executives are based at corporate headquarters, but are located wherever it makes sense from a day-to-day business perspective.

The company has also instituted considerable competition within the company. Each profit center knows how all the others are doing, and managers can move their operations to new sites within the company if they are more efficiently run.

CEO Percy Barnevik has pursued a strategy of empowering his entire work force for the fifteen years he has run ABB. Each team is thus encouraged to "own" its share of the business, because, in the end, it is responsible for its center's profit and loss statement. As a result, the units have become more flexible in the way they design the power plants they build and have slashed delivery time. Sune Karlsson, head of that division, put it this way:

Our most important strength is that we have 25 factories around the world, each with its own president, design manager, marketing manger, and production manager. These people are working on the same problems and opportunities day after day, year after year, and learning a tremendous amount. We want to create a process of continuous expertise transfer. If we do, that's a source of advantage none of our rivals can match. (Peters 1992: 51)

ABB is typical of the success stories Peters and others have encountered. It is a world leader in all its business areas, despite having operations spread around the globe and having incorporated a dozen or so other companies in the last few years. As Peters' book went to press, Barnevik was developing a plan to reduce the time it took to fill orders by half.

### Sausage

There is now evidence that such practices can work in any kind of organization. I became convinced of that when I learned about two different sausage manufacturers, which are as far from the stereotype of a new age company as you can get.

The first is Johnsonville Foods and the remarkable saga of its turnaround under the leadership of Ralph Stayer, who inherited the company from his father in 1978 (Peters 1992: 237–245; Stayer 1990; Simons 1995). Although the company was doing well, Stayer wasn't enjoying his work. Then, he realized, most of his employees weren't either. Even more worrisome was the fact that the workers weren't interested in taking any kind of initiative; after years of top down management they were used to following orders from the Stayers. If the company was to withstand competition from larger national companies, it was going to have to change. In Stayer's words:

I tried to picture what Johnsonville would have to be to sell the most expensive sausage in the industry and still have the biggest market share. What I saw in my mind's eye was definitely not an organization where I made all the decisions and owned all the problems. What I saw was an organization where people took responsibility for their own work, for the product, for the company as a whole. If that happened, our product and service quality would improve, our margins would rise, and we could reduce costs and successfully enter new markets. (Stayer 1990: 3)

Stayer may have envisioned what that company would be like, but he couldn't make it happen. Gradually, and painfully, Stayer realized that he was the biggest problem and that any fundamental change had to start with him. He told Tom Peters, "If anything needed fixing, it was me" (1992: 238). After firing a few of his managers, he realized that he was sending mixed messages, telling people they should take initiatives and make their own decisions but holding onto almost all the levers of power within the company himself.

Like Tom Chappell, Stayer then set in motion a radical restructuring of his company, in this case into self-managed[1] teams. Each handles its own personnel, training, budget, and quality control decisions and is expected to work with all the others in developing new ideas and strategies for the corporation as a whole. All front line supervisory positions have been eliminated. Top executives coordinate and guide, but issue next to no orders.

To use a term one finds throughout studies of such companies, Stayer gradually gave his workers "ownership" of their jobs. They, not their supervisors, took over quality control (which seems to have meant tasting each batch of sausages). Complaints and suggestions were passed on to the workforce. Soon, workers were beginning to complain about colleagues who weren't working hard or well. Stayer and his colleagues turned the problem back to the workers, telling them they had the authority to work it out. Eventually, teams of workers took on almost all traditional personnel functions, from hiring to training to, when necessary, firing.

Workers have also been given an important stake in the success of the company. As in almost any of the examples I could have included here, Johnsonville has an extensive profit sharing plan, in this case with an individual's share determined by how well he or she has performed during a six month period.

Within five years, Stayer could see results typical of the companies that have gone through this type of managerial revolution. Profits, sales, and equity

[1] His use of this term is interesting, if for no other reason than it is the same one used to describe decentralized forms of socialism championed by some marxist groups on the far left in France which I studied in the 1970s and 1980s (Hauss 1978).

all were up. More importantly, Stayer and his staff had created a flexible, "learning" organization that could effectively adapt to dramatic changes, as it was then able to do when a larger company asked Johnsonville to supply sausage as one of its subcontractors. The new deal essentially meant doubling the size of the staff and its production. In 1980, the company could not have handled the stress; in 1985, the whole company pitched in.

It took a long time for Stayer's ideas to catch on, because it takes a long time to develop trust in what has traditionally been an adversarial or at best a grudging relationship. That leads to the second sausage story.

In May 1993, Baltimore-based Parks Sausage Co. went through a bitter strike (Kerber 1993). The strike came on the heels of years of losses which imperiled the company itself and led management to demand a wage cut of seventy-five cents an hour. The workers ultimately agreed to a fifty cent cut in wages in exchange for the creation of a labor-management committee which would have some say in the way the company was run.

Unlike many companies these days, Parks did not hire those euphemistically named "replacement workers" during the strike, but used management employees to staff the production lines. It was a mind opening experience for the managers, who learned just how unpleasant making sausage can be.

That led to an even broader realization on both sides that the fate of the company hung in the balance and that the traditional adversarial relationship was actually harming both management and labor. It is still an open question whether or not the new found cooperation between business and labor will be able to save Parks, but the committee and improved labor-management relations in general at least gives it a chance.

That kind of albeit tentative cooperation is more and more common in labor-management relations in the United States. On July 26, 1993, the Clinton administration's Labor and Commerce Departments convened a meeting of five hundred top business, labor, and academic leaders in Chicago. The meeting and the joint sponsorship themselves were unusual. This Conference on the Future of the American Workplace was designed to show that labor-management conflict frequently eroded efficiency and competitiveness and, with them, jobs. Secretary of Labor Reich argued that empowering workers by bringing them into the decision making process about everything from corporate strategy to the organization of work itself would lead to a stronger company and a happier work force. Participants heard about a cooperative program at the US West, which had given workers many such powers. They heard, too, about such companies as Inland Steel Industries and the L-S Electro-Galvanizing Company in which unions had agreed to forego pay increases and even accept some reductions in the work force in exchange for more say in corporate decision making and more profit sharing.

No one argued that the Conference was a celebration of a new age in American labor-management relations. Almost all participants acknowledged that few companies have made many moves in these directions. Even the most enthusiastic participants skirted most issues involving a more equitable distribution of income and wealth or whether such a system could really generate many more jobs in a still sluggish economy.

Nonetheless, Conference organizers felt it gave unprecedented national exposure to some experimental ideas which hold out considerable promise for the American economy. President Clinton perhaps put it best in his closing comments, "The most interesting thing that you said is that what turned out to be good for the company turned out to be good for the employees" (Uchitelle 1993: D1).


### Reinventing Government

During the period between his election and inauguration, Bill Clinton hosted what came to be known as the "policy wonk" conference on government and the economy in Little Rock. Those few wonks among us in the general public who watched the proceedings were treated to a series of presentations, some painful and some optimistic, but none deviating much from the conventional wisdom until David Osborne began to talk about *reinventing* government, about experiments that made the public sector more effective *and* less expensive by introducing entrepreneurial and market oriented practices. The word got out, and sales of the book he had written with Ted Gaebler (1992) became something of a best seller (in wonk circles that is) when it was reprinted in paperback a couple of months later.

While leftists traditionally have trouble with words like "entrepreneur" or "market," it was hard to fault the liberal credentials of these two men. In the first few pages, Osborne and Gaebler make it clear that they believe in government and that only government can provide many, if not most, social services. And, even when the private sector can provide them, the government first must set explicit goals and standards those firms must live up to.

They also make it clear that only dramatic change will produce that kind of government in the 1990s and beyond. In the first two pages of their acknowledgments, they honor their intellectual debt to Peter Drucker, the management theorist who has called for fundamental change longer and more evocatively than any of his colleagues, and then liken their reinvention to *perestroika*, which Gorbachev hoped would lead to a profound "restructuring" of all aspects of Soviet social, economic, and political life.

The new administration leapt onto the reinventing bandwagon. On March 3, President Clinton announced the creation of a National Performance Review (NPR) that would study the federal bureaucracy and then make a series of recommendations six months later. He appointed Vice President Gore to chair the NPR; Osborne served as a major consultant.

When the NPR's report was issued on September 7, the Congress and the media focused their attention on the 252,000 jobs and $108 billion it proposed cutting. The report (Gore 1993) itself dug far deeper and emphasized longer term personnel and managerial changes, which promise much more as does its subtitle, *Creating a Government That Works Better and Costs Less*. In his introduction, Gore explicitly drew on the corporate revolution discussed above. Not coincidentally, Tom Peters was called on to write the Foreword.

The ideas contained in both the Osborne-Gaebler book and the NPR report would revolutionize service delivery, if not policy making itself, because they have such obvious parallels with what we saw in the private sector. Steering rather than micromanaging government. Clear missions that drive an agency's actions. Empowering workers. Putting customers first. Anticipating problems in order to engage in preventive care. Giving everyone involved in the delivery and receipt of government services some degree of ownership in their success.

### America Works

Typical of the kind of program they applaud is America Works, a for profit employment agency doing business in New York City and Hartford, Connecticut. It is probably as committed as any of the "new age" companies to its social and political mission, but it deals with a very different clientele, mostly young unemployed women who otherwise would have next to no hope of pulling themselves out of abject poverty (Scott and Rothman 1992: 22–34; Osborne and Gaebler 1992).

America Works is responding to the fact that most conventional anti-poverty and job training programs have had a marginal impact, especially in improving the lot of the poorest of the poor. It is also responding to the fact that it costs the taxpayer a lot, about $24,000 a year in payments and support services, to provide for a family which is dependent on the social service system in New York. Meanwhile, benefits are high enough and available jobs at fast food outlets and the like are dull and low paying enough that many people simply resign themselves to a life on welfare.

America Works is committed to building a partnership between the state and the private sector and providing incentives to the otherwise hopeless from which all benefit. Over the last decade, the program has placed about twenty-five hundred poor people, mostly women, in permanent jobs which offer not only a decent wage but also the possibility for professional advancement.

The America Works approach is quite simple. It starts by putting its clients through a rigorous training program that lasts about six weeks. During that time, they learn practical skills like word processing and also get an introduction to what it takes to succeed in a major corporate office. The training also helps the clients learn to make presentations and, more generally, enhances their self-esteem.

Once the worker completes the training period, America Works places her with a company for a four month trial period. During that time, AW pays a modest salary to the employee and bills the company enough to cover its expenses. Afterward, the company picks up the full salary and benefits package for its new employee. If the employee stays on the job a full year (which about 90 percent of them do), the company can then claim a $1,000 tax credit for providing jobs for the long term unemployed. It is only at that point that America Works gets paid by the state, about $4,000 in Connecticut and $5,300 in New York for each worker placed.

Some critics are skeptical and claim that America Works works only because it does so much screening of applicants that it only takes the few people who are likely to succeed. From the evidence available on the company, that does not seem to be the case. Most of its clients had long bouts of unemployment and seemed to have few prospects for the future when they started the program.

Why, then, does this program work where so many others have failed? To begin with, like Head Start and other relatively successful social service programs, it provides direct services and skills which its clients can use indefinitely rather than just financial support which tides them over in the short run. Perhaps even more importantly, America Works has tried to create a system in which everyone has clear and personal incentives. The employer gets some tax and salary breaks along with a well-trained employee. The state saves money. And, of course, the client gets a job. America Works itself may have the biggest stake in making the system work for each and every client, since it makes no money unless the employee succeeds. In short, America Works uses markets and all the other tools of capitalism in building a program that the most liberal of liberals has to laud.

There are questions about how broadly such a program could be applied, especially in reaching out to people who are not as ambitious for themselves and their families as the women America Works tends to attract. America

Works itself has taken great pains not to grow too quickly, and few other entrepreneurs have shown much interest in establishing comparable programs in other cities and states.

Nonetheless, there is reason to believe that similar programs can make major inroads in getting millions of people out of the social service system. Some programs are private, like those of the Southshore and other banks (which operates a lot like the Grameen Bank discussed in Chapter 10) which target loans at job-creating enterprises in "deteriorating" neighborhoods (Scott and Rothman 1992: 91–102). Others involve the public sector, including a number of experiments in which tenants in public housing are given literal and figurative "ownership" of their buildings. With their new stake in their property and some financial help from agencies like HUD, they have been able to make their buildings safer and more pleasant places to live. Some have even been able to spin off day care programs or businesses that, for instance, provide maintenance and fix-up services for other run-down projects *and* provide jobs for the often absent fathers of the children growing up in those units (Osborne and Gaebler 1992: esp. chs. 2 and 10).

On balance, however, it is hard not to be pessimistic. Some critics always believed that the Clinton administration never intended reinventing government to be anything more than a rationale for slashing the federal payroll. Whatever their initial intentions, the program has turned into little more than a political football in the fight between the administration and the Republican Congress. The more far-reaching proposals have already been all but forgotten. Many top federal executives are worried that the reforms will go too far too fast (*The Public Manager* 1993) and stretch already overworked government employees beyond any reasonable limits. Despite what we have learned from the private sector, the review occurred with a minimum of involvement by rank and file civil servants above and beyond the meetings Gore held with federal employees at most agencies, some of which were televised on C-SPAN.

Moreover, while there will be some immediate savings as the federal government pares down its workforce, all the other changes envisioned here will take a long time to accomplish, because they really involve changing the culture in which government officials work. It took the better part of a decade to turn the automobile industry around, and it is only a tiny fraction of the size of the federal government. What's more, neither the American people nor their elected officials are known for their patience or their ability to think in long run terms, especially these days.

Despite all these problems, I would suggest that it is no accident that these ideas have found their way into government now. That it took longer than in the private sector is not surprising, since government does not have to respond as quickly or as fully to market pressures. On the other hand, it is also not surprising that they have found their way into the governments of most industrialized democracies, because their impact on the private sector has been so dramatic.

## WHY ALL THIS WORKS

It would be easy to read this chapter as a naive paean to fashionable business management theory. It is not meant to be that at all.

There are plenty of examples in which these approaches have not worked. Many of the companies that claim to have "greened themselves" really haven't. I have friends who work in the paper, ceramics, and other industries as well as the federal government in which TQM and other such methods have failed, often abysmally. I helped preside over the death of a once thriving food co-op in which we practiced just about all these techniques—or so we thought.

Most of those failures actually reinforce the implications of this chapter. In some cases, like our food co-op, we first let the enterprise get into such deep trouble that nothing could have saved it. More typically, however, the efforts failed because they proved to be little more than window dressing. In most cases, the bosses didn't learn Ralph Stayer's lesson: Let go so the employees can take control of their own work. The organization may have officially adopted a program like TQM. However, one key element was missing, a strong commitment to new thinking at the top of the organization.

Still, so many have succeeded that there must be something to these methods. Indeed, it seems to be the case that whenever something along these lines has been adopted throughout the organization, dramatic improvement in performance has occurred (*Economist* 1994b).

To see that, let's turn briefly to one more company, Ben and Jerry's. As I was drafting this chapter, a student loaned me a copy of *GQ*, not a magazine I normally read. In it, Joe Queenan (1994) tells a remarkable story. Five years earlier, he had written an article attacking Ben and Jerry for being a pair of publicity seekers. They ran such a small operation that they weren't making much of a difference by giving away 7.5 percent of their pre-tax profits; all they were doing was promoting themselves and their high-priced ice cream.

In between, Queenan had fallen ill and embarked on a spiritual quest for the meaning of life which had got him nowhere until he met a friend who said he had his life transformed by visiting the Ben and Jerry's factory in Vermont. With his normal cynicism, Queenan headed north to what has become the largest tourist attraction in a state known for its tourist attractions. He was, as he had been told to expect, "surprised by joy." He saw workers who loved making ice cream, who participated in the management of the company, and who were wildly enthusiastic about the causes Cohen and Greenfield championed. He also fell in love with the ice cream. He ends his article this way:

As my tongue snakes around 1.3 cents' worth of roasted almond, I feel a wave of indescribable joy come over me, reckoning that some .21 of a cent of my money will now go to support the Burlington Emergency Shelter fund. I cannot be sure what the Burlington Emergency Shelter actually does, but as my teeth grind into a tough little nugget of almond, I think of the homeless people who will perhaps have a roof over their head because of my efforts. I have never had this experience eating Häagen-Das. (1994: 222)

## REFERENCES

Argyris, Chris (1993). *On Organizational Learning.* Cambridge: Blackwell.

Chappell, Tom (1993). *The Soul of a Business.* New York: Bantam.

DeVos, Richard (1993). *Compassionate Capitalism.* New York: Dutton.

Drucker, Peter (1993). *Post Capitalist Society.* New York: Harper Business.

*Economist* (1994a). "Re-engineering Europe." 26 February, 63–64.

*Economist* (1994b). "Re-Engineering Reviewed." 2 July, 66.

Gore, Albert (1993). *Creating a Government That Works Better and Costs Less: The Report of the National Performance Review.* New York: Plume.

Hamel, Gary, Yves L. Doz, and C. K. Prahalad. "Collaborate with Your Competitors—And Win." *Harvard Business Review,* January, 133–139.

Hauss, Charles (1978). *The New Left in France: The Unified Socialist Party.* Westport, Conn.: Greenwood.

Hawken, Paul (1993). *The Ecology of Commerce: A Declaration of Sustainability.* New York: HarperCollins Business.

Kerber, Ross (1993). "Solving Problems Together: Parks Sausage to Chart Future with Management-Labor Panel." *Washington Post,* Business Section, July 26, 1, 14, 15.

Makower, Joel (1993). *The E Factor: The Bottom-Line Approach to Environmentally Responsible Business.* New York: Times Books.

Moore, Curtis, and Alan Miller (1994). *Green Gold: Japan, Germany, the United States and the Race for Environmental Technology.* Boston: Beacon Press.

Myers, Norman (1993). *Ultimate Security.* New York: W. W. Norton.

Osborne, David, and Ted Gaebler (1992). *Reinventing Government: How the Entrepreneurial Spirit is Transforming the Public Sector.* New York: Plume.

Ottman, Jacquelyn (1992). *Green Marketing.* Lincolnwood, Ill.: NTC Business Books.

Peters, Tom (1995). *The Pursuit of Wow.* New York: Knopf.

———. (1992). *Liberation Management: Necessary Disorganization for the Nanosecond Nineties.* New York: Knopf.

————. (1987). *Thriving on Chaos*. New York: Knopf.

Peters, Tom, and Nancy Austin (1985) *A Passion for Excellence*. New York: Random House.

Peters, Tom, and Robert H. Waterman (1982). *In Search of Excellence*. New York: Harper and Row.

Public Manager (1993). *Special Issue on the National Performance Review*, Winter.

Queenan, Joe (1994). "I've Seen the Lite." *GQ*, April, 216–222.

Roddick, Anita (1991). *Body and Soul: Profits with Principles—The Amazing Success Story of Anita Roddick and the Body Shop*. New York: Crown.

Scott, Mary, and Howard Rothman (1992). *Companies with a Conscience*. Secaucus, N.J.: Carol Publishing Group.

Senge, Peter (1990). *The Fifth Discipline: The Art and the Practice of the Learning Organization*. New York: Doubleday/Currency.

Simons, Robert (1995). "Control in an Age of Empowerment." *Harvard Business Review,* March, 81–88.

Stayer, Ralph (1990). "How I Learned to Let My Workers Lead." *Harvard Business Review*, November–December.

Uchitelle, Louis (1993). " 'Empowering' Labor Held Key to More Jobs." *New York Times,* July 27, D1, D9.

# 12

# IN THE GLOBAL INTEREST*

After Rio, the world will never be the same.

—Tim Wirth

It is hard to be optimistic these days. To be sure, the possibility of a major nuclear war has receded dramatically. On just about every other front, however, the 1990s seem as fraught with danger as any other period, including the Cold War.

If that were the way things had to be, nothing discussed in Chapters 10 and 11 would matter here. Luckily, there is another and more promising side to the "real world" in the mid-1990s.

Despite all the disheartening news, there is a lot of cooperative problem solving going on. There are now more supranational intergovernmental organizations (IGOs) than national governments. Cooperative international initiatives such as the Montreal Protocol have allowed us to make major progress on a number of environmental issues. A range of treaties and agreements are breaking down the restraints national borders and policies have had on international trade and development.

Some of it is occurring through the United Nations, which is playing a greater, if not always more effective, role on a number of global issues. As of January 1995, there were thirteen active United Nations peacekeeping or

*With Angela Harkavy

observation operations. (Karns and Mingst 1994). In the long run, it may prove more important that countries are looking to the UN as a force to help solve other, non-military problems.

Some of it is occurring in ways not wholly consistent with the normative case being made in this book. While many of us may not want to admit it, the allied response to the Iraqi invasion of Kuwait was an unprecedented example of international cooperation, albeit one which ended up in war. More generally, the major powers are increasingly looking for collective responses to regional security threats. That even holds for the United States, which sought United Nations approval for a potential invasion of Haiti in July 1994, the first time it has ever done so when contemplating intervention in the western hemisphere.

Some of it has been around for a long time. Years ago, the nations of the world developed ways of regulating and managing the growing flow of travelers, mail, and telecommunications across international borders with hardly a trace of difficulty or tension.

I don't want to make this case too strongly. Confrontation, not cooperation, is still the norm, especially when contentious issues are involved. We've also certainly made far less progress on this front than we have at either the individual or organizational levels.

That should hardly come as a surprise. International disputes are more difficult for all the reasons scholars steeped in realism tend to stress. They often involve a lot of very different actors, the stakes are often very high, and there is nothing like an international state or other such body which can routinely adjudicate disputes.

Nonetheless, examples of extended and effective cooperation exist, which we could build on during this period of unprecedented change when there is no distracting, overarching geopolitical threat like that of a thermonuclear holocaust during the Cold War. We can "learn" at the international as well as the individual or organizational level. Doing so will not take us wholly beyond confrontation. That will probably never happen, but it would be an important step in that direction.

## STATES, ANARCHY, SECURITY, AND REGIMES

Realists have dominated the academic study of international relations for most of the last half century. As we saw in Chapter 6, they paint a bleak, or at least a pessimistic, picture of an anarchic world in which states try to protect themselves and compete for scarce resources, often leading them to war. Cooperation, especially over an extended period of time, is difficult if not impossible.

Over the last quarter century or so, international relations experts have begun paying more attention to economic and, now, environmental issues which has led them to acknowledge that there are some important instances of cooperation, though rarely, as they see it, in "high politics." A lot of ink has been spilled in trying to figure out why states cooperate under some, but not all, circumstances (see, for instance, Stein 1990, Grieco 1990; Baldwin 1993; Brown 1992, 1994, Miller 1994). In exploring the roots of cooperation, most of these scholars remain more realist than not, but they do question two of the key principles underlying realism, the ironclad assumptions about international anarchy and the sovereignty of the nation state.

None would go as far as Teilard de Chardin and claim that the age of the nation state is past. Nonetheless, these observers see plenty of examples in which states have (usually quietly) ceded some of their sovereignty to supranational bodies like the European Union or seen some of their sovereignty eroded by non-governmental entities like the World Bank or the major multinational corporations.

For our purposes, the most important example of this type of cooperation is the international regime. Regimes have been on the intellectual radar screen at least since the emergence of OPEC, but have only achieved significant attention from mainstream scholars in the 1980s and 1990s.

In the most widely cited early article on the subject, Stephen Krasner defined regimes as "sets of implicit or explicit principles, norms, rules, and decision-making procedures around which actors' expectations converge in a given area of international relations" (Krasner 1983: 2). International relations experts and government officials rarely say it this bluntly, but when "actors converge in a given area of international relations" that really means they are making joint decisions in which they hand over some of their sovereignty to whatever institutions or procedures or institutions they are converging on. Similarly, though the experts are loath to put it this way, the existence of "norms" and "rules" means that regimes not only have established procedures for making decisions, but at least rudimentary mechanisms for enforcing them. In other words, regimes take on at least some of the characteristics of a state and thus at least peck away at international anarchy.

Renée Marlin-Bennett has taken these abstract concepts and made them more concrete for people interested in international trade:

Companies and countries can conduct trade in today's world because people engaging in international trade understand the rules (regulations, laws, and customs) for doing to. A US businesswoman who wishes to export goods obtains the necessary licenses from the US governmental agencies that license her operations and the enterprises that purchase her products. Rules that direct her to do these things, rules made available to her by her legal advisor or through international trade associations or governmental export promotion programs are among the rules that constitute international trade regimes. (Marlin-Bennett 1992:21)

Regimes exist for a whole host of issues. Most deal with economic or environmental matters (Young 1989, Haas 1990). Some are rather simple and non-controversial, like the International Sugar Agreement. Others are extensive either in terms of the issue or the countries they cover, like the NAFTA or the GATT agreement. There are even some covering issues of international security. Most observers, for example, consider that the Nuclear Non-Proliferation Treaty of 1968 established a regime.

It is important to stress the two key common denominators all regimes share. First, they bring nation states together into some form of collective or joint decision making process. Second, they include some mechanisms for enforcing whatever decisions are made.

Many realists respond by saying that regimes are far from becoming the international state that could overcome anarchy. They're right, of course. In any regime, states pursue short term national interests as well as the broader, common interests that transcend national boundaries. And, few regimes have effective tools for compelling their members to abide by their decisions.

In making that case, however, the realists miss the two most important aspects of regimes for our purposes.

First, they forget that even the most stable, powerful, and legitimate nation states face these very same problems domestically. No nation state can fully escape anarchy at home, as the inability of the US government to enforce everything from its laws regarding speeding to the use of handguns suggests. No government ever completely escapes anarchy, but regimes are a step in that direction, and some are probably as effective in enforcing their decisions as, say, the British or French governments of the early nineteenth century, not to mention sheriffs on the American frontier.

Second, one should not assume that regimes mark the end point in the evolution of transnational cooperation. There is every reason to believe that as policy makers learn more about how regimes work, we'll get better at developing them just as our ancestors did at building nation states from the seventeenth century on. As was the case then, there will be fits and starts. As we will see in exploring the European Union below, regimes can suffer degenerative setbacks, just as most nation states have. But, and this is the central point, regimes are an important mechanism for resolving international problems that could become more and important as we are forced to confront the transnational, overlapping issues in the global crisis in which self-interest and national interest increasingly become common interests. As Seyom Brown put it, "cooperative regimes are fully consistent with and the most rational responses to the security dilemmas facing modern great powers under the anarchic nation-state system" (1994: 36; also see Talbott 1992).

So, are regimes the same thing as world government, which realists and most other mainstream policy makers scoff at? Perhaps. Perhaps not. There is no a priori reason why regimes will have to lead to a single world government in which the traditional nation state disappears. In fact, current trends suggest that the most plausible model includes a multi-level system in which supranational institutions exist alongside national ones, in much the same way that sub-national ones function in tandem with national governments today.

In sum, the analyses of regimes simply suggest that we can "learn" from our increasingly interdependent world and become more cooperative. It is far too early to try to anticipate what kind of cooperative arrangements which actually handle the vast majority of the transnational issues would be like—or even if they would be much like today's regimes. After all, the opposition leaders in the American colonies or in France at the time of the Bastille could not anticipate what their post-revolutionary institutions were going to be.

## THE NEW EUROPE

The cover of the August 13, 1994, *Economist* carries a headline which reads "Europe's Dash for the Future." The only problem is that the accompanying cartoon depicts a snail with the European Union flag on its shell looking down an infinitely long path.

Since the signing of the Maastricht Treaty in the fall of 1991, little has gone right for people who support more European integration. Public support for the treaty and for giving Brussels more power in general plummeted. The Exchange Rate Mechanism, which kept the twelve countries' currencies in balance with each other, collapsed.[1] its first attempt to forge a common non-economic foreign policy, the then European Community failed to bring the fighting in the former Yugoslavia under control.

[1] There is an inescapable awkwardness to writing about European integration which reflects the changes which have taken place in its major institutions, especially in the 1980s and 1990s. Its official title has been the European Union since the ratification of the Maastricht Treaty. Before that, it was the European Community. With the accession of Finland, Sweden, and Austria, one should also speak of the "fifteen" and not the "twelve" (or "nine" or "six") any longer. Here, I've used terminology consistent with the time period I was writing about.

However, those and other problems should not keep us from seeing just how far Western Europe has come. Barely fifty years ago, the continent went to war, something it did rather frequently. Anyone who argued then that Franco-German war was impossible or that their most serious disputes would be over trade policy would have been branded a hopeless visionary—or worse. Today, it is hard to imagine what kind of issue might lead the democracies in the West to fight each other again.

Moreover, the Europeans have created a number of supranational institutions to which they have given significant decision making power, the most important of which is the European Union (EU). At the very least, these institutions demonstrate that people can create institutions to which nation states can turn over at least some of their sovereignty. In some ways and at some times, too, those institutions reflect the kind of cooperative problem solving discussed in the last few chapters. As with everything else, I don't want to overstate the case, because the EU and Europe as a whole still face many daunting problems. I simply want to point out the potential for more cooperative and transnational problem solving one can see in today's western Europe.

## Integrating Europe

The idea of an integrated Europe is not a new one (Ross 1995, Dinan 1994; Sbragia 1992; Colchester 1992; Delamaide 1994). Leaders from the Romans through Hitler tried to unite the continent, primarily through the use of force, most recently under Hitler's Third Reich. It is probably no coincidence that it took the devastation of World War II plus the tensions and threats of the Cold War to permit the first peaceful and apparently promising attempt at integration.

The first serious discussions of a peacefully united Europe occurred following the horrors of World War One, but fared as poorly as most of the plans for world government and collective security in the 1930s. The aftermath of the next war, however, would prove very different.

This time, the superpower rivalry sparked the creation of NATO and the Warsaw Pact, and all but a handful of European states ended up in one or the other. Though the causal connections are less clear and more indirect, the post-war situation also made more economic cooperation possible as well. The US chose to administer the Marshall Plan through a new international institution, which has since evolved into the Organization for Economic Cooperation and Development (OECD). The war and its aftermath also opened the door for a new group of politicians, like Jean Monnet (see Chapter 13), who, for a variety of reasons, had come to believe that the countries of Europe could not afford to go to war again and thus had to solve their problems cooperatively.

Their first major success came with the creation of the European Coal and Steel Community (ECSC) in 1951 by France, the German Federal Republic, Italy, Belgium, Luxembourg, and the Netherlands (Table 12.1 lists the major turning points in the history of European integration). Coal and steel were vital industries for Europe's recovery, and much of the coal deposits and steel factories were located in a relatively small area, but which also included parts of five of these countries (all but Italy). Though limited in scope, the ECSC created four institutions, a bureaucracy, a decision making body based in national governments, a court, and a rudimentary parliament, which remain the core of the much larger EU today.

The ECSC exceeded all expectations. The six thus were able to speed up plans for further integration and agreed to the Treaty of Rome which created the European Economic Community (EEC) and the European Atomic Energy Community (Euratom) in 1957. Most notably, the Treaty called for the elimination of all tariffs and other barriers to the free flow of goods and services over the next decade.

**Table 12.1**
**Turning Points in European Integration**

| Date | Event |
|------|-------|
| 1951 | Creation of the ECSC |
| 1957 | Treaty of Rome |
| 1961 | First rejection of British entry |
| 1965 | Formation of the EEC |
| 1966 | Creation of Common Agricultural Policy |
| 1973 | Britain, Denmark, Ireland join |
| 1981 | Greece joins |
| 1985 | Spain and Portugal join |
|      | Delors named Commission president |
|      | Single European Act passed |
| 1989 | Collapse of communism in Eastern Europe |
| 1991 | Maastrict Treaty signed |
| 1995 | Finland, Sweden, Austria join |

After that, progress slowed almost to a standstill. French President Charles de Gaulle vetoed Britain's application to join in 1961, worrying that French interests would be diluted in a larger and/or more powerful EC, a position which, ironically, British Prime Ministers Margaret Thatcher and John Major would themselves take a quarter century later. With the economic slowdown which began in the late 1960s, national governments in general proved reluctant to take many risks, especially ones which might entail giving up some of their country's control over its own destiny.

There was some movement. Britain, Ireland, and Denmark did join in January 1973 (Norwegian voters defeated its entry in a referendum). A few new programs, like the ill fated Common Agricultural Policy, were agreed to. Gradually, the governments allowed more decisions to be made using a complicated system of qualified majority voting, rather than requiring unanimity, the device de Gaulle had used to block British entry. Then, in the 1980s, the EC took a major step by admitting Greece, Spain, and Portugal with their far weaker economies and new, shaky democracies.

Nonetheless, the prospects for further integration were not good, prompting some observers to talk about "Eurosclerosis." By the early 1980s, groups of leaders within the EC and some of the member countries realized that it was going to have to "deepen" or take on new responsibilities if the European economies as a whole were going to pull out of what was then a decade long period of stagnation. In particular, a commission headed by the Italian Paolo Cecchini estimated that if remaining non-tariff barriers to trade were removed, it could spark an additional 5 percent growth per year community wide.

Support for more reform built, especially following the selection of the prominent French Socialist Jacques Delors as president of the Commission and passage of the Single European Act (SEA) in 1985. The act called for the elimination of trade barriers over the next seven years (e.g., border controls within the EC, national licensing of many professions which limited the mobility of labor, even the use of different types of plugs on electrical appliances). It also strengthened many of the Community's institutions by, for instance, officially sanctioning the semi-annual summit meetings between the members' chief executives and reducing still further the number of issues which would be subject to the unanimity rule. Eurosclerosis was replaced by Euphoria.

That sense of optimism was enhanced by the collapse of communist regimes in Eastern Europe in 1989 and then in the Soviet Union two years later. French President François Mitterrand, German Chancellor Helmut Kohl, and Delors pushed for yet more integration, even before the provisions of the SEA were fully in place.

That led to the adoption of the Maastricht Treaty by the twelve late in 1991. The Treaty gave the EC authority to act in a wide variety of areas, including monetary policy, foreign affairs and national security, fisheries, transportation, the environment, health, justice, education, consumer protection, and tourism as well as those laid out in the Treaty of Rome and the SEA. It created European citizenship which means that people could live, work, and vote in elections for the European Parliament in any member country. It committed the Community to creating a central bank and common currency in stages so that both would be in place no later than 1999. In an attempt to appease the concerns of many national politicians, the Treaty also endorsed the principle of subsidiarity which holds that the EC should act only in policy areas where objectives "cannot be sufficiently achieved" by national governments or could be "better achieved" at the supranational level. There was even an important symbolic change. Upon ratification, the EC's name would become the more powerful sounding European *Union*.

As has often been the case with European integration over the years, the optimism did not last long. At the time, ratification of the treaty was not seen as a major stumbling block, and it was expected to go into effect on January 1, 1993, to coincide with the completion of the internal market as called for in the SEA. The sharp recession of the early 1990s, Germany's commitment to keeping inflation down while it rebuilt the old Democratic Republic, and the EC's difficulties in forging a common and effective policy for dealing with the former Yugoslavia all led to a dramatic and rapid decline in support for Maastricht and integration in general. First, the Danish population rejected the treaty in a referendum, and the French almost did the same.[2] Euroskeptics in John Major's own Conservative Party imperiled ratification in Britain, which only occurred in the end because Britain had insisted on provisions which would allow it to opt out of some of the social and economic institutions envisioned in the treaty. Meanwhile, the Exchange Rate Mechanism (ERM) which coordinated the members' currencies collapsed. This, among other things, made creation of a common currency by the end of this decade highly unlikely. Finally, in one of the most embarrassing setbacks, the British vetoed the candidacy of Belgian Prime Minister Jean-Luc Dahaene as the replacement for Delors whose second term ended in 1994.

## The EU and Supranationality

At least five elements in the evolution of the EU and its supranational aspects warrant our attention here.

[2] After gaining a few minor concessions, the Danes later ratified the treaty.

First and most obviously, it shows us that the nation state is not the largest or most inclusive governmental organization people can create. While no one would mistake the EU for a United States of Europe even as powerful as the United States was under the Articles of Confederation, it does have some rudimentary elements of a state. Most notably, the governments of the fifteen member countries have ceded a good bit of their sovereignty, especially over industrial, agricultural, and high technology policy making. To be sure, politicians in their right minds never talk about how they have given up any control over their own country's destiny. But that is, in fact, what they've done.

Take one example which might seem trivial at first glance. Member governments have typically bought almost all of the goods they use from domestic producers, which is true of just about every government (think, for instance, about how few states, counties, and cities in the US buy foreign cars). The SEA, however, has provisions on government procurement which forbids member governments from giving preference to domestic producers. Governments will probably get around some of these restrictions. It will likely be a long time before you see a French president in a Mercedes limousine or a German chancellor in a Citroën. Nonetheless, other purchases, which account for about 10 percent of member states' GNP, will now have to be made from a pool of all European suppliers.

More generally, the Commission has become an ever more important institution, representing Union-wide interests. The Council remains the more powerful decision making body, at least for initiating broad new programs and policies. But, the Commission has a number of all important tasks in developing everything from the concrete language of those policies to their enforcement. If that weren't the case, there would be no reason for European, Japanese, and American firms to have at least ten thousand lobbyists in Brussels, one for every 1.3 Commission employees (Facchinetti 1994).

That leads to the second characteristic of the EU. Like a nation state, it can enforce its decisions. The European Court of Justice (ECJ) has jurisdiction over broad areas of economic life. It can intervene if the EU itself, member states, or private corporations are found to have violated its laws or decrees. Over the years, the ECJ has overturned policies, actions, and/or laws at all three levels, often with sweeping implications.

Among the most important and illustrative of the ECJ's decisions was the famous *Cassis de Dijon* decision of 1979, which opened the legal door to both the SEA and Maastricht. Cassis is a liqueur which one adds to white wine to make the smooth, sweet, and potent drink, kir. It is made only in the Dijon area of France. A German firm wanted to import cassis on the assumption that kir would be as popular there as in France. The German government banned it on the grounds that it contained too little alcohol to qualify as a liqueur by German standards, but too much to be considered a wine. The court found for the importer, ruling that if cassis met French standards for being a liqueur, it should meet German ones as well and that such arbitrary differences constituted an illegal impediment to trade in the internal market. The court thereby began the development of the notion of "mutual recognition" which holds that except under the most unusual of circumstances (like the licensing of lawyers), member states had to recognize the standards developed by other member states. As a result, the Commission could avoid the impossibly cumbersome task of harmonizing standards across national lines. If one national government asserted that a good or service met its standards, that standard had to be accepted by all others as well.

Third, the EU has shown signs of becoming the kind of learning organization that organizational management theorists discussed in Chapter 11 so favor. Because the EU is a complex organization in which national and supranational interests overlap and, at times, clash, it is more cumbersome and changes more slowly than a smaller or more streamlined corporation.

Nonetheless, EU officials have tried to restructure the organization and its operating principles to cope with changing circumstances. Most recently, that has involved the adoption of the idea of subsidiarity.

As the then EC took on more tasks and responsibilities, especially with the SEA and Maastricht Treaty, it was subjected to considerable criticism for trying to take on too much at the expense of the national governments. After a year or two of carping from the British and others, Delors and his colleagues came to realize that there was a good bit of truth to those criticisms. As a result, they incorporated subsidiarity into the Maastricht Treaty.

Subsidiarity's origins lie in the Christian Democratic philosophy which had been an inspiration to the young Delors. In its current form, it commits the EU to only taking on the functions that are best handled at the supranational level. All others are to be left as the responsibility of national and/or sub-national governments. This is, in other words, one of the very few instances in history in which an increasingly powerful government body chose to turn over some responsibilities to "lower level" authorities, because its leaders realized that the changing economic environment made that a preferable outcome.

Fourth, the growth of the EU as a whole is a political response to the economic and cultural changes already going on in Europe. By the 1980s, economic life in Europe was already heavily integrated. Economic zones and regions had little in common with the political units defined by national boundaries. As early as the 1950s, the ECSC made sense because the coal and steel industries already straddled the boundaries of Germany, France, and the Benelux countries along the Rhine.

Today, so many companies have merged and are doing business Europe-wide that national boundaries are at best an impediment to economic growth in a community which Darrell Delamaide (1994) sees as being composed of all or part of nine "superregions." Each has its own economic core. For example, his "Mitteleuropa" stretches from the southern parts of the Nether-lands and Belgium eastward into Poland and is the industrial heartland of the continent. The "Atlantic Coast" includes the British Isles, the western coast of France, Portugal, and Spain, and the shoreline of the North Sea, where trade with North and South America is far more important.

It's hard to tell if this idea of a superregion makes sense. It's also hard to tell how much of this is a product of European integration or how much would have occurred without it. Nonetheless, there is little question that Europe is integrating socially and culturally as well as economically. Political integration lags behind, but it is occurring as well, albeit in fits and starts. And, if Delamaide is right, it is occurring along smaller, regional lines as well as within the EU as local governments in France and Spain, on the one hand, or the Baltic States, Poland, and Germany create inter-governmental authorities to regulate trade (for a more far-reaching argument about the obsolete nature of nation states, see Ohmae 1995).

Fifth and perhaps most important of all, we often forget the most remarkable fact about European integration and western Europe in general. It has achieved what Kenneth Boulding (1978, 1988) called "stable peace." One can never rule war out between any two countries. Nonetheless, it really is hard to imagine what kind of conflict could take such historical rivals as France and Germany back to the battlefield.

Of course, there is conflict between France and Germany and all the other western European democracies. What makes 1995 different from 1895 or 1795 or 1695 is that their leaders have developed far more effective mechanisms for resolving their differences short not only of war but even of the credible threat of war.

Again, one cannot read too much into the role European integration and the EU, in particular, have played in all this. Obviously, the Cold War and the division of Europe was an important factor as well, probably more important at first than anything happening on the economic front.

Finally, further European integration is a virtual certainty. There is little doubt that the EU will continue to "broaden" or expand, perhaps admitting a few eastern European countries before this decade is out. The "deepening" of Europe or giving its institutions more power seems more problematic at the moment, given the current recession, the uncertainties on European currency markets, and other woes. Nonetheless, as the reality of an ever more integrated European economy and society continues to unfold, it seems likely that the political world will have to do the same as well. As Yale's David Cameron put it,

Certainly, the states will retain control over the Community through the Council of Ministers. And their leaders may often rail against and occasionally succeed in stalling the movement toward an integrated Europe. But over the longer term, the institutions and powers of the Community will continue to expand and certain policy making powers, heretofore vested in the member states, will be delegated or transferred to, or pooled and shared with, Community institutions. As a result, the sovereignty of the member states will increasingly and inevitably be eroded. (1992: 73)

## ENVIRONMENTAL POLITICS

More than in any other policy area, national leaders understand that environmental problems will require cooperative solutions. Developing countries cannot resolve their financial and technological problems without help from the North, and industrialized countries cannot save the environment by or for themselves.

Though we obviously have a long way to go, there has been a lot of progress on at least two fronts. First is the proliferation of international environmental regimes, which have had considerable success most notably in reducing the production of CFCs. Second was the remarkable 1992 Rio Summit on the Environment and Development which stands as a symbol of the growing influence of the United Nations.

In neither of these cases will we see the kind of supranational sovereignty or enforcement capabilities the European Union has at its disposal. On the other hand, we will see clearer examples of the way governments and other actors can cooperate and plan for the medium to long run.

### Environmental Regimes

International relations experts have not been studying regimes for very long, and thus all conclusions they have reached have to be viewed as tentative and preliminary. Nonetheless, two conclusions are already clear (Young 1989; Litfin 1993; Lipschutz and Mayer 1993).

First, nation states are by no means the only players. Typically, they are the formal signatories to the agreements which have been reached. However, the impetus for creating the regimes has often come from two other types of actors, existing international organizations (IOs) and non-governmental organizations (NGOs).

Generally speaking, these groups have played an extremely important role in regime formation and maintenance. To take but one example, the International Atomic Energy Agency (IAEA) and the Natural Resources Defense Council were both involved in monitoring the Chernobyl nuclear power plant disaster of 1986 and the attempt to clean up the plant and the surrounding region afterward.

More generally, the United Nations Environment Programme (UNEP) has been a major force in getting environmental issues onto the political agenda since it was formed in 1972. Other IOs like the World Bank and the GATT have had to address the environmental implications of their actions, most of which were directed primarily at non-environmental goals.

The record of the NGOs is in many ways even more impressive, because there are so many more of them and they have more latitude in what they choose to do. They have, for instance, been major players in protecting the rights of indigenous peoples, setting up international forums, lobbying national governments, sharing and spreading information, and even convincing private companies such as McDonald's to stop or reduce their polluting practices.

Second, IOs and NGOs are, virtually by definition, motivated by something other than a single nation's interests. Groups like Greenpeace or the World Wildlife Fund are organized worldwide and at least see themselves as representing global interests regarding particular issues. Moreover, these groups have expertise on environmental issues which is still in relatively short supply in most national governments. Precisely because they are not politicians who have to make day-to-day policy choices, the NGOs are better able to develop plans and strategies for the longer term.

The international community has created dozens of these regimes, often through the auspices of the UNEP. Among the issues covered are the regulation of nuclear reactors, the protection of endangered species, maritime pollution, the transportation of hazardous waste, whaling, "transboundary air pollution" more commonly known as acid rain, and the management of Antarctica.

Perhaps the most famous and important of these regimes is the one dealing with CFCs and the damage to the ozone layer. The UNEP first raised the question of regulating CFCs and the ozone in 1975 and 1977, when researchers established the link between the two (Porter and Brown 1991: 75–78). At that point, an extended period of study began, involving a coordinating committee established by the UNEP and hundreds of scientific and environmental organizations around the world.

By the early 1980s, a fairly common political pattern had emerged. The northern industrialized states were willing to accept considerable regulation of CFC emissions. Domestic pressures had already led to the search for alternatives. The United States had already banned the use of CFCs in aerosol cans in the US. Companies were beginning to shift production of CFCs to the LDCs.

Most of the LDCs, on the other hand, were reluctant to slow, let alone stop, their production for economic reasons. Not only did the CFC-related industries provide jobs, but they also held out the possibility that the people in their countries could enjoy the benefits of a more modern and affluent economy.

The coalition of governments, IOs, and NGOs that were "out front" on this issue, however, understood that any serious attempt to reduce CFC emissions would have to include all the major producing countries, including the former Soviet Union and the LDCs. As is often the case with regime formation, they started slowly.

The year 1985 saw agreement on the Vienna Convention, which simply committed the countries to study the problem and share what they had learned. As the evidence on the dangers kept coming in, momentum to reach an agreement mounted.

Finally, most of the major producing countries (plus some others) agreed to the Montreal Protocol in 1988. It was a compromise, as all such agreements tend to be. Nonetheless, it established a framework for the gradual reduction and then elimination of CFCs and other ozone-destroying chemicals. At first, the burden was to be placed on the industrialized countries. They were obligated to cut their CFC production in half by 1996, eliminate most such emissions by 2000, and share technologies for alternatives with the LDCs. In the meantime, the LDCs were actually allowed to increase CFC production in the short run before, they, too, could take advantage of those alternatives and phase out production as well. Further agreements reached in London in 1990 sped up the timetable for the major industrialized countries, most notably the United States.

Before we move on, note that international environmental regimes are no panacea in at least five respects.

First, they take a long time to develop. It will be fifteen years before the regime for protecting the ozone layer is fully implemented.

Second, because regimes do take so long to do their work, they actually allow for more pollution to be produced, in this case for a quarter century. The Montreal and London protocols could do nothing to reverse the damage that will continue to be done by CFCs which reached the ozone layer before the protocols went into effect.

Third, in some ways, this was a relatively easy regime to establish. There were relatively few major producing states. Alternative technologies were already in the pipeline. A win-win solution wasn't all that hard to envision or convince member countries to accept. That's not always the case, as we'll see in the next section when we consider the United States' role at the Rio Summit. As most of the people who have written applaudingly about environmental regimes point out, quite often a single country or group of countries constitutes a "veto coalition" who doom a regime to impotence because they refuse to participate in it or force other members to water down provisions so much that they are essentially ineffective.

Fourth, regimes only cover a limited set of problems. The Montreal Protocol is probably the most extensive of them, yet it, like all the others, does little to address the synergisms that are such an important part of the overlapping nature of the global crisis as discussed in Part One.

Finally, many regimes often don't do all that much to diminish the power of the nation state. In fact, if one recent, and sympathetic, observer is right, they may strengthen its role as the dominant actor in global political life.

The current flurry of cooperative environmental institution-building has emerged very much within the confines of traditional practices of sovereign-state diplomacy Thus, rather than deep-structural change, the patterns of explicit environmental politics reflect a marked tendency toward *re-structuring* (in the sense of reproducing) rather than restructuring (in the sense of fundamentally altering), the modern, sovereign, capitalist features of the current world order. International regimes legitimize new regulatory capacities and tasks for states, extending state sovereignty in important new directions. (Conca 1993: 310)

That said, regimes are one of a number of steps that people and countries have already turned to for solving problems which can only be solved transnationally and cooperatively. There are plenty of other experiments being tried along similarly cooperative lines: debt-for-nature swaps, transferable pollution credits, aid projects aimed at sustainable development, and more.

Are these or regimes the answer in and of themselves? Of course not.

Do they show us that we can make progress by cooperating? Of course they do.

## The Rio Summit

The degree to which transnational institutions could be used to solve environmental and related issues was driven home by the 1992 United Nations Conference on Environment and Development (UNCED), more popularly known as the Rio Summit (for a summary of activities and the full texts, see Johnson 1993).

For some environmentalists, the Summit was a disaster. The speeches and actions of the leaders who assembled at Rio were overwhelmingly shaped by the way of thinking outlined in Chapter 6. The United States took the bulk of the criticism for its insistence on a weakened global warming treaty and its refusal to sign the agreement on biodiversity. Critics, in particular, focused on the Bush administration's reluctance to look beyond what it took to be the short term economic self-interest of American energy and bio-technology firms and their employees.

The United States was not the only country singled out for criticism. Oil producing nations insisted on language which did not directly link petroleum with global warming and other environmental problems. There was plenty of rhetoric but not much commitment, including what seems for now to have been considerable political sleight of hand. Thus, the Italian government claimed it had reduced its carbon dioxide emissions, when in fact it had simply purchased power abroad and used accounting mechanisms to make the country appear to have changed. Similarly, the Japanese government pledged to reduce its emissions by building forty new nuclear power plants by 2010 even though political realities there make the construction of those plants all but impossible.

There was also substantial "we versus they" thinking, especially in the critical debate between North and South. In fact, very little progress was made toward reaching agreements that included concrete goals, obligations, and monitoring on the part of both sets of nations. Instead, there was a lot of finger pointing, with northern leaders complaining about the South's continued destruction of much of its ecosystem and their southern counterparts blaming the North for its failure to provide enough aid and its arrogance in not allowing their countries to pursue the kind of economic growth (and the related pollution) that has given the advanced industrialized democracies such a high standard of living. In the meantime, both sides did little, each waiting for the other to take the first step in initiating compromise solutions.

However, the summit was by no means the disaster its sharpest critics made it out to be. Like its predecessor in Stockholm a generation earlier, the fact that it occurred and drew most of the world's leaders is a sign of how important environmental issues have become. And, while one might have wanted more wide ranging agreements, the fact that treaties on biodiversity and global warming were signed, the sweeping Agenda 21 plan drafted, the UN Sustainable Development Committee created, and the Global Environmental Facility expanded all set precedents and opportunities for future activists and politicians to build on. Perhaps most importantly of all, it led world leaders from around the world to see the synergisms and the overlap among the problems and begin getting the "distance" then Senator Gore wrote about.

At that first summit in 1972, the UN explored the state of the world environment, generated the Stockholm Declaration on the Human Environment, and laid the ground work for creating UNEP. However, environmental problems did not stay near the top of the list of international priorities for long. They returned following the 1987 publication of the UN's Brundtland Commission report, *Our Common Future* (World Commission on Environment and Development 1987), which linked environmental and developmental issues for the first time in an official document. As we have already seen, it came at a time when traditional Cold War tensions were drawing to a close and global attention was being drawn to other issues which had not been on center stage but which could also no longer be ignored.

Two years later, the United Nations General Assembly decided to hold a new conference on the environment and development in Rio de Janeiro in the summer of 1992 and marked its recognition of how much trouble the world was in and how those troubles reflected its interdependence. Among other things, it called for a conference which would:

- discuss the continuing deterioration of the eco-system
- recognize the global nature of many environmental problems
- explore the link between environmental problems and underdevelopment
- stress the need for international cooperation
- develop strategies for dealing with these and other problems

The UNCED turned out to be the largest inter-governmental conference ever held. The decisions made (and avoided) and the ability (or the lack thereof) to enforce the agreements reached there will go a long way toward determining the future of life on this planet.

After two and a half years of negotiations and preparation, representatives from 174 governments, including 118 heads of state, convened for the two-day summit, held around a huge round table especially constructed for the meeting.

The Rio conference was not only a major historical event but also an illustration of changes in international economic and political relations, because it succeeded in putting interdependence squarely on the world political agenda, creating an integrated strategy for dealing with the environment and development, establishing a set of principles to serve as guidelines for the solution of North-South conflicts, and beginning to allot countries and regions responsibilities for the transition to sustainable development. While much of what happened at Rio remained at the level of principle and may turn out to be little more than the rhetoric of what international relations experts call "declarative policy" for now, it marked a major turning point in recognizing the problems brought on with interdependence and charting a collective and cooperative response to them.

The rest of this section outlines its major decisions and declarations, many of which were legally binding on the governments represented at Rio.

The **Rio Declaration on Environment and Development** is a set of twenty-seven principles designed to govern the economic and environmental behavior of both nations and individuals and was adopted by consensus. Even if it lacks many teeth for enforcement, it went farther than any such document in history, "recognizing the integral and interdependent nature of the Earth, our home" (Preamble), "makes a detailed commitment towards the planet," calling on "[s]tates [to] cooperate in a spirit of global partnership to conserve, protect and restore the health and integrity of the Earth's ecosystem" (Principle 7). Over the often heated objection of the United States, the Declaration also calls for a "precautionary approach" in which countries respond to problems before they become too serious or the full scientific community reaches agreement. Over the equally strenuous opposition of many authoritarian regimes in the Third World, it included the principle of public participation and at the very least guaranteed all people access to full information about environmental problems that affect them.

**Agenda 21** is an equally remarkable document which lays out an integrated strategy for human activities in all areas of economic and environmental life. It attempts to cover all areas where environment and development intersect and major social groups are affected, sustainable development, combating poverty, changing consumption patterns, demographic change, resource conservation, protection of the atmosphere, slowing deforestation, managing fragile ecosystems, promoting sustainable agriculture, promoting biodiversity, enhancing the role and protecting the rights of indigenous peoples, women, and children, and more (Johnson 1993: 125–133).

The delegates agreed to a number of institutional changes, most notably by committing themselves to the creation of a high level Commission on Sustainable Development. That decision was later ratified by the General Assembly, and the CSD was created in 1993. In Rio, much controversy between developing and developed nations made the negotiations difficult until the last moment. Many delegates and NGOs wanted the Commission to report to the top political body in the UN, the General Assembly. Most major industrialized governments opposed this approach as being incompatible with the objective of revitalizing the Economic and Social Council (ECOSOC) and insisted, successfully, that the new Commission report to it. The NGOs, in return, succeeded in insuring that the chapter of Agenda 21 on Institutional and Legal Matters call for an expanded role for themselves in the Commission.

The CSD has already held several meetings and done much work in its role of overseeing the implementation of Agenda 21. After the Earth Summit more than forty countries had created National Councils or Commissions on Sustainable Development and National Reports on their performance will be reported to the CSD. A new Undersecretary General (currently Nitin Desai, who had been Deputy Secretary General for the summit) was named and given the job of overseeing the CSD and coordinating all UN efforts to promote sustainable development.

The summiteers also adopted two **Conventions on Biological Diversity and Climate Change**. The Biological Diversity Convention asserts that primary responsibility for setting up protected areas rests with the individual states but regards indigenous peoples and rural groups as the first beneficiaries, as the ones whose patterns of sustainable use have preserved these ecosystems for centuries. The Framework Convention on Climate Change calls on industrialized nations to return to their 1990 levels of greenhouse emissions by the year 2000. It provides for a conference of the parties to take subsequent steps and for at least two reviews before the year 2000.

Both conventions were highly controversial and took years to negotiate. The Bush administration refused to sign the one on biological diversity and forced the negotiators to water down provisions in the other on climate change. As of this writing, the Clinton administration has joined upwards of 150 countries in signing them and the processes of ratifying and implementing them are well under way.

As noted earlier, the Rio Summit remains controversial, and interpretations of it vary tremendously. Nonetheless, at the very least it did three things. First, it put interdependence squarely on the global political map. Second, it brought the governments and leaders of the world together and helped them reach unprecedented agreement on a strategy for achieving sustainable development. Finally, it created more momentum for political, social, environmental, and economic cooperation afterward.

The United Nations itself emerged from Rio far stronger at least on environmental issues. The new Undersecretary General's office headed by Nitin Desai has become a major force in coordinating global development and environmental programs. Desai, himself, is probably the second most powerful person in the UN as a whole. Secretary General Boutros Boutros-Ghalli has become even more outspoken in his support for stronger United Nations institutions and enhanced world governance in general.

The momentum extends beyond the UN itself. An ad hoc "Commission on World Governance" was formed in Stockholm in 1991. It charged a smaller group under the leadership of Maurice Strong (Secretary General of the Rio Summit) and former Soviet President Mikhail Gorbachev with the task of developing an Earth Charter, which will be presented to the United Nations no later than 1997.

As Tim Wirth put it in the statement which begins this chapter, the world will never be the same after Rio. Indeed, his own job as Undersecretary of State for Global Affairs probably wouldn't exist had the Rio Summit not been held and focused world attention on the issues arising from interdependence.

As with everything else in this book, one cannot make too much of any one event or trend. The Rio Summit alone will not produce a world that has moved beyond confrontation. It has, however, given us important new insights into what can be done as well as to what has to be done. For that reason alone, we are likely to feel its impact for years to come.


## IS THE AGE OF THE NATION STATE PAST?

As I stated in the introduction, Part Three has been the most speculative part of a speculative book. The examples presented in these last four chapters cannot be seen as anything more than tentative first steps on what at best will be a long and uncertain journey. At most, they are examples of what people could do if we become serious about making the shift to new thinking.

For the purposes of this chapter, the central issue is the nature and future of the nation state. The state remains the primary political unit in just about all areas of political life, a life which is still marked by confrontation and violence. Although states are still reluctant to sacrifice any sovereignty to supranational entities or become more cooperative in their dealings with each other, the pace of change and the global crisis are making movement on this front more urgent. As the "gaps" depicted in Figures 1.1 and 1.2 and all the discussion since have suggested, we live in an interdependent world, a reality we lag far behind in our geopolitical lives.

The very nature of the global crisis shows us that no nation can solve its problems alone. The inexorable trend of world events toward increased contacts and interdependence and the growing diversity of problems are forcing us to consider more global responses to what are clearly global challenges. Only concerted action and a cooperative effort can work, as I hope this chapter and this book have demonstrated.

That is a daunting task. We are still a long way from making such cooperation and anything approaching world governance the norm. Like most other

IOs, the United Nations has become more powerful in recent years; there is even serious discussion today about creating a permanent, volunteer, UN-led peacekeeping force.

But, it is still *very far* from gaining the kind of autonomous power to act and enforce its actions in ways we associate with a state and governance. The initiatives described in this chapter are important first (perhaps better "baby") steps in that direction. Perhaps the next ones can be taken through existing institutions like the EU, international environmental regimes, and the United Nations. Perhaps they can be taken while maintaining the nation state within some larger but still loose global organization(s) short of the formal world government that realist international relations experts find so unrealistic and unappealing. Perhaps we will have to start from scratch and build entirely new institutions if we are to close that gap.

In ending, I remain convinced of two things. First, as this book as a whole has tried to show, business as usual and the conventional wisdom aren't working. We need to try dramatically different approaches to solving our problems in our families, communities, regions, and nations, as well as the world as a whole. Second, as I have tried to document in these last three chapters, we have taken enough of those baby steps at all those levels to at least plausibly argue that such change is possible, though we clearly have a lot to learn in getting past these first initiatives. The main organizer of the Rio Summit, Maurice Strong, tells the story of a meeting between Henry Kissinger and Zhou Enlai. While discussing revolution, Kissinger asked, "What do you think were the principal results of the French Revolution?" He reports that Zhou replied with a benign smile, "It's too early to tell."

By that logic, it is much too early to tell how far these initiatives can take us, let alone what other obstacles and problems we might find along the way. It is not too early to see the urgency and the need.

## REFERENCES

Baldwin, David A. (1993). "Neoliberalism, Neorealism, and World Politics." In David A. Baldwin, ed., *Neorealism and Neoliberalism: The Contemporary Debate*. New York: Columbia University Press, 3–29.

Boulding, Kenneth (1978). *Stable Peace*. Austin: University of Texas Press.

————. (1988). "Moving from Unstable to Stable Peace." In Martin Hellman and Anatoly Gromyko, eds., *Breakthrough: Emerging New Thinking: Soviet and American Scholars Issue a Challenge to Build a World Beyond War*. New York/Moscow: Walker/Novosti, 157–167.

Brown, Seyom (1992). *International Relations in a Changing World*. Boulder, Colo.: Westview.

————. (1994). "World Interests and the Changing Dimensions of Security." In Michael T. Klare and Daniel C. Thomas, eds., *World Security: Challenges for a New Century*. New York: St. Martin's, 10–26.

Cameron, David R. (1992). "The 1992 Initiative: Causes and Consequences." In Alberta Sbragia, ed., *Euro-Politics: Institutions and Policymaking in the "New" European Community*. Washington: Brookings Institution, 23–74.

Colchester, Nico (1992). "Into the Void: A Survey of the European Community." *The Economist*, July 11, 1992.

Conca, Ken (1993). "Environmental Change and the Deep Structure of World Politics." In Ronnie Lipschutz and Ken Conca, eds., *The State and Social Power in Global Environmental Politics*. New York: Columbia University Press, 306–326.

Delamaide, Darrell (1994). *The New Superregions of Europe*. New York: Dutton.

Dinan, Desmond (1994). *Ever Closer Union?* Boulder, Colo.: Lynne Rienner.

Facchinetti, Ronald (1994). "Why Brussels Has 10,000 Lobbyists." *New York Times*, August 21, Section 8, 9.

Gore, Albert (1992). *Earth in the Balance*. New York: Plume.

Grieco, Joseph (1990). *Cooperation among Nations: Europe, America, and Non-Tariff Barriers to Trade*. Ithaca: Cornell University Press.

Haas, Peter (1990). *Saving the Environment: The Politics of International Environmental Cooperation*. New York: Columbia University Press.

Johnson, Stanley (1993). *The Earth Summit: The United Nations Conference on Environment and Development (UNCED)*. London: Graham and Trotman/Martinus Nijhoff.

Kaplan, Robert (1994). "The Coming Anarchy." *The Atlantic* (February).

Karns, Margaret F., and Karen A. Mingst (1994). "Maintaining International Peace and Security: UN Peacekeeping and Peacemaking." In Michael T. Klare and Daniel C. Thomas, eds., *World Security: Challenges for a New Century*. New York: St. Martin's, 188–215.

Kidder, Rushworth (1993). *Shared Values for a Troubled World*. San Francisco: Jossey-Bass.

Krasner, Stephen (1983). "Introduction." In Stephen Krasner, ed., *International Regimes*. Ithaca: Cornell University Press, 1–23.

Lipschutz, Ronnie and Judith Mayer (1993). "Not Seeing the Forest for the Trees: Rights, Rules, and the Renegotiation of Resource Management Regimes." In Ronnie Lipschutz and Ken Conca, eds., *The State and Social Power in Global Environmental Politics*. New York: Columbia University Press, 246–276.

Litfin, Karen (1993). "Eco-regimes: Playing Tug of War with the Nation-State." In Ronnie Lipschutz and Ken Conca, eds., *The State and Social Power in Global Environmental Politics*. New York: Columbia University Press, 94–118.

Marlin-Bennett, Renée (1992). "Contending Trade Regimes in a Posthegemonic World." In Chronis Polychroniou, ed., *Perspectives and Issues in International Political Economy*. Westport, Conn.: Praeger, 21–37.

Miller, Lynn (1994). *Global Order: Values and Power in International Relations.* 3d ed., Boulder, Colo.: Westview.

Ohmae, Kenichi (1995). *The End of the Nation State: The Rise of Regional Economies.* New York: Free Press.

Porter, Gareth, and Janet Welsh Brown (1991). *Global Environmental Politics.* Boulder, Colo.: Westview.

Ross, George (1995). *Jacques Delors.* New York: Oxford University Press.

Sbragia, Alberta M., ed. (1992). *Euro-politics: Institutions and Policymaking in the "New" European Community.* Washington: Brookings Institution.

Stein, Arthur A. (1990). *Why Nations Cooperate: Circumstance and Choice in International Relations.* Ithaca: Cornell University Press.

Strong, Maurice (1993). "Beyond Rio—Problems and Prospects." *Colorado Journal of International Environmental Law and Policy* 4, Winter, 21.

Talbott, Strobe (1992). "The Birth of the Global Nation." *Time,* July 20, 70–71.

World Commission on Environment and Development (1987). *Our Common Future.* New York: Oxford University Press.

Young, Oran (1989). *International Cooperation: Building Regimes for Natural Resources and the Environment.* Ithaca: Cornell University Press.

# 13

# EPILOG

The only real hope of people today is probably a renewal of our certainty
that we are rooted in the Earth and, at the same time, the cosmos.
                                                        —Vaclav Havel

Jean Monnet was a remarkable man. In his long career, he was everything
from a brandy salesman to the primary architect of both the French
economic planning system and European integration. In a professional life
that spanned two world wars (which, perhaps not coincidentally, he could not
fight in because of ill-health), he came to see the need to replace the bloody
fighting of trench war and blitzkrieg with a new form of transnational
economic cooperation.

As such, Monnet is often seen as an idealist and visionary. That is apparently
not how he saw himself. Instead, as he put it in his memoirs, which he wrote
at age 90 (so much for ill-health), he saw that there was an important task that
had to be done and simply dedicated himself to doing his part.

I am not an optimist. I am simply persistent. If action is necessary, how can one say
that it is impossible, so long as one has not tried it? Very often firm determination and
a simple idea have their best chance when indecision is rife. There can be no progress
without a certain disorder, or at least disorder on the surface. To organize events that
strike me and occupy my thoughts lead me to general conclusions about what has to

be done. Then circumstances which determine day-to-day events suggest or supply the means of action. (cited in Smith 1992: 47; Duchesne 1994)

Monnet thus deserves our attention in concluding this book on two levels.

First, as much as any single person in modern history, he symbolized what the book has been about: the practical, realistic need for and opportunity to replace confrontation with cooperation. He made what seemed impossible possible. In the early 1940s, when Monnet first started building support for a united Europe, the idea that the prospect of war between Germany and France could be all but eliminated was unimaginable. A half century later, it was reality.

Monnet isn't the only reason European integration has progressed so far. But, he was an important participant in the process, someone whose dogged commitment and pragmatism were every bit as important as the vision of a united Europe he had in the first place.

Second, he demonstrates the point made throughout the last third of the book that individuals can make a tremendous difference in producing change. Few people will ever have the kind of impact he did. That said, we should not miss the important lessons in his story.

To begin with, a surprising number of people who have made a major impact started out as relative "nobodies." Monnet himself only had a high school education when his father sent him off to the frontiers of western Canada to represent their modest brandy company. Martin Luther King, Jr., was a young, relatively unknown minister who seized the opportunity presented by the Montgomery bus boycott, itself begun by an even more "normal" person, Rosa Parks who refused to give up her seat in the front of the bus. The same could be said for Mohandas Gandhi, who first developed his philosophy and strategy of non-violence while serving as an attorney for the Indian community in South Africa. Vaclav Havel, whose words begin this epilog, was a "mere" playwright who spent much of the generation between the Prague Spring and the Velvet Revolution in prison.

It's not just a case of obscure people who become global celebrities. Take the case of two teenagers from Maine. Samantha Smith was a junior high school student who sent letters to President Reagan and General Secretary Andropov urging them to disarm. When Andropov agreed to meet with her, Smith got a lot of publicity and helped spark a tremendous increase in youth exchange programs. Her tragic death in an airplane crash a few years later prompted the creation of a foundation that bears her name and continues the work she began. The other was a high school student who sewed a simple canvas bag, took it to the supermarket, and suggested that the company sell them as reusable grocery bags. After a while, the company agreed and also began offering a few cents off each time a customer reused any bag. Within a few years, both the bags and the discount were standard offerings in supermarkets up and down the east coast.

In their own ways, everyone from Jean Monnet to those teenagers from Maine reveal to us a piece of ourselves and how we are a part of the Earth and cosmos Czech President Havel referred to in accepting the 1994 Liberty Award. If I'm right, in the constant learning that comes from asking the two questions they all ask(ed), "Who am I?" and "Who are we?" lies the potential for moving beyond confrontation.

This book has covered a lot of ground and, I hope, been good food for thought. I assume that many readers will disagree with the basic argument about the crisis or the response to it and that most who accept my basic premises will have had trouble with major points I have made along the way. On the other hand, there is a simple conclusion virtually all of us can share. It is most briefly summed up on the coffee mug I use in my office. It bears a picture of a tabby cat holding up the world and the caption, "fragile, handle with care."

## REFERENCES

Duchesne, François (1994). *Jean Monnet: The First Statesman of Interdependence*. New York: W. W. Norton.
Smith, Geoffrey (1992). "Euro-What?" *World Monitor*, December: 44–49.

# INDEX

**About the Author**

CHARLES HAUSS, the author of four other books, is a member of the Public and International Affairs Department at George Mason University (USA) and is also currently a Visiting Research Fellow at the University of Reading (UK).

ISBN 0-275-94615-0

90000>

EAN

9 780275 946159

HARDCOVER BAR CODE